7-26-74

The State, the Enterprise and the Individual
An Introduction to Applied Microeconomics

The State, the Enterprise and the Individual
An Introduction to Applied Microeconomics

Margaret Sharp

A HALSTED PRESS BOOK

John Wiley and Sons
New York

Published in the USA by Halsted Press, a
Division of John Wiley & Sons, Inc., New York

ISBN 0 470-77890-3
Library of Congress Catalog Card No 73-10892

Printed in Great Britain

1817368

To Tom, with love

Contents

CONTENTS

CONTENTS

Author's preface

This book took its form from a lecture course which I gave for several years at the London School of Economics. The lecture course was for second year students studying for a general paper in applied economics. These students were not specializing in economics, but in government, international relations, sociology and so on, and were obliged to take a paper in economics as part of their examination under the BSc (Econ). From this audience comes the emphasis on policy problems; they were interested in real issues not hypothetical ones. From them too derives the literary exposition, for many shied away blankly from anything mathematical. Algebra, in so far as it was introduced, had to be verbal algebra. For my part I was anxious to impart to this audience a sense of the unity which the theoretical framework of welfare economics gives to the consideration of microeconomic policy issues, and without which it is often difficult to understand the economist's approach to this sort of problem. In this respect the book has become something of a theme and variations: the theme of welfare economics is discussed in the first chapter and the subsequent chapters are a series of variations upon this theme.

I hope that this book will be of use not only to the non-specialist, general course student in economics, but also to a wider lay audience to whom it may help to explain both the contribution and the limitations of economics in these policy fields.

As with any textbook, this has been through successive drafts and I am indebted to many of my colleagues at LSE for invaluable help and criticism. I should like in particular to thank Christine Whitehead, Basil Yamey, Lucien Foldes and my editor Brian Henry for their advice and suggestions, and also my husband Tom, who has patiently worked through numerous drafts with a civil servant's eye for logic and detail and an unfailing fund of common sense. I am, of course, entirely responsible for errors and faults that remain.

London School of Economics, December 1972.

The State, the Enterprise and the Individual
An Introduction to Applied Microeconomics

I

The framework – the elements of welfare economics

1.1 Introduction

This book is a series of studies in applied economics. Planning, corporate behaviour, anti-trust, cost benefit analysis, the social services – each chapter will stand substantially on its own. Yet there is a common theme which links them together. All these chapters are about problems of applied *micro*economics – the functioning of parts of the economic system and their contribution to the performance of the system as a whole, in contrast to macroeconomic issues where the emphasis is upon the overall performance of the system.

There is a distinct body of economic theory involved here which is called welfare economics. This is less well known than the Keynesian national income analysis which underlies the consideration of issues of macroeconomic policy, for it is not usually included explicitly in introductory economics courses. In such courses microeconomics covers the price system – the way in which the price mechanism can co-ordinate the activities of individual agents, consumers and producers, within the economy. Welfare economics goes beyond the mechanics of the system and asks whether the way in which these actions are co-ordinated is 'good' or 'bad'. Some welfare economics is implicit in introductory courses – competition is usually represented as 'good' and monopoly as 'bad'. Yet to arrive at such conclusions involves introducing ethical judgements and, as we shall see, ethical judgements are at the base of welfare economics. In this respect welfare economics is unsatisfactory, for it does not provide us with any clear cut 'objective' answers but throws us back upon the ethical premises from which it originates and for this reason many economists choose to ignore it and to concentrate instead upon the mechanics of the system – upon positive economics. The fact remains however that in approaching many problems in applied microeconomics the economist does fall back, implicitly or explicitly, upon the welfare economics model. This is his starting point. The model is extended, amended, qualified and transposed, sometimes beyond all recognition. Yet the model is still there and to be able to grasp the economist's approach involves an understanding, at least at an intuitive level, of its main elements. The purpose of this first chapter is to provide readers with such an understanding. This in turn provides the framework for the rest of the book, which picks up and explores a variety of applications.

1.2 The concept of welfare

Economists seek to analyse and to understand the workings of the economic system with the ultimate purpose of trying to improve its functioning. But improve it to what end? A variety of objectives are advocated – full employment, stable prices, economic growth, social justice, balance of payments equilibrium and so forth. We shall be looking at some of these later in the chapter. The classical economists however had a much more straightforward answer to this question. For them the purpose of improvement of the economic system was to advance the welfare or happiness of the community, which in a utilitarian fashion they defined as being to promote the greatest happiness of the greatest number. Such an objective presupposes that the community or group is clearly demarcated. This may be straightforward enough – we are usually interested in the welfare of people rather than of inanimate objects, such as machines or land, or, for that matter, of animals (although the welfare of any of these may bear upon human welfare and thus be of concern to us). Further, such is the force of nationalism that, when we talk of the community, we usually mean a national community rather than the global community.

However, this utilitarian objective also presupposes that welfare is something that can be measured in either monetary or physical terms. It is this aspect which causes most difficulty. The classical economists thought that welfare was something tangible which could be measured on some absolute scale, just as one can measure quantities of rice or wheat. Given this measure of each person's welfare, the calculation of community welfare was just a matter of adding up the total of individuals' welfares within the community.

Unfortunately this is not so. Welfare or happiness is something which, like pain, we know to exist but cannot measure with any accuracy. As an individual I can judge for myself when I am 'better off' and when I am 'worse off', just as I know when something hurts more or less. Moreover, if I am rational (in the sense of acting consistently with my aims and objectives), I will always, given a choice, choose that opportunity which offers me the greatest welfare. Thus, if I choose A in preference to B, it is a fair deduction that I consider my welfare to be higher in A than in B. On this basis we can say something about individual welfare. From the choices they make we have some idea about when people judge themselves to be 'better off' or 'worse off', just as we can gauge in some degree when in illness people feel better or worse. The difficulty comes in trying to make comparisons between persons. I may know that you are in pain, but I cannot gauge precisely how much pain you are in. We have no measure of the intensity of pain, and cannot compare except on a very superficial level the relative pain suffered by different persons. So too we have no method of comparing the relative welfares of individuals. I may know that some change in circumstances makes you better off but, given a similar change in circumstances for your neighbour, I am not in a position to say that you are 'more' better off than they. The lack of any absolute scale for measuring relative welfare and the consequent impossibility of making interpersonal comparisons of welfare means that we cannot calculate community welfare by totting up the total of individual welfares. We have nothing more than a collection of individual welfares which are measured on a variety of 'personal' scales and are not therefore comparable.

The social welfare function

People do however make judgements about relative levels of welfare. If you are poor and your neighbour is rich, I may judge your welfare to be increased more than that of your neighbour by, for example, an increase of both your incomes of £1 per week. Such a conclusion involves the explicit introduction on my part of an ethical judgement – I think that poor people gain more from a given increase in income than rich people. There are no objective grounds for this opinion, and some might dispute it – the poor man may spend the money on gambling while the rich spends it on books. But if we are prepared to introduce such ethical judgements, we can make interpersonal comparisons of welfare and therefore add up individual welfares to measure group welfare. Interpersonal comparisons of welfare, and therefore the measurement of group welfare, are not impossible, but they cannot be made without the introduction of judgements of an ethical nature.

The method chosen for combining individual welfares is sometimes called a *social welfare function*. It is an attempt to arrive at a generally accepted system of weights to be applied to individual welfares in order to aggregate them into a measure of group welfare. The difficulty is to reach any general consensus on the weighting system to be used, for this is where the ethical judgement is introduced. Many but not all would accept the notion that the poor gain more from a given increase in income than the rich, which argues for greater equality in the distribution of income and for weighting the gains to the poor more highly than those to the rich. Few however are unanimous in their views and, where there is no unanimity, there is no uniquely correct method of combining or compromising between individual views. A simple example serves to illustrate this point. Suppose three people wish to go to the theatre. If all three wish to see the same play there is no problem. But should one differ in preference from the others then what criterion for choice should prevail? Accept the preference of the dissenter? Abide by majority rule? Look to second preferences? There is no correct criterion for choice.[1] For society as a whole

[1] See K J Arrow *Social choice and individual values* John Wiley & Sons Inc New

any weighting system that is chosen to combine individual welfares (any social welfare function) is therefore to some extent arbitrarily 'imposed', even if imposed by a democratically elected government which may be ousted from power when a majority disagrees with its decision.

The Pareto criterion

Clearly the more detailed the set of ethical judgements incorporated in the social welfare function, the more difficult it is to arrive at a 'community view'. There is more likely to be agreement on ethical propositions of a fairly broad kind. One such proposition is that called the Pareto criterion. Working from the basis of individual welfares, the Pareto criterion states that for the community as a whole a change which makes at least one person better off and no-one worse off constitutes an improvement in the welfare of the group; and conversely if some are made worse off and none better off then group welfare diminishes. The Pareto criterion is thus a form of social welfare function, but one based on what might be called 'the least offensive' proposition. Where some gain and none lose there is an overall gain. Where some lose and none gain there is an overall loss. But if some lose and some gain, which would involve comparing the relative loss of those losing with the relative gain of those gaining, the Pareto criterion cannot tell us what has happened to group welfare. We can only make judgements where the gains or losses have been all one-way.

It is worth noting some of the features of the Pareto criterion at this stage for it forms the basis of 'traditional' welfare economics. First, as we have seen, it is an ethical proposition, even if one of a broad general nature with which many would go along. It is however *independent* of the distribution of income. The distribution of income is the share of community income received by each member of the community. Given this, as long as some gain and none lose, be the gainers rich or poor, the Pareto criterion for an improvement in welfare is satisfied. It applies equally to a society where the distribution of income is egalitarian and to one where it is highly unequal. The Pareto

York 1951 for an exposition, in terms of mathematical logic, which brings out very clearly the limitations of trying to gauge social welfare in terms of social choice.

criterion is not concerned about the equity of the shares going to different members of society but with the *allocation of resources*, that is whether there is potential within the economic system for re-organizing the use of resources so that some can be made better off without making others worse off. As we shall see, it is possible to derive a set of rules which satisfy the Pareto criterion and these rules too are independent of the distribution of income. They are rules for allocating the resources of the economic system, labour, capital and natural resources, in such a way that, given the initial distribution of income, there is no potential for further improvement. When these rules are satisfied there is said to be an efficient allocation of resources. From this derives one of the fundamental features of traditional welfare economics – the dichotomy between questions of income distribution and questions of resource allocation. To move from questions about whether we are using our resources efficiently to questions about what constitutes a 'good' or a 'bad' distribution of income requires the explicit introduction of an ethical judgement, or set of ethical judgements, side by side with the Pareto criterion. Although the Pareto criterion is, as we have seen, a broad ethical proposition, it seeks to isolate itself from further incursion into the world of ethics, to derive by a process of logical deduction from the initial premise a set of 'scientific' rules relating to the allocation of resources, and to allow ethical notions of what constitutes a 'good' or a 'bad' distribution of income to be introduced separately.

A further feature of the Pareto criterion deserves noting. As we have seen, it seeks to aggregate individual welfares into a concept of group welfare. There are two implications of importance here. First, seeing the group as the aggregation of the individuals who compose it, implies an *individualistic* concept of society, in contrast to Hegelian-based philosophies where the group is seen to have a 'spirit' of its own. Secondly, the definition of individual welfare which we have adopted is based on the concept of choice – if I choose A in preference to B then I am better off in A. There is no attempt to question individual preferences – as a consumer I decide what is good for me. This is the notion of *consumer sovereignty*. Likewise the concept of efficiency in the allocation of resources, derived from the Pareto criterion, is based upon consumer sovereignty. We are

6

anxious within given production constraints to allocate resources in accordance with consumer preferences, but do not question these preferences.

The Pareto criterion is thus an attempt to introduce a broadly acceptable ethical proposition which enables us to overcome the impasse of interpersonal comparisons and to 'say something' about group welfare. From this premise it is possible to derive by a process of logical deduction a series of propositions about the allocation of resources within the economy. It is worthwhile following this path for the moment to see precisely what these propositions are. Let us not forget however that this relates only to the allocation of resources within the economy – how much should be produced, of which goods, with which factors of production – and that we have to introduce separately notions relating to the distribution of income. We shall be returning to income distribution later in this chapter.

1.3 The efficiency rules derived from the Pareto criterion

Production efficiency

The Pareto criterion states that a change which makes at least one person better off and no-one worse off constitutes an improvement in welfare. If we can produce more of any output with the same inputs then, because they would have the same or equivalent amount as before, it would be possible to make some people better off, by giving them more output, without making others any worse off. More output from the same inputs is a 'good thing'. It is important therefore to know whether as a community we are using available inputs, factors of production, to produce the maximum possible output of goods and services, or whether by reshuffling inputs between uses we could secure a greater output.

When a factor of production can be used to produce more than one commodity, then maximum output from that factor can be obtained when the value of its marginal product is the same in all uses. If it were not, total output could be increased by switching the factor from an occupation where it is less productive to one where it is more productive. For example, if the marginal product of a factor were 4 units of output in one

7

occupation and 6 units in another, then switching one unit of the factor into the latter occupation would result in a net gain of 2 units of output. Thus, assuming diminishing marginal productivity in both industries, it is worth switching factors between occupations until the value of their marginal products is equal. When this is achieved, no more output can be obtained by switching factors from one occupation to another and maximum production has been achieved with given inputs. This rule can be generalized to relate to many factors (inputs) and many commodities. To secure maximum output from given inputs, the ratio of the marginal products of any two factors (inputs) used in the production of a commodity shall be the same in the production of any commodity in which the factors are used.[1]

This is then our *production efficiency rule – the ratios of the marginal products of any two factors should be equal in all occupations.* When this rule is satisfied, society is producing on what is termed the *production possibility frontier.* A position on the frontier represents a position where factors are being used to produce the maximum possible output. This is illustrated in figure 1.

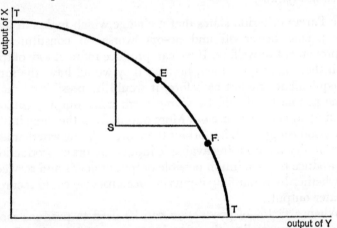

Figure 1. The production possibility frontier. Given the availability of factors of production, T.T is the locus of points of maximum potential output–of maximum possible production. E and F are both points of maximum potential output; S is below the frontier and is not a point of maximum potential output.

[1] For general proofs and more detailed elaboration of these efficiency rules derived from the Pareto criterion see any of the standard texts on welfare economics mentioned in the bibliography at the end of this chapter.

A position such as S, below the production possibility frontier TT, is sub-optimal, for merely by shuffling factors (inputs) between occupations we could produce an output such as E where more of both X and Y are being produced. E however is an optimal position for there exist no further opportunities, by reshuffling inputs, to increase output of at least one product without simultaneously decreasing output of the other – it is a position of maximum possible output.

However it is apparent that there is not just one point of maximum output but a whole series of such points, which form the production possibility frontier. Switching factors from one occupation to another at E need not push production to a sub-optimal position, but could change the composition of output, for example we might move from E to F. Both positions are production efficient and therefore on the production possibility frontier. Moving from E to F means an increase in the output of Y, but a decrease in the output of X. What this illustrates is the well-known concept of *opportunity cost*. Once we are on the production possibility frontier we cannot obtain more output just by reshuffling inputs. We cannot obtain something for nothing as we do when we move from a sub-optimal to an optimal position. If we want to increase the output of Y then we must sacrifice some output of X, because we must shift

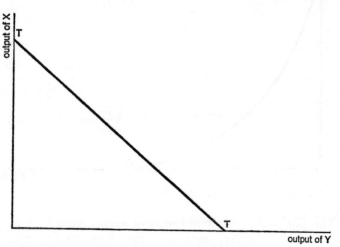

Figure 2.   Production possibility frontier with constant opportunity cost.

9

factors of production from producing X to producing Y. The amount of X which we have to give up for the extra output of Y is the opportunity cost of this extra output. The slope of the production frontier thus represents the opportunity cost of X in terms of Y, and Y in terms of X, that is the amount of X which at the margin has to be sacrificed for the production of an extra unit of Y. When opportunity cost is constant, the production possibility frontier has a constant slope, i.e. it is a straight line as in figure 2.

The production possibility frontier illustrated above in figure 1 represents a situation where, as more of one output is produced, opportunity cost rises because increasing amounts of factor inputs are required to produce an extra unit of that output. This is often regarded as the 'normal' situation. Another possibility is that increasing the production of one product requires a smaller and smaller sacrifice of the other, a situation of increasing returns to scale. In this case the production possibility frontier is curved but in the opposite direction, convex to the origin as in figure 3.

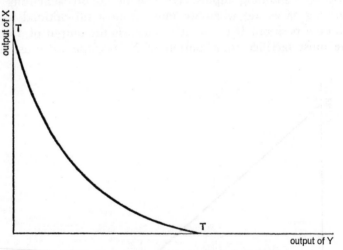

Figure 3.   Production possibility frontier with increasing returns.

The production possibility frontier is also referred to as the transformation curve, and its slope (opportunity cost) is referred to as the marginal rate of transformation, $\mathrm{MRT}_{\mathrm{X\ and\ Y}}$

of one good for another, or sometimes the marginal rate of substitution in production of one good for another, $\text{MRS}_{\substack{\text{X and Y.} \\ \text{production}}}$

Distributive efficiency[1]

It is important whatever the total volume of goods and services being produced that this should be allocated among consumers in such a way as to make them as well off as possible. It should not be possible to make consumers better off merely by re-shuffling goods and services between themselves. Assume here that incomes, the amount people have to spend, are fixed. If Mrs Jones, who likes biscuits, is given cake, while Mrs Smith, who likes cake, is given biscuits, then the two of them could be made better off by mutual exchange. Following Pareto, if consumers could be made better off by exchange, in which presumably no-one accepts a deal which makes him worse off, then there is room for improvement in the allocation of re-sources. When there is no scope for such exchange then the economy is said to achieve *efficiency in distribution* just as it achieves production efficiency when there is no possibility of increasing output by reshuffling factors of production between occupations.

The distributive efficiency rule is analogous to the production efficiency rule. Let us go back to our example. If Mrs Jones values biscuits for cakes at a rate of 1 to 2 and Mrs Smith values them at 2 to 1, then the exchange of a packet of biscuits for a cake would make both parties better off. Mrs Jones assesses her gain of a packet of biscuits at twice her 'loss' of a cake, while Mrs Smith values her gain at twice her 'loss'. As long as their relative valuations differ, exchange is to their mutual advantage. There will come a point when this is no longer the case. Mrs Jones, while preferring biscuits, may like to keep some cake in the house for visitors, and likewise Mrs Smith may like to keep some biscuits in reserve. When Mrs Jones values cake in terms of biscuits at the same rate as Mrs Smith, there will be no gain

---

[1] The notion of distributive efficiency is quite distinct from that of the distribution of income. The latter refers to the relative share of community income going to different persons. Distributive efficiency takes the distribution of income as given and considers whether consumers are spending their incomes so as to secure the maximum possible satisfaction from their expenditure.

from further exchange, and there will be an 'optimal distribution' of cakes and biscuits between them. For the economy as a whole an optimal distribution of goods and services is obtained when the marginal rate of substitution between any two goods is the same for all consumers. The marginal rate of substitution is the relative subjective valuation of one good in terms of another. In the above example Mrs Jones's relative valuation of biscuits for cakes of 1 to 2 indicates that she would be willing to substitute 2 cakes for one packet of biscuits, while Mrs Smith's marginal rate of substitution is 2 packets of biscuits for one cake. As more and more of one good is acquired, we assume that the relative valuation, the marginal rate of substitution between it and other goods, falls. As we have seen, it is when their relative valuations are the same, when their marginal rates of substitution between the two goods coincide, that there is no further gain from exchange and there is an optimal distribution of the two goods between them.

Generalizing the *distributive efficiency rule* is therefore that *for any two goods or services all consumers*[1] *should have the same marginal rate of substitution.* Just as in the case of production efficiency, this does not lead to one unique optimum position but to a series of optimal positions which vary according to the initial distribution of income. For each initial income distribution, there will be a different distributive efficiency point.

The optimal conditions of production and exchange

The simultaneous satisfaction of the production efficiency conditions and the distributive efficiency conditions leads to what is termed an 'optimal' allocation of resources. This means that we want *both* to be on the production possibility frontier *and* to achieve distributive efficiency *at the same time*. We can achieve this when the slope of the production possibility frontier is the same as the common marginal rate of substitution in consumption between the two commodities. In figure 4 E is an optimal production point, for at E the common marginal rate of substitution in consumption, shown by $MRS_{X \text{ and } Y}^{\text{consumption}}$ is the same as the slope of the production possibility frontier TT.

---

[1] More correctly, all consumers who consume both goods or services.

This is not so at F where the two slopes diverge. If we produced at F, the extra amount of X which could be produced for any reduction in the output of Y would be more than required by people to compensate for the loss of Y output, and therefore by shifting production towards E, ie producing more X and less Y, some people could be made better off without others being made any worse off. At E there is no further scope for this. The extra amount of X produced for each unit of Y production is exactly the same as the extra amount of X which

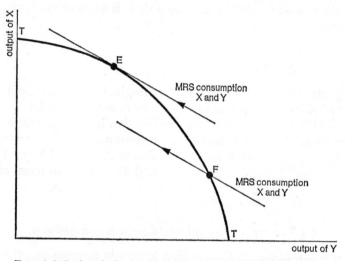

Figure 4. Optimal production is achieved when the common marginal rate of substitution in consumption (shown by MRS consumption X and Y) is the same as the marginal rate of substitution in production (shown by the slope of the production possibility frontier).

is required to compensate consumers for the loss of a unit of Y.

The rule for production optimality therefore requires that *the slope of the production possibility frontier, the marginal rate of substitution in production, is equal to the marginal rate of substitution in consumption between the two commodities.* Now the slope of the production possibility frontier represents, as we saw earlier, the opportunity cost of producing one good in terms of another. Similarly the common marginal rate of substitution in consumption represents the relative subjective valuation placed by consumers on one good in terms of another, or the relative benefit which consumers feel they gain from the possession of one good. By equating the marginal rates of substitution in production and consumption in this way, the optimality conditions really require that the opportunity cost of production of any commodity should be equal to the relative benefit which society gains from consuming it – that its cost to society should equal the benefit that society gains from it.[1] And this is what it all boils down to, the intuitively very reasonable rule that, at the margin, cost should equal benefit; that no resource or commodity should be used in one way if there is another use for it of greater social value.

The optimality rules

Opportunity cost of X in terms of Y (or Y in terms of X)	Marginal rate of substitution in production of X and Y	Marginal rate of substitution in consumption of X and Y	Marginal social benefit of X in terms of Y (or Y in terms of X)
=	=	=	

1.4 The optimality rules and perfect competition

Now it can be shown that, subject to certain assumptions, these rules for achieving optimum efficiency are satisfied under conditions of perfect competition. We shall be returning to the assumptions later for they are important. In the meantime let us consider briefly why perfect competition satisfies the optimality rules. In perfect competition:

a all inputs and outputs are sold at prices which are determined in the market by the forces of supply and demand;
b these prices are the same for all buyers and sellers, and no buyer or seller can in any way influence them;

[1] For the present we are assuming that there is no divergence between personal, subjective, costs and benefits and social costs and benefits – that what is true of the individual is true also of society. This is a major assumption to make and we shall examine below, see p. 17, the complications that arise when we drop it.

c any firm can enter, or leave, the production of any commodity at these prices if it finds it profitable to do so.

The production efficiency rule and perfect competition

The profit maximizing entrepreneur will equate the price he pays for an input with the value of its marginal product. Under perfect competition the prices of all inputs will be determined in the market for all users; the value of the marginal product of any input must therefore be the same in all uses. From this it follows that the ratio of the marginal products of any two inputs, factors, will be the same in all uses. Thus our production efficiency rule will be met in perfect competition.[1]

The distributive efficiency rule and perfect competition

If a consumer behaves optimally, ie tries to secure maximum benefit from his income, he will buy commodities in quantities such that his relative valuation of the two goods, the marginal rate of substitution between them, is equal to the ratio of their prices. Since these prices are the same for all consumers, the marginal rate of substitution between any two commodities must be the same for all consumers.

Production optimality and perfect competition

The profit maximizing entrepreneur will equate marginal cost with price. In perfect competition marginal cost equals opportunity cost. Moreover, we have seen that consumers will equate their relative valuation of the benefit derived from any two goods with their price ratios. Thus on the production side

[1] Given two inputs i and j in the production of outputs x and y, the production efficiency rule requires that
$$MP_{ix}/MP_{jx} = MP_{iy}/MP_{jy}$$
For the profit maximizing entrepreneur:
$$P_i = MP_{ix}.P_x = MP_{iy}.P_y$$
$$P_j = MP_{jx}.P_x = MP_{jy}.P_y$$
where P_i and P_j, the prices of inputs, and P_x and P_y, the prices of outputs, are determined in the market and are the same for all entrepreneurs. Therefore
$$P_i/P_j = MP_{ix}/MP_{jx} = MP_{iy}/MP_{jy}$$
and $MP_{ix}/MP_{jx} = MP_{iy}/MP_{jy}$

$$\frac{P_x}{P_y} = \frac{MC_x}{MC_y} = \text{Marginal rate of substitution in production of x and y}$$

And on the distribution side

$$\frac{P_x}{P_y} = \frac{\text{Marginal benefit x}}{\text{Marginal benefit y}} = \text{Marginal rate of substitution in consumption of x and y}$$

Since both producers and consumers face the same set of product prices

$$\begin{matrix}\text{Marginal rate of} \\ \text{substitution in} \\ \text{production x and y}\end{matrix} = \frac{P_x}{P_y} = \begin{matrix}\text{Marginal rate of} \\ \text{substitution in} \\ \text{consumption of x and y}\end{matrix}$$

and the optimality rules will be satisfied.

This result, that under certain assumptions the equilibrium conditions in competitive markets correspond to the Pareto efficiency requirements, is of prime importance to welfare economics. It is for this reason that perfect competition is called 'perfect' and why one learns so much about it; not because it represents a realistic picture of what goes on but because it represents a norm which can, perhaps, be used to measure the performance of the economy. Before we jump too hastily to this conclusion, let us go back to the assumptions which have to be met if perfect competition is to satisfy the Pareto efficiency conditions. Without the satisfaction of these assumptions, perfect competition is a necessary but not sufficient condition for allocative efficiency, that is, an optimal allocation of resources.

1.5 The assumptions underlying the optimality of perfect competition

There are three important assumptions which have to be satisfied if we are to uphold the optimal properties of perfect competition.

Increasing returns to scale

Increasing returns to scale may be present over the whole production range or over a part of it as a result of, for example, indivisibilities in equipment. Indivisible equipment means that instead of an infinite array of different types of equipment suitable for each of an infinite range of production levels there are certain minimum size items of equipment such that plant can be expanded only by finite size ranges; capital equipment becomes 'lumpy'. Once plant is installed, short run average cost falls up to capacity levels as fixed costs are spread over increasing output levels. Marginal cost will be below short run average cost until capacity is exhausted, when it will start rising steeply. The classic example of an indivisible expenditure is that of a bridge. Once built the marginal cost of an extra person using it is zero, until capacity is reached and congestion causes marginal social costs to rise steeply.

When increasing returns are present average cost will be falling, and marginal cost will be below average cost. There will be no stable profit maximizing equilibrium position within a competitive market, for the larger producers will oust the smaller, and market structure will tend towards monopoly. The presence of increasing returns to scale means therefore

i that we cannot have perfect competition; and
ii that within a market framework, price will not be equal to marginal cost.

For the optimum conditions to be satisfied it is therefore necessary that increasing returns to scale are absent.[1]

Externalities

So far in this analysis we have assumed that there is no divergence between social and private costs and benefits; that the

[1] Strictly speaking this is not an assumption *additional* to perfect competition, for, as we have seen, the presence of increasing returns to scale rules out the existence of a competitive equilibrium. The optimal conditions as stated above are all first order conditions. This means that where the production possibility curve is convex to the origin, they are consistent with a constrained minimum position. Second order conditions, which require the slope of the production possibility frontier to be increasing at the point of tangency, are therefore necessary, but even these are consistent with a local maximum where a portion of the production possibility frontier is convex. What are referred to as 'total conditions' (which include the possibility of introducing a new product or ceasing to produce an existing good) are required for a genuine optimum position. These require that for all movements, large or small, from the optimum in question no other position can be reached at which everyone is better off. See JR Hicks 'The foundations of welfare economics' *Economic Journal* 1939 p 704.

costs and benefits experienced by individual consumers and producers are the same as the costs and benefits experienced by society as a whole. Where this is so, as we have seen, the profit maximizing entrepreneur, or utility maximizing consumer, in promoting his own interests necessarily promotes the interests of the rest of the community. Unfortunately this is frequently not the case. There may be times when the decisions taken by an individual or a group affect the welfare of others, the effects of their decisions spilling-over to affect those who are 'external' to the decision taking machinery. (Hence the name externalities by which such divergences between social and private costs and benefits are frequently known.) Such spillovers arise because producers and consumers cannot act independently of each other; because there are inter-dependencies in both production and consumption. On the production side, there may be *external economies* of production which lower costs to other producers as the output of one firm expands. An example here is lower raw material costs arising from the exploitation of economies of scale in their production (eg car production requires increased output of sheet steel which is subject to substantial economies of scale; increased car output by one company may lower the production costs not only for itself but also for rivals). *External diseconomies* of production arise when production of one commodity raises costs to others, such things as the oft-quoted examples of pollution costs imposed by smoking factory chimneys, or of travel delays and pollution caused by traffic congestion. *Consumption externalities* arise when the consumption of a commodity by one person affects the welfare of others. For example, playing a transistor radio loudly may give pleasure to some people, and therefore make them better off than before, but may annoy others, and thus make them worse off. Vaccination not only prevents you from getting smallpox, but reduces the probability of others contracting the disease. Buying a new car may annoy some of your neighbours, but give pleasure to others. And so on. Examples are not hard to find, for we are surprisingly seldom completely independent of decisions taken by others. The difficulty posed by the existence of externalities is that, since we are concerned to maximize social welfare, it is important that decisions taken within the economic system are taken on the basis of social costs and benefits, and not private costs and benefits. Yet it is the private costs and benefits that in the normal working of the market mechanism confront the decision taker.

Marketability

The third assumption that is necessary if perfect competition is to meet the optimality criteria is that all goods should be market-able, which means that all goods and services should be of a kind that can be allocated through the market mechanism. There does however exist a category of good, called *public goods*, which by their nature will not be provided by the market mechanism. There are two important characteristics of public goods. One is that they are 'indivisible' in the sense that, once provided, they shower their benefits indiscriminately upon all comers, and it costs no more to provide for 1,000 than for one person. This means that unlike private goods 'more for you means no less for me'. The concomitant of this characteristic is that it is impossible to exclude from benefit those who are not willing to pay the price of it. Public goods are closely allied to externalities, for it might be said in their case that the spillover effects are total. It is perhaps easiest to give an illustration. Take street lighting. Once a street lamp is erected we cannot pick and choose who may benefit from it; anyone passing under-neath on a dark night will benefit. Moreover, we do not have to erect more lamps to light the street as it gets busier. In these circumstances, the rational, as distinct from the altruistic, individual would not be prepared to state a price that he would pay towards the erection of street lighting. If street lighting is to be erected, he will benefit from it whether he has contributed towards it or not. Why then should he be so foolish as to con-tribute? If all take this line then the market system will not of its own accord provide street lighting, for a private company would not on this basis find enough backers to make the project worth while, even though all would admit that in general street lighting was a 'good' thing and that it would add to social welfare. This is the crux of the matter. Where there is a good whose benefits cannot be reserved for those who will pay for them, the rational individual will not be willing to state his preferences and render himself liable to payment according to benefit, and the market will not therefore provide the good, even though its provision would increase social welfare. Lighthouses are often quoted as the supreme example of a public good, but defence, police, sanitation, roads, and many other public services have public good characteristics, although not all of them are 'pure' public goods in the sense that 'more for you means no less for me'.

1.6 The world of 'second best'

These three assumptions underlying the optimality conditions are important, for unless they are met neither the marginal rules of the optimality criteria nor the presumptive 'perfection' of perfect competition are valid. Moreover it is clear from our brief discussion above that the three assumptions are unlikely to be met in practice. Economies of scale and indivisibilities in plant or equipment are frequently encountered, which in turn means that production units are too large to be compatible with a competitive environment. Externalities are frequently encountered, for neither as producers nor consumers are we independent of others, and thus actions which we take are going to affect others whether we like it or not. Finally, as we indicated, there is an important category of goods, public goods, which is not marketable. Therefore the third assumption cannot be upheld.

It is sometimes suggested that the non-compliance of the economic system with these assumptions should be regarded as 'distortions' and that it might be possible to adjust the system to eliminate these 'distortions'. A complicated system of taxes and subsidies might be used to eliminate the structural effects of increasing returns to scale and to ensure that many firms could co-exist within a market framework. More frequently it is suggested that taxes and subsidies should be used to align private costs with social costs and private benefits with social benefits. Thus the factory belching smoke would be taxed according to the amount of damage caused by the smoke, the motorist taxed according to his contribution to congestion and pollution costs, and subsidies paid to rural bus services which fail to cover their costs but which provide a valuable service for the

THE ELEMENTS OF WELFARE ECONOMICS

old and the poor in rural areas. Again, it is an accepted role of government, even with a *laissez-faire* framework, to provide public goods. If these 'distortions' could be corrected in these ways then, it is argued, the market system would bring about an optimal allocation of resources in a Pareto sense. This is the essence of the case for *laissez-faire*. The government's role is restricted to correcting 'distortions' and ensuring the existence of a competitive framework (eg preventing the establishment of monopolies by 'unfair' trading practice etc); the rest is left to the market.

So simple a solution is really not possible. For example, it is doubtful whether we could ever quantify with any accuracy the myriad of taxes and subsidies which would be necessary to correct the 'distortions'. As we shall see when we discuss cost benefit analysis in chapter 7, externalities frequently involve widely dispersed effects among the population and it is not feasible to attempt to take account of them all. Even if measurement were feasible, the resultant system of taxation and subsidy might be so complicated as to be administratively impracticable. Again, where government activity which is not self-financing is envisaged, as for example in the provision of public goods or in the subsidization of enterprises which are subject to increasing returns to scale, it is never clear how such activities should be financed. The only method of taxation that does not upset the 'marginal equivalences' (ie which does not 'distort' the system itself by causing the prices of goods, services or leisure in the case of income tax, to be shifted away from their marginal social cost) is lump sum *per capita* taxation – poll taxes. These offend against the canons of social justice to a much greater extent than income or expenditure taxes offend against the canons governing the allocation of resources, and it is never seriously suggested that we should finance government activity by a system of poll taxes. Yet, unless we are prepared to contemplate them, the very means by which the government seeks to correct the 'distortions' in the economic system will itself create a further distortion.

Here lies the rub. We cannot correct for all 'distortions' within the system. There will always be some constraint that prevents their removal, administrative constraints which prevent the imposition of a highly complicated tax and subsidy system, political constraints which prevent the use of poll taxes, etc. This means that we cannot hope to operate in the 'first best' world which meets the optimality criteria, but that we inevitably operate in what is termed a *second best* world.[1] By this we mean that, if one of the optimality conditions is not fulfilled in one or more sectors of the economy, then we cannot make the best of a bad job, neglect this and blithely proceed to equate price with marginal cost in all other sectors. In these circumstances the 'optimal' conditions for the economy as a whole are altered. For example, consider the optimal price/ output position of a nationalized industry in an economy where, in all other industries, price exceeds marginal cost. As compared with the 'optimal' situation under perfect competition, those industries where price is above marginal cost will have a restricted output and thus employ fewer factors. This means that factor prices are lower than they would have been had perfect competition prevailed, which in turn means that an industry required to equate price with marginal cost would produce *more* than it would have done in the perfectly competitive situation. This does not help to correct the 'distortion', rather it over-corrects for the initial disturbance. To achieve a 'proper balance' in such circumstances does not require moving as far as this: the optimal solution requires that prices in this industry too be set above marginal cost. The above example is a simple one in which price exceeded marginal cost in all industries but one. By contrast, if some industries were competitive, some monopolistic and others subsidized, the rules would be far from simple. For each set of circumstances a different set of rules is appropriate.

The general theory of the 'second best' is thus of immense importance. No longer is there any presumption that the rules appropriate to the perfectly competitive world are the right ones for the world which we find around us. But its importance is negative, since it does not tell us what to do. Within a second best world there is no generalized set of rules which can be laid down which relate to the optimal allocation of resources. What

[1] It is unfortunate that the use of language in these circumstances reinforces the presumption of 'goodness' in the competitive equilibrium solution. We talk about it as 'perfect' competition, the non-fulfilment of the assumptions about increasing returns, externalities etc as 'distortions', and the world with which we in fact have to deal is called 'second best'.

constitutes a good or a bad allocation of resources cannot be laid down in advance, but has to be judged in the light of circumstance.

1.7 Allocative efficiency, equity and growth

Allocative efficiency and the distribution of income

Where does all this get us? The theory of the 'second best' may destroy the presumption that all we have to do is to try, as far as possible, to reproduce the conditions of perfect competition in certain sectors of the economy, but it does not destroy interest in allocative efficiency as one of the objectives of the economic system. If we can gain 'something for nothing' it is still worthwhile. We want to use techniques of production to produce as much as possible with given inputs. We want the labour force to be employed in jobs where they are producing as much as possible. Moreover we recognize that it is of no use producing goods and services which nobody wants, and so are anxious to use the resources at our disposal to produce those goods and services which people value most. These objectives remain; it is the rules of the game that change in the second best world. What is more, we have to tailor the rules to the terrain on which the game is played.

The other factor that we need to recognize is that we are very seldom in a Pareto type situation in which some gain and none lose. Most changes in the economic system involve some people being made better off while others are made worse off. For example, shifting from an average cost pricing system in a nationalized industry to a peak and off-peak tariff means that off-peak users will be 'gaining', in the sense that they will be paying less for the same consumption, but peak users will be 'losing', in that they will be being asked to pay more for the same consumption. While such a change may be considered beneficial on grounds of allocative efficiency (see chapter 6 for a discussion of pricing policies in nationalized industries), it is also necessary to consider the implications of such a change on the distribution of income. We need to consider equity side by side with efficiency.

As we saw earlier, the Pareto criterion explicitly excludes situations where some gain and some lose. Only if we can isolate distributional changes from allocational changes can the Pareto criterion, and the concept of allocative efficiency which derives from it, be of any use. For this reason, most economists do try to separate the issues – to follow the traditional dichotomy between allocation and distribution. Indeed some go further and imply that distributional considerations do not matter, for income can with ease be redistributed through the tax/benefit system in accordance with desired objectives on the distributional front, and that attention need only be focused on allocative issues. This view is much too simple and ignores some of the complications of the second best world. It is impossible to ignore the distribution of income. Allocational and distributional considerations are interdependent. Unless we really contemplate poll taxes, redistribution will have to take place through the taxation of income or expenditure, which itself alters the 'marginal equivalences' of the Pareto optimality conditions. Similarly attempts to alter the allocation of resources through monopoly policy, taxation, subsidies, etc, also affect the distribution of income. Added to this is uncertainty – uncertainty on the part of the government as to how people will react to policies it pursues, and uncertainty by people themselves as to how they will be affected. To secure a 'desired' distribution of income may require a series of adjustments as the economy moves by a process of successive approximation to the 'desired' position, adjustments which affect both allocation and distribution. But it is not always administratively feasible to make such a series of adjustments. Policies cannot be altered at will to take account of the out-turn of events. For example, social security benefits cannot be increased and then cut back again. So the government has to work by a process of approximation which may involve conflict between these objectives. On other occasions it may be felt that the most effective means of achieving distributional objectives are those which openly flout the price mechanism as the method of allocating resources, for example by providing education on health services free of charge. We shall be looking in greater detail at this conflict of objectives in chapter 8 below.

If we accept that it is not feasible to separate allocational from distributional considerations, and thus to ignore the distribution of income, then we need a method of taking account of both objectives. One method is to go back to individual welfare and to identify for each individual the gains and losses from any change. In order to be able to aggregate these individual welfares, we need to introduce some system of weights between individuals in the form of a 'social welfare function'. We discussed this briefly at the beginning of this chapter. Implicit in many policy decisions is some such system of weights, for example within the EEC the gains and losses to the farming community count heavily; at a period of unemployment gains and losses to those living in regions of particularly high unemployment are of particular importance. However, although much is written about the need to formulate an explicit social welfare function in these circumstances, few attempts have been made to derive an operational form of such a function. In most instances when the notion is employed, as for example in cost benefit analysis, a simple and straightforward form has been employed which gives equal weight to all gains and losses, implying in effect that distributional considerations do not matter. (See chapter 7.) As with so many of the grandiose notions of welfare economics, the 'social welfare function' proves in practice something of a broken reed. Yet if you reject the idea that allocation and distribution can be separated and put in different pigeon holes, it is difficult to escape from some form of social welfare function. The alternative is nihilism.

Allocative efficiency and macroeconomic objectives

At the beginning of this chapter we listed a number of objectives of economic policy, full employment, stable prices, economic growth, social justice, balance of payments equilibrium. With the exception of social justice – the distribution of income – we have so far considered none of them. Rather we have been at pains to explain and explore the microeconomic concept of efficiency and to suggest that it still has some role to play, although not the predominant role that some have ascribed to it. It might be useful, at this juncture, to give some brief indication of the link between these two sets of objectives.

In a general sense all these objectives can be thought of as being embraced within the concept of social welfare – they are all seen to promote social welfare – and where conflict arises between them they can be 'traded-off' one with another. In another sense, these macroeconomic objectives can be seen as 'special cases' arising from the microeconomic objectives. Full employment for example is a pre-requisite of allocational efficiency. Yet, as Keynes showed, in a world where prices and wages do not respond readily to market pressures (a 'second best' world where institutional forces constrain the full working of the price mechanism) an unemployment equilibrium is a real possibility, and the policies necessary to cure unemployment may conflict with allocational objectives. Another objective, price stability, is sought primarily for distributional reasons, the adverse distributional effects of inflation on fixed incomes being one of the main arguments in favour of price stability – although one ought perhaps to add that in a world of fixed exchange rates (another 'second best' constraint) the balance of payments, and with this price stability, becomes a prime objective of policy. In all these cases where conflict arises one has, within the framework of something like a social welfare function, to assess the gains and losses involved in the pursuit of one objective as compared with another.

ECONOMIC GROWTH AS A POLICY OBJECTIVE: Growth comes into a slightly different category. By growth is meant an increase in real output, stemming both from increases in inputs and from the increased productivity of inputs. Clearly, when growth means we are producing more for given inputs, it meets the Pareto criterion for an improvement in welfare, since with the fruits of growth we can make some people better off without making others worse off. Growth stems from investment – investment in physical capital (machines, buildings etc) and investment in human capital (education and training, etc). Investment means the sacrifice of present consumption for future consumption. As individuals we have a certain natural preference for present consumption over future consumption. We have a certain rate of time preference. The higher our rate of time preference, the greater the 'reward' we require for the sacrifice of present consumption, that is the higher the rate of interest we require to be paid on our savings. An optimal allocation of resources implies an optimal division of income between consumption and saving. This in turn implies an optimal rate of investment, the yield on investment at the margin being equal to the marginal rate of time preference. (This ignores problems arising from indivisibilities and externalities, which can and do arise in this field.) Implicit therefore in an optimal allocation of resources is an optimal rate of growth. Growth therefore can be seen as a dynamic extension of the static welfare conditions which we elaborated earlier. Growth in this sense means dynamic efficiency.

Yet there is a sense in which it is useful to identify growth as a separate policy objective. This is because governments have it in their power to intervene in the savings/consumption decision and to channel resources into investment and growth. Thus governments sometimes take positive views on what they consider to be an appropriate rate of growth for the economy and seek to influence the allocation of resources to that end. In this sense the pursuit of growth *per se* can conflict with both allocational efficiency and distributive goals. As regards allocative efficiency, investment may be pushed beyond the point where it yields a return equal to the social rate of time preference. In other words, society would be 'better off' with more consumption and less investment. It is interesting that when it comes to the 'inter-temporal' allocation of incomes (that is, questions of the choice between jam today or jam tomorrow), consumer sovereignty is treated in so cavalier a fashion. The explanation would seem to be that, since nobody has any real idea what rate of interest represents the social rate of time preference, it is always possible to argue that it is lower, or higher, than the level implicit in the allocation of resources between investment and consumption, and thus that society should undertake more, or less, investment than currently. See below chapter 7, p 222 for a more detailed discussion of the notion of the social rate of time preference.

Moreover, the pursuit of growth in terms of the growth of real national product may ignore the externalities of growth which seldom enter into national accounting procedures. Fumes, noise, the use of rivers and lakes as sewers, the ravaging of the countryside by opencast mining, electricity pylons and so forth are not costs which enter into the calculations of Gross National Product, yet their absence substantially improves the quality of life. To eradicate these forms of pollution requires resources. It means producing motor car engines which do not emit carbon monoxide fumes; it means producing quieter aeroplane engines, building sewage works, restricting opencast mining and putting electricity cables underground at considerable expense, etc. Resources devoted to these ends might instead be devoted to producing more goods and services. Which is the greater gain for society – a faster rate of increase in the production of material goods and services or an improvement in the quality of the environment? Do we devote resources to making good externalities, to moving closer to the production possibility frontier or shifting it outwards but remaining well within its bounds? Here is a very real conflict between objectives, and one to which there is no easy solution.

1.8 Summary and conclusions

As a framework for the rest of the book, this chapter has aimed to acquaint the reader with some of the more general ideas and jargon of welfare economics.

We began with the concept of welfare, and the difficulties in moving from a notion of individual welfare to that of social welfare. To do so requires the explicit introduction of a set of social objectives, a social welfare function, so that we may aggregate individual welfares together. But to decide what set of social objectives are appropriate is a matter of ethics, not economics. In an attempt to minimize the ethical element, economists have adopted the Pareto criterion. This is a broad ethical proposition which states that, where the gains or losses are all in one direction – some gain but none lose; or some lose but none gain – then we can claim unequivocally that there is a gain or loss to social welfare. Building upon this premise by a series of logical steps it is possible to derive a set of conditions which define optimality, in the sense that when they are met no-one can be made better off, ie gain, without someone else being made worse off, ie lose. Since the Pareto definition explicitly excludes consideration of changes which involve some gaining and some losing, changes which involve a redistribution of income, these optimality conditions exclude such situations and relate only to the allocation of resources. They relate to allocative efficiency in the sense of getting the most out of what we have, whether purely by reshuffling factors between jobs, goods between consumers or producing a different product mix. The basic rule for allocative efficiency which emerges from these optimality conditions is that, at the margin, society should equate the extra benefit it gets from the acquisition of a commodity with the extra cost of producing it.

It can be shown that these optimality conditions are satisfied in a state of perfect competition, provided however that three assumptions are met. These relate to the absence of increasing returns to scale and indivisibilities, the absence of externalities and the marketability of all goods. The nonfulfilment of these assumptions in itself requires the model to be amended for the 'distortions' they create. If such amendment cannot be made and the optimality conditions are violated, even in only one sector of the economy, then the optimality rules no longer hold as a general rule. We are plunged into a 'second best' world where the presumptive optimality of perfect competition is lost. We have to judge each case on its own merits.

Once we move away from the narrow field of circumstances which satisfy the Pareto definition and consider situations where some gain and some lose, we are back with trying to work with some kind of social welfare function. In a somewhat nebulous fashion we can look upon this as a complex function incorporating a number of objectives which, where they conflict, have to be 'traded-off' against each other. Thus the state can be seen to pursue a variety of objectives, prime amongst which are allocative efficiency, equity (the distribution of income) and growth, with full employment and stable prices as subsidiary objectives which can be embraced by the first three.

What conclusions can be drawn from all this? Welfare economics sets out to provide a theory of economic policy and we end up with no such theory. Time and again it wriggles around one logical impasse, only to run into another. The Pareto definition enables it to escape from the problem of interpersonal comparisons of welfare, and to build the edifice of the optimality criteria, only for this to be toppled by the general theory of the second best. The social welfare function presents a method of overcoming problems by balancing gains against losses but, while viable in principle, it proves something of a broken reed in practice. We are left with the necessity to judge each situation on its own merits, and to accept the arbitrariness of any standard we apply. It is not surprising that economists have fled in nihilism from welfare economics and devoted themselves to the politically neutral ground of positive economics – to studying the mechanics of the system rather than attempting to make prescriptive recommendations.

Yet even if one casts the whole creation into the waste-paper basket, the tradition of welfare economics dies hard. As a mode of analysis, economists have inherited much from it. Thus, for example, cost benefit analysis derives from first the treatment of indivisibilities, secondly the notion of a social welfare function and thirdly the measurement of externalities. The provision of the social services can be seen partly as an attempt to redistribute income in accordance with social objectives, but partly too as an attempt to overcome problems associated with externalities and the provision of public goods. Present concern with the environment and pollution is the recognition of the existence of important externalities arising from industrial development, and an attempt to make good some of the divergences that exist between private and social costs and benefits. And so forth. The examples are numerous. The economist's approach to such problems borrows implicitly both in analysis and terminology from welfare economics.

In the rest of the chapters in this book, which are a series of chapters about aspects of microeconomic management, we shall be picking up as recurring themes some of the issues that have arisen in this chapter; the distinction between allocation and distribution, the concept of allocative efficiency and the problems posed by the world of second best, the problems of indivisibilities, increasing returns to scale, externalities and public goods, and the difficulties of trying to formulate a social welfare function. We suggested at the beginning that this first chapter provides the general framework into which the later chapters in this book slot. It may be useful to conclude this chapter with some indication of how the following chapters fit into this framework.

Chapter 2 looks at the economic organization of the command economy, where resources are allocated through the planning machine rather than the market system. It explores not only the institutional organization of the economy, but also looks at what is meant by 'efficiency' within a command framework and how far it is possible to promote allocative efficiency simulating market conditions within a socialist framework.

Chapter 3 picks up the theme of planning from chapter 2 and examines the role of planning within capitalist economies. It is to some extent the odd man out amongst these chapters. Planning within capitalist economies is seen to be a macro-economic rather than a microeconomic exercise, there being no attempt to use the planning machinery to allocate resources as in the command economy. The purpose of planning is seen to be primarily one of securing stability in growth, but a distinction is made between negative and positive planning, positive planning being concerned to take a positive view on the appropriate rate of growth for the economy and to secure a switch of resources into the investment sector in line with the growth objective.

Chapter 4 is closer to the central theme. It begins with an examination of the profit maximization assumption and some of the alternative theories of business behaviour that have recently been discussed. From this it proceeds to look at how market conduct is influenced by different structural features. In this chapter we shall be looking at how important a part indivisibilities and increasing returns to scale play in the industrial structure of a capitalist economy, and at the nature of the 'second best world' in which we in practice find ourselves.

Chapter 5 returns to the theme of the second best, and looks at the evolution of policy for the control of monopolies and restrictive practices in the US and the UK. How far has policy in this field been influenced by the perfectly competitive ideal? How far has it adapted itself to the second best world?

Chapter 6 looks at the nationalized industries. Here indivisibilities are of considerable importance and appropriate pricing and investment rules in the face of these indivisibilities and the generally second best world are examined. Externalities are also an important consideration, especially for some of the industries, and we consider appropriate methods of taking account of their presence.

Chapter 7 continues on the theme of externalities and examines two methods of taking account of externalities in decision making, namely cost benefit analysis and the possibility of imposing a congestion tax on motorists.

Chapter 8 looks at the social services as a redistributive mechanism, concerned on the one hand to alleviate poverty and on the other, together with the tax system, to promote greater equality in the distribution of income. Consideration is given to how effectively they fulfil these objectives and to some of the 'allocational' issues which arise from these attempts at redistribution, and in particular whether redistribution in cash is preferable to redistribution in kind.

Further reading

AC PIGOU *The economics of welfare* Macmillan London 4th edition 1932. This is the classic text on welfare economics; reading it is an enjoyable if somewhat lengthy task.

J DE V GRAAF *Theoretical welfare economics* Cambridge University Press 1957 paperback edition 1967. A brilliant, terse treatment of modern welfare economics, whose very terseness makes it fairly difficult reading. It is really recommended only for those who wish to explore further some of the theoretical and logical complexities of the subject.

ROBERT DORFMAN *Prices and markets* Foundations of modern economics series Prentice Hall Englewood Cliffs NJ 1967. This is basically an elementary microeconomics text. Chapters 7 and 8 contain an excellent introduction to the concept of efficiency within the context of the market economy.

FM BATOE 'The simple analytics of welfare Maximization' American Economic Review March 1957. Reprinted in W Breit and HM Hochman (eds) *Readings in micro-economics* Holt, Rinehart and Winston New York 1968. A more advanced treatment of the analytical aspects of welfare economics.

EJ MISHAN 'A survey of welfare economics 1939–59' *Economic Journal* 1960. Reprinted in *Survey of economic theory* American Economic Association and Royal Economic Society Macmillan

London 1965. A comprehensive treatment of the development of modern welfare economics.

DM WINCH *Analytical welfare economics* Penguin Modern Economics Texts Penguin Books Harmondsworth 1971. A very good introductory text to welfare economics.

2

Resource allocation in the command economy

2.1 Introduction

The concept of welfare which we elaborated in the previous chapter is an individualistic one, derived from the utilitarian philosophy in which the state is the totality of individuals who compose it and its role that of promoting the greatest happiness or welfare of its members. This utilitarian philosophy can be contrasted directly with philosophies which regard the state not as a collection of individuals but as possessing a rationale in itself. The economic system adopted by the state reflects the underlying political philosophy. In those countries where the state is seen as possessing a 'spirit' of its own, it is the state, not the individual consumer, who is sovereign. Fascism for example sees the role of the state as one of self-enrichment to enable it to wage war against other states for the greater glory of the state itself, the interests of individual citizens being subjugated to this end. Similarly, the aim of the mercantilist state was the accumulation of wealth for the glory of the state.

The most publicized alternative to utilitarian democracy is that of the Marxist-Leninist system of communism. Here also the state is seen as an end in itself rather than as a means to an end, although it nominally serves the 'real' interests of individuals and is predicted ultimately to wither away. This difference in the view of the role of the state creates difficulties when we try to compare the economic system which has evolved in the communist world with our own economic system. For

34

example, we judge efficiency on the basis of consumer sove-reignty; we are making 'efficient' use of our resources when, subject to technical production constraints, we organize produc-tion to go as far as possible to meet consumer preferences. But this concept of efficiency is not appropriate in a world in which it is the state and not the consumer who is sovereign. Efficiency then can be judged only in the light of the objectives of the state: we cannot transpose the standards we use to judge the perfor-mance of our own economic system to other systems. For this reason this chapter concentrates upon the organization of the communist economic system, and does not seek directly to make comparisons between the two systems.

Market socialism   **1817368**

The economies of communist countries are often called 'socialist' economies. It is misleading to contrast socialism with the market system, since the distinctive feature of socialist economic systems is the common or state ownership of the means of produc-tion and distribution as distinct from the private ownership of these assets in the capitalist system. Socialism is about the ownership of wealth and the distribution of income, a theme that has been common to many socialist groups in western democracies from the Guild Socialists to the Fabians. The type of economic organization adopted is a different matter entirely. Indeed socialism is compatible with a market or a non-market system.

In the 1930s certain economists turned to socialism as a means not only of achieving equality in the distribution of income but also of achieving a better allocation of resources. They argued that there were certain inbuilt constraints within the capitalist system which would prevent the achievement of an optimal allocation of resources and in addition that the capitalist system was basically unstable. If the state, rather than its constituent members, made the consumption/investment decision, then such instability could be avoided and a more optimal growth path achieved.

The type of economic system proposed by these economists, of whom perhaps the best known is Lerner,[1] is known as market

[1] A P Lerner *The economics of control* Macmillan New York 1947.

35

socialism. The market system was to be retained both as a means of transmitting consumer preferences and of allocating resources. They argued that not only was the utilitarian based welfare analysis applicable to the socialist state but that the optimal resource allocation conditions were more likely to be achieved in such a society, since it would be open to the state to remove some of the obstacles to their fulfilment that are found within the capitalist system. The markets for goods and services were to be entirely free allowing prices to fluctuate according to supply and demand, and the managers of the firms owned by the state were to be instructed to maximize profits. Given small independent units competing with each other in this way, perfect competition could be simulated and the optimality conditions met. One member of this group of economists was Lange.[1] His ideas were more centralist than Lerner's, and he emphasized the difficulties involved in achieving a free market in investment goods, given that all firms were owned by the state. He argued however that accounting prices which simulated free market prices could be achieved by trial and error and, given these, the managers of enterprises need only be instructed to minimize costs and to equate price with marginal cost. If, because of the existence of increasing returns to scale, this resulted in losses (since when there are increasing returns to scale, marginal cost is below average cost and the enterprise cannot cover total costs if price is set equal to marginal cost) then the enterprise should receive a subsidy from the state. As we shall see in chapter 6, these ideas have had a substantial influence on thinking relating to nationalized industries.

Another important aspect of the ideas of both Lerner and Lange was that responsibility rested on the state to maintain a high level of employment. In so far as the level of investment generated through the socialist 'market system' was insufficient to do this, the state was to generate further investment expenditure: investment decisions were to be guided not just by consumers' wishes expressed through the market but also by the central planning authority, whose job it was to ensure macroeconomic balance within the economy. With this 'Keynesian'

[1] See O Lange *On the economic theory of socialism* in B E Lippincott (ed) *On the economic theory of socialism* University of Minnesota Press Minneapolis 1938.

exception, which is now commonly accepted as a part of the role of the state even in capitalist countries, the advocates of market socialism put emphasis upon the achievement of an efficient allocation of resources – efficient in the sense of using the economic system to go as far as possible towards meeting consumer preferences. Consumer sovereignty and the concept of efficiency based upon consumer sovereignty is as important, or even more important, to market socialism as to a capitalist market system.[1]

Market socialism therefore is the extension of individualism to a socialist framework. It is a far cry from the practice of most communist countries today. But its interest extends beyond the bounds of an academic exercise and, as we shall see, some communist countries including the USSR are moving in directions influenced by market socialism.

Administrative socialism

If one puts market socialism at one extreme, at the other extreme comes what one might call a 'pure administrative system'. The pure administrative system implies the physical rationing of goods and services, both to consumers and to producers, and the allocation of resources through the rationing system. In a world in which consumer preferences were known and stated, and where all this information was processed on giant computers alongside information about available resources and techniques, it might be possible to contrive a rationing system which achieved *de facto* consumer sovereignty. Although we now have computers of a size to cope with it, such a process is really inconceivable since consumers clearly are not in a position to supply an elaborate ranking of their preferences. It is worth noting in passing that an administrative system,

[1] The writings of Lange and Lerner can be regarded also as an elaborate exercise to rebut other economists writing in the 1930s, economists of the school of Von Mises, Hayek and Robbins, who were arguing at that time that because there was no free market in investment goods socialism was incapable of achieving an efficient allocation of resources. There is of course no such obstacle to a free market, as current experience in China demonstrates, and it is now generally acknowledged that within a socialist framework it is not inherently impossible to simulate the conditions of perfect competition, and thus to meet the optimality conditions. It cannot therefore be claimed that perfect competition within capitalism is the only way in which the Pareto optimality criteria can be satisfied.

whether or not it achieves consumer sovereignty, is splendidly amenable to securing other objectives, for example, strategic objectives in time of war.

Within this spectrum, ranging from market socialism to the pure administrative system, lies the type of economic system found in practice in communist countries. The archetypal system is that established in the Soviet Union in the 1950s, a system which was adopted also by most European communist countries. Inevitably it has been amended and reformed, and different countries have moved along different paths. Within the Soviet Union however its essential structure has not been changed radically. The bulk of this chapter is therefore devoted to examining the organization of the Soviet economy. At the end of the chapter we shall look briefly at the variant upon the Soviet system that has developed in Hungary and at the very different system developed in Yugoslavia.

2.2 The Soviet economic system

In the USSR the system adopted has been neither that of pure administrative socialism nor of pure market socialism, although there have been periods when conditions have come near to both these extremes. The 1939–45 war period saw an economy in the USSR which came close to being a pure administrative economy, with the almost total rationing of all goods and services to both producers and consumers. By contrast the period 1921–8, the period of Lenin's New Economic Policy, was a period when the market played a substantial part in the allocation of resources within the economy. Generally, the economic system has fallen half-way between these two extremes. Consumers have been given freedom of choice, in so far as there has been relatively little rationing of consumer goods, but decisions as to the balance of production between consumption and investment and the allocation of raw materials and producer goods, have been administrative, that is, made by central planners with scant regard paid to consumer wishes as expressed in the market for consumer goods.

The prices of consumer goods have been 'free market prices' to the extent that they are based on estimates of demand in relation to supply and aim to clear the market. If a good does not sell, the price is dropped until the market is cleared. But once fixed prices are seldom raised when there is excess demand and thus queues form. Resources for the production of consumption goods have been severely restricted and demand has tended to exceed supply. Thus prices for consumer' goods have in general tended to exceed production costs by a substantial but variable margin, the surplus, euphemistically known as 'turnover tax', going to the state and used to finance investment in heavy industry. The price received by the production unit, the enterprise, is based upon production costs and does not reflect this variable turnover tax element. It does not vary therefore according to supply and demand conditions: there is no market feedback to the enterprise, only to the administration. Thus, although there has been consumer 'freedom of choice', in so far as consumers have been free to spend their earnings as they will on the consumer goods provided, there has not been consumer sovereignty, for what is produced has not been directly influenced by consumers nor have investment decisions been guided by what is selling well in consumer markets. Again the labour market also has an element of freedom. Wages are fixed centrally, but workers, with the exception of agricultural workers, have been free except in periods of war socialism to take any job that they please. This means that actual earnings have tended to vary somewhat from job to job and from area to area.

However, in spite of this freedom of choice, the basic allocation of resources is administrative. Decisions as to how much of which type of good shall be produced, where and with what factors of production are taken centrally. These decisions are incorporated into plans, and the planning machinery of the USSR has become the real mechanism through which resources are allocated. It is worth while looking a little more closely at this planning machinery.

The planning machinery

There are two important types of plan in the USSR, the medium term plan, usually spanning five years, and the short term plan, which relates only to one year ahead.

The medium term plan embodies the major objectives of the

politicians and planners. The first five year plan was launched by Stalin in 1928 as a part of his drive to replace the market economy of the New Economic Policy era with a highly centralized command economy. Since 1928 the Soviet Union has been guided by nine successive five year plans.[1] The five year plan establishes a target rate of growth and examines the implications of this on available resources and the division of these resources between the major macroeconomic sectors, namely investment, defence, public consumption and private consumption. The core of this plan is the investment plan. This determines the future output of the different sectors. Details are also given of many of the larger construction projects, such as dams or power stations.

Traditionally, in the five year plans, priority has been given to defence and the investment goods sector, and consumption has come a very poor third behind these two.[2] Recently there has been some sign of change. Inflationary pressures and production difficulties during the 1965–70 plan period meant that in the event, contrary to plan, the rate of growth of consumer good production began to exceed the rate of growth of the investment good sector, and in the five year plan for 1971–5, for the first time ever, the planned rate of growth of production of consumption goods marginally exceeds the target for the rate of growth of investment goods (44–48 per cent for consumption goods, compared with 41–5 per cent for investment goods).[3]

The five year plans are above all a set of policy objectives. They have no legal force: nor do they relate to individual

[1] The plan for the years 1959–65 was in fact a seven year plan. The ninth plan, covering the years 1971–75, was published belatedly early in 1971.

[2] See section 2.3 below on 'Objectives and efficiency in the Soviet economic system'.

[3] See article by V Zorza *Guardian* 19.2.71. These figures provide the basis for the claim that the new plan will give a new deal for the consumer in the Soviet Union. Zorza comments 'But this is the propaganda message that has accompanied every five year plan in the past. The results have been less impressive. Since the death of Stalin, every five year plan has been a compromise between the demands of heavy industry and the military lobbies on the one hand and the consumer goods lobby on the other. If the military lobby was unable to get its way in drafting the plan, it usually succeeded in changing the figures more to its own satisfaction while the plan was in operation. That is why the target figures for output of various commodities given in the new document are far from conclusive.' This warning proved apposite. The consumption targets have been abandoned: not, however, to military priorities, but in the wake of the poor harvests of 1971–2.

enterprises. By contrast, the one year plans are plans drawn up ultimately for each individual enterprise and constitute a legally binding set of directives to the individual enterprise. The one year plans are the real method of allocating resources within the Soviet Union. These plans, based on the general objectives written into the five year plans, are drawn up by Gosplan USSR, the central planning authority, which is a vast organization with divisions at the national, provincial and district level. Side by side with Gosplan are other hierarchies. On the one hand are various other state commissions, which co-ordinate such things as materials allocation, construction and research and development, of which the most important is Gosnab responsible for physical allocation of those materials and equipment subject to central allocation, and a substantial proportion of such commodities are centrally allocated. Clearly, there has to be co-ordination between these various commissions to make sure that planned material inputs, new buildings, etc, will be available for enterprises, or, in the event of non-availability, that plans are adjusted accordingly.

In addition to these state commissions, there is the 'executive' hierarchy of ministries which are responsible for the running of the enterprises; for making sure the plan proposals are implemented, for the appointment of managers to the enterprises, for the collection of data from the enterprises, and so on. This executive hierarchy has in general been organized on the basis of industrial sectors with a central ministry for each sector which, like Gosplan, also has its regional divisions, co-ordinating the activities of an industry or a group of industries and ultimately the individual firms.

The whole organization of production and distribution is therefore a huge bureaucratic machine consisting of overlapping pyramids of responsibility. There is remarkably little horizontal contact between the echelons of the various pyramids. For example, requests for an alteration in a raw material allocation emanating from the firm itself, will be passed up through the ranks of the ministry concerned, over to Gosnab where it will be passed down through the hierarchy to the official concerned with material allocation for the enterprise, who will then pass the reply back up through Gosnab and it will be received by the firm after having been passed back down the ministry hierarchy. A similar process will then have to be repeated with Gosplan to change plan commitments, in the light of raw material allocations. It is no wonder that on the unofficial payroll of each enterprise there exists a class of person known as a 'pusher' whose job it is to oil these bureaucratic wheels and where possible to keep them turning sweetly in the interests of the enterprise for which he works.

It is Gosplan's task to translate the objectives of the five year plans into detailed sectoral plans, which are then used by the ministries as the basis of plans for individual enterprise. The five year plans are often drawn up in physical terms – a target output of so many tons etc – and it is for Gosplan to co-ordinate the plans for the different sectors; to integrate output, supplies, deliveries, etc within and between sectors.

As regards the enterprise, it is one of Gosplan's tasks to ensure that the plans drawn up are internally consistent, that is that raw materials and intermediate goods will be available to meet production targets. This requires co-ordination with the materials commission Gosnab, but such co-ordination can go awry and frequently enterprises are not able to get resources which they have been allocated in the plan, or are allocated insufficient resources to meet commitments. This provides yet another role for the 'pusher', who will negotiate direct with enterprises producing the raw materials or machinery etc, and ensure that supplies are despatched to his parent enterprise, sometimes in its own trucks. Where the pusher is not successful the result can be idle capacity and a failure to meet output targets, which in turn may mean that an enterprise further along the line is unable to obtain the supplies it has been allocated and so on. Production bottlenecks are a major problem in communist countries.

The enterprise

The production unit in the Soviet Union is, misleadingly enough, called the enterprise or firm.[1] It is usually a single plant, although in recent years there has been some tendency to encourage some amalgamation of management of establish-

[1] Misleadingly, because it is not strictly analogous with its capitalist counterpart.

ments producing the same products. In charge of the enterprise is a manager who is traditionally given very little freedom of manoeuvre. The plan fixes his output, inputs, raw materials needed, numbers employed and total wages bill; the prices of inputs and the prices of outputs are also fixed. Given planned output (usually expressed in terms of gross value of output; since the prices paid to the firm are also fixed, this amounts to a target in terms of physical output) planned profits, or on some occasions planned losses, are also fixed. Bonuses are paid to management and workers when planned output is exceeded, and there is therefore an incentive to produce as much as possible, more or less irrespective of production cost, quality or sales potential. All production goes to the state at prices based upon input costs plus a 'profit' margin. The government in effect acts as wholesaler, distributing output from enterprise to retail outlets, or in the case of producers' goods to other firms. It buys at a fixed price from the producer and sells at a fixed price to retail outlets. If it has to drop the price in order to sell the good, it is the government not the firm who stands any loss. Similarly, where there is excess demand and retail price is high in relation to costs, the effect is 'cushioned' by the variable turnover tax, and the excess profits do not go back to the enterprise. There is therefore, no incentive to the firm to tailor goods to consumers' taste – whether to produce more of a good, or a better quality product – for the enterprise does not confront the consumer directly, and does not know how well or badly, the product sells.

Isolating the producer from his market in this way and providing incentives to produce as much as possible in physical terms has led to some odd situations. The chandelier plan was expressed in tons, so all chandeliers were unnecessarily heavy. There has been a constant shortage of children's clothing since clothing manufacturers found it easier to fulfil their plan target, expressed in terms of roubles, that is gross value of output, by producing the larger and therefore more expensive sizes. Restaurants show a preference for producing expensive dishes because their targets are expressed in terms of gross turnover. Nail manufacturers produce heavy nails when their target is expressed in terms of weight, and small nails when it is expressed in terms of quantity. There are numerous examples which are quoted not only by Western observers of the Soviet economy[1] but also by the Soviet people themselves, and constant changes are made in the 'success indicators' in order to try to produce a more rational result. For example, enterprises who produce an array of sizes of a commodity, and whose plan target is expressed in terms of gross value of output, find themselves also with an 'assortment' target, so many of each particular size. Experiments have been made in using 'value added' rather than gross value of output as the plan target, but this led to unnecessarily expensive processing, and so has been changed to a type of piece-work system where there is a 'normal' value of output for each process. The incentive is to get below the 'norm', but this in turn has distorted the product mix by efforts to produce items for which the maximum 'normed' value can be achieved for least cost. Each alternative presents its own problems. The result is that, in spite of much criticism and discussion within the Soviet Union, the 'gross output' indicator remains the predominant plan indicator.

The system also has an inbuilt resistance to innovation because the enterprise seeks to avoid anything which destroys established norms and routine, for if something goes wrong and they do not fulfil their plan targets it is the managers and the workers who suffer. Thus innovation tends to be imposed from above by the planners, who insist that the enterprise moves over to new techniques. There is little pressure for innovation coming from the enterprise itself.

Nove has neatly summed up the relationship between the manager, the enterprise and the plan, 'The problem is one of reconciling a system designed to secure obedience with instructions with what might be called 'micro-rational' behaviour on the part of the enterprises within the area of their (ie the managers') responsibility.'[2] The plan is essentially a set of instructions to the enterprise; although to our way of thinking it leaves very little freedom of manoeuvre to the managers, it frequently does as we have seen leave room for manoeuvre on easier and more difficult ways of fulfilling the plan targets.

---

[1] See A Nove *The Soviet Economy* George Allen and Unwin London chapter 6 1968 3rd edition.

[2] A Nove *op cit* 2nd edition 1965, p. 171. This sentence does not appear in the 3rd edition.

Since reward is given for plan fulfilment, the incentive is to fulfil the target in the easiest way possible.

The reforms of 1965

In 1965 fairly radical reforms were introduced giving enterprise managers in consumer goods industries considerably more initiative, and to some extent decentralizing decision-taking within the system. Targets continued to be expressed in terms of gross value of output, but the price paid to the producer was varied according to the ease with which the goods were sold, and in some cases producers were put into direct contact with retailers. This gave enterprises some feedback from the market which had previously been lacking. Managers were also given more initiative on investment decisions and for the first time an interest charge was made on investment funds tied up in the enterprise, giving an incentive to the enterprise to economize in the use of capital, for making capital a 'free' good encouraged the use of capital intensive methods of production, even though labour was in many instances in relatively abundant supply and capital was scarce.

These reforms were a move in the direction of 'Libermanism', so called after the Soviet economist Liberman who at that time advocated the more extensive use of profit as a success indicator within the economic system, and freer contact between producers and consumers.[1] It amounted to the introduction of an element of the market mechanism in the allocation of resources; a move away from administrative allocation through the plan and towards market socialism. But so far the moves have been minimal; many of the initial experiments introduced in 1965 were abandoned fairly rapidly, and the inflationary pressures that built up in the period 1965–70 in the Soviet economy were blamed by conservatives in the regime on these managerial reforms which they claim has kindled wage inflation. At their best however reforms can be regarded only as an attempt at a rather superficial patching up of a system that was obviously not working perfectly. It is worth remembering that since

[1] Translations of some of Liberman's articles at this time are to be found in *Problems of economics* Vol VIII 1965 Nos 2, 3, 4. Although a considerable influence over the development of one school of Soviet economic thought at this time, Liberman has subsequently recanted his 'liberalism'.

1958 more attention had been given in the USSR to the production of consumer goods, and that by the mid 1960s the worst shortages of the post-war period were over. Moreover the Russians were also beginning, if only through the medium of television, to have much more contact with the outside world. All this meant that as consumers they were becoming choosy and were no longer always prepared to buy goods of inferior quality, even at low prices. This increasing consumer discrimination manifested itself by the mid-1960s in the form of accumulating stocks of goods which could not be disposed of. The system was not working perfectly and the reforms of 1965 were an attempt, and not a very successful one, to patch it up.

Prices

It would be difficult to go much further in implementing Liberman's ideas and introducing a greater element of the market mechanism without a more rational price structure. Following Marx, prices in the Soviet Union have traditionally been based upon labour costs, Marx's (v), plus a surplus (m) or profit, which goes to the state. The price received by the enterprise for its product, the factory wholesale price, is based upon the average costs of production of all enterprises producing that commodity plus a profit margin, a part of which is usually retained by the enterprise, the retained element being greater when planned production targets are exceeded. Costs here exclude any charges on basic capital or rent payments, the main element being labour costs and material costs, the latter in turn being based upon labour costs at earlier stages of production, so that ultimately all costs are derived from labour costs. The profit margin varies immensely from industry to industry. Given the policy that the prices of basic raw materials should be low, profit margins in these industries have tended to be low, even negative. (Granted the inevitable variation in production costs between enterprises, the use of *average* cost pricing often means, when the profit margin is low, that enterprises whose costs are higher than average make a planned loss.) Profit margins have tended to be highest in the food and consumer goods industries.

Retail prices, as we have seen, are fixed at a level which

clears the market, except where there is some social reason for goods to be priced highly (eg vodka) or cheaply (eg children's clothing). There is however, both at the wholesale and the retail level, a great reluctance to change prices (perhaps because it requires action by the full bureaucratic machine), which has led to a tendency to underprice goods and to accept queues and waiting lists as a normal phenomenon. The difference between the wholesale price plus the distribution costs and the retail price charged is the turnover tax. This too varies a great deal from good to good, both reflecting conscious policy and demand and supply conditions. The low priority accorded to investment in consumer goods means that turnover tax is high on items such as textiles and clothing. By contrast, in spite of considerable shortages, consumer durables, particularly cars and television sets, were deliberately underpriced in the 1950s. This variation in the incidence of turnover tax means that, in relation to costs of production, some retail prices are much higher than others, but since turnover tax 'mops up' the surplus, the producer is insulated from the consumer and price variation does not perform its 'market' function of transmitting changes in consumer tastes and preferences to manufacturers.

Now if the market is to be used to allocate resources 'efficiently', in the sense of getting as much as possible out of what we have, then, as we have seen in the last chapter, the prices charged for goods and services should reflect opportunity or resource cost. This means, *inter alia*, regarding capital not as a free good but as a scarce resource, whose price will depend upon its scarcity. It is of little use decentralizing the decision making process in certain sectors unless the price which the managers use as guide lines for their decisions reflect resource costs. For example it is useless giving consumer-good producers greater initiative over investment, if the price they pay for investment goods is likely to lead to an even more inefficient decision than Gosplan's. There is a certain element of all or nothing about this. It is no good trying to patch up the Marxist system with bits from the rag-bag of capitalism, for it may well lead to an even worse mess. It is perhaps for this reason that the reforms introduced in 1965 have generally fizzled out, the system shifting fairly rapidly back to its traditional path.

The agricultural sector in the Soviet economy

There is one sector of the Soviet economy which is to some extent isolated from the full rigours of the command economy. This is agriculture where, although some 35 per cent of total production comes from large state farms, analogous to the state enterprises of the manufacturing sector, the majority of farms are organized on a co-operative basis in collective farms. Although most of the output of these collectives is subject to direct command, each farm having output quotas for the different products which have to be delivered to the state, in other respects the planning authorities do not maintain very tight control over the farms, and the chairman of the collective and his colleagues have more initiative over financial matters etc than the managers of the state enterprises. Moreover any surplus produced over and above the quotas that have to be delivered to the state may be sold by the collective farms in the 'free' markets which are found in most towns and where the prices fetched are usually higher than those paid by the state. This provides an important extra source of revenue to the collective farms.

Each household in the collective farm is entitled to a small private plot. At times this too has been subject to compulsory deliveries, partly to prevent it from becoming too profitable and thus occupying too much of the peasants' time. The peasant reckons to feed his family largely from his own small holding, but again any surplus may be sold on the free market, which has led to a good deal of very intensive farming of these small holdings. In all, these private holdings contribute today some 34 per cent of global output in the agricultural sector in the Soviet Union. Since global output includes bought-in current industrial inputs, which are much greater in the state and collective sectors, the contribution to the net output of the private sector may be as much as 40 per cent[1] – a surprisingly high proportion.

Hence in the agricultural sector the 'command' economy is limited and direct contact between consumer and producer a more common feature. At times, particularly for livestock and

[1] P J D Wiles, unpublished work.

dairy produce, the private sector has been of very considerable importance (in 1950 for example 75 per cent of milk produced and 89 per cent of eggs came from private production), but its contribution has diminished somewhat in recent years, largely as a result of deliberate reforms introduced by Kruschev and aimed at limiting the amount of time and effort devoted by the peasants to their private holdings. Although these reforms, which were badly mishandled, have been rescinded by Kruschev's successors, the private sector has not regained its previous position.

2.3 Objectives and efficiency in the Soviet economic system

The difficulty that confronts a western economist in trying to judge the performance of the Soviet economy is that it is based not upon consumer sovereignty – the idea of trying to meet consumer wishes as nearly as possible – but upon planners' sovereignty, and unless one knows what the planners are seeking to achieve it is impossible to tell whether they have organized the economy effectively to achieve this end. Our concept of efficiency in the economy is inextricably tied up with the fundamental philosophy which underlies our system. Hence it is no good pointing out that the Soviet system produces only red lampshades, whereas consumers would like to have other sorts of lampshades, and regarding this as a mark of inefficiency in the system, for the system is not fundamentally concerned with doing what consumers want. It is necessary to transpose our standards of judgement and seek to assess how far the Soviet economy has been successful in achieving what its planners have sought to achieve.

What objectives then have Soviet planners sought to achieve? A formal expression of these objectives comes in the five year plans and from these it is possible to identify the major goals of the planners; a fast rate of growth, a rapid increase in military power including nuclear weapons and space research, universal education with emphasis on widespread training in technical and scientific skills and the achievement of self-sufficiency within the communist trading bloc, Comecon. Foremost amongst these objectives has been that of a fast rate of economic growth. Here the ultimate goal may be that of full communism, the society of abundance, but the most immediate goal has been to equal and surpass the United States in terms of *per capita* production and consumption.

In line with this objective of a rapid rate of growth has been the emphasis on investment and the low priority given to the rate of growth of private consumption, (although as we noted above when discussing the five year plans, the most recent plan has put more emphasis on the rate of growth of private consumption; moreover ultimately investment yields its fruits in terms of goods and services – it is consumption postponed rather than consumption forgone). The rate of investment in the Soviet Union has varied between 25 and 30 per cent of GNP, a rate equalled among capitalist countries only by Japan and to be compared with a rate of between 20 and 25 per cent of GNP in the US and continental Western Europe. Within the investment goods sector, considerable emphasis has been given to heavy industry, the steel, chemical, electricity, oil and engineering industries, rather than to the consumer goods industries or for that matter agriculture. As a result the growth rate in the Soviet Union has been fast, during the 1950s it averaged about 7 per cent per annum,[1] and although it slowed down in the 1960s to between 5 and 6 per cent per annum this is still a fast rate of growth by any standard. But it has been unbalanced growth, with the heavy goods sector leading the consumer goods sector. Hence the juxtaposition in the Soviet Union of an extremely advanced and sophisticated technology, which produces the space spectaculars, with primitive production methods in other sectors, notably agriculture.

This unbalanced growth has been deliberate policy. Soviet industrialization should be seen not as a smooth continuous process, but as a discontinuous series of leaps forward. The process is a highly political one involving what Nove calls the Soviet habit of 'campaignology'. The five year plans should be seen as a series of forward leaps, each involving a campaign to break some particular bottleneck. But the very process of breaking bottlenecks, creates new ones, like improving stretch after stretch of a trunk road, and the next plan involves a campaign to break these, and so on. Nove sees in this 'campaign-

[1] A Bergson *The economics of Soviet planning* Yale University Press New Haven 1964.

ology' a method of stimulating growth in an economy where 'there is no built-in growth-inducing force where the intervention of authority, and the targets set by authority, must act as a substitute for the automatic functioning of the profit motive'.[1] Such a strategy for growth has necessarily to reject ideas of 'optimization' in a narrow economic sense or any attempt to achieve a balanced advance on all fronts. Rather the economy is deliberately lunged from point to point in an attempt to break the bottlenecks, the 'interlocking vicious circles' which prevent movement forward.[2]

All this puts a new dimension on the meaning of efficiency. Where development is stimulated by government action which deliberately eschews the market mechanism, the marginalism of traditional welfare economics has no part to play. What to our eyes might seem obvious inefficiencies, for example the comparative neglect of the agricultural sector in the Soviet Union, may become logical in the light of the aims pursued.

Efficiency and consistency

Nevertheless, whatever disclaimers we may make about our ability to judge the system, the Soviet economy is not, on its own admission, without problems. There are two major issues with which the planners have been grappling. One is that of how to pursue their objectives at least cost in terms of human and material resources. At the microeconomic level this problem exhibits itself in the difficulties experienced in the choice of 'success indicators' within the enterprise, and in trying to get enterprises to adopt new techniques of production. At the macroeconomic level, it can be seen in the clear waste of resources that has occurred on some of the prestige projects, and in over-ambitious sectoral plans. This is the problem of securing efficiency in the narrow, production efficiency sense. How do you get the most out of resources that are available?

[1] A Nove *op cit* p 305.
[2] This phrase comes from A D Hirschman, the French economist who belongs to the so-called 'unbalanced growth' school and advocates a strategy for economic development based on deliberately creating tensions within the economy, which act as a stimuli for change. A D Hirschman *The strategy of economic development* Yale University Press New Haven 1958.

If such wastage had not occurred, a similar rate of growth could have been achieved with far less cost in human and economic terms.

The other major problem with which the planners grapple is that of securing consistency in planning, the problem of striking 'material balances' so that demand and supply for inputs and outputs match each other both between and within sectors; for example, so that the planned production of steel is not held up by lack of supplies of coal or iron ore; so that the production of machines is not held up by a shortage of components. The planning authorities attempt to secure consistency in their plans by drawing up what amounts to a second plan of 'material balances' side by side with the target output plans. This is a process which proceeds in various time dimensions. For the five year plans, output targets need to be adjusted and modified in the light of policy decisions and inconsistencies thrown up in the planning process, so that the final plan presents a co-ordinated and consistent programme of development. Within this framework, the investment plan ensures (on paper) that capacity necessary for the achievement of planned output is available when required. Similarly it ensures that the iron, steel, machinery, etc necessary for the creation of this capacity is also available. In the shorter term, the problem of consistency is that of allocating available supplies. We discussed earlier the supply allocation system through Gosnab (see p 41) and some of the problems and difficulties that develop on this front. Some of these reflect errors made in striking material balances at earlier planning stages, some the sheer complexity of the organization required for the physical allocation process. The bottlenecks and ensuing idle capacity which emerge make it clear that the Soviet planners have by no means overcome the problems of consistency, in either time dimension.

These problems of securing efficiency and consistency arise because the command economy relies upon bureaucracy to process the flows of information and to adjust plans and targets accordingly. Bottlenecks and inconsistencies arise within capitalist economies, but these matter less for such inconsistencies tend automatically to provoke remedial action from within the system. Where bottlenecks arise, prices and profits rise and capacity is expanded either by existing firms or by new entrants. If the market mechanism is working reasonably well, the feedback is automatic and does not depend upon the processing of bureaucracy. Viewed purely as a cybernetic system, concerned with processing information flows, the price mechanism offers some clear advantages.[1]

The use of input-output analysis and linear programming

There are two techniques which have been developed which can go some way to helping Soviet planners overcome these problems of efficiency and consistency. These tools are input-output analysis and linear programming. Both have been taken up and developed in the Soviet Union by a school of very able mathematical economists who, somewhat in opposition to Liberman, look to securing a better allocation of resources, not through the market, but through mathematical simulation of the market mechanism with computers, and the allocation of resources in accordance with the results of this exercise through administrative machinery. They are however essentially mathematical techniques as applicable to other economies as to the Soviet economy. Let us look in somewhat more detail at the main characteristics of these two techniques.[2]

INPUT–OUTPUT ANALYSIS: The central idea behind input–output analysis is that much of the production of a modern economy is in the form of intermediate goods, and in turn the output of these intermediate goods is substantially determined by the demand for final products. A change in the output of some final product, say cars, implies changes in the outputs of intermediate goods, steel, glass, rubber, etc, used in the manufacture of the final product. Input–output analysis is essentially

[1] We shall be exploring in chapters 4 and 5 some of the factors which limit the efficiency of the market mechanism in this respect.

[2] It is not intended to present here more than a very brief description of these techniques. Readers who would like to know more of them may like to refer to the following for an elementary introduction to the concepts, G L Shackle *Economics for pleasure* 2nd edition chapter 9 Cambridge University Press Cambridge 1968. For more detailed coverage W J Baumol *Economic theory and operations research* Prentice Hall Englewood Cliff New Jersey 3rd edition 1971 (chapters 4 and 5) and R Dorfman, P Samuelson & R Solow *Linear programming and economic analysis* McGraw Hill New York 1958.

a study of the patterns of inter-industry and inter-sector dependence.

Its characteristics are probably best understood by means of a simple example. Let us assume that the economy consists of only two sectors, an agricultural sector and a manufacturing sector. Then it is possible to illustrate their activities in the following way

	column 1 agriculture	column 2 manufactur-ing	column 3 final demand	column 4 total output
output input				
row 1 agriculture	50	350	100	500
row 2 manufacturing	80	40	120	240
row 3 labour	20	80	0	100

Row 1 represents the agricultural sector. Total output is 500 units, of which 100 go direct to the consumer, eg vegetables and fruit, 350 units go to be manufactured, eg wheat to be made into flour and bread etc, wool for cloth, and 50 units goes into agriculture itself, fodder and seed etc. Row 2 represents the manufacturing sector. Total output is 240 units, of which 120 goes to the consumer (bread, cloth etc) 80 to agriculture (agricultural machinery, fertilizers etc) and 40 units to manufacturing itself (machinery). Row 3 represents the labour inputs into each sector necessary to produce the outputs. Of a total of 100 units, 20 to go to agriculture and 80 to manufacturing.

Now let us suppose that we wish to double total output of agricultural goods. In order to produce 500 units of agricultural output, it has required (column 1) an input of 50 units of agricultural output, 80 units of manufacturing output and 20 units of labour. If we assume that these proportions are fixed, doubling output to 1000 units of agricultural output will require a total input of 100 units agricultural output, 160 units manufacturing output, and 40 units of labour. Alternatively, we could say that each unit of agricultural output requires an input of 1/10 (50/500) units of agricultural output, 4/25 (80/500) units of manufacturing output and 1/25 (20/500) units of labour. These represent the input proportions displayed by the above table, and we can use them to calculate inputs needed for different output levels if we think they are likely to remain constant – which we are doing when we assume that we can double output by doubling inputs. However, any increase in agricultural output is going to increase the demand for manufactured goods. Unless this increase is to be met by lessening final demand, this in turn will mean an increase in demand for agricultural goods, and so on. We would have to dodge from sector to sector making adjustments first to one and then to the other, gradually getting closer to consistency between two sectors.

A much simpler way than this trial and error method, which becomes extremely complicated if more than two sectors are introduced into the analysis, is to make use of these fixed proportion figures, input–output coefficients, and form the complex of these inter-sectoral relations into a matrix, a set of linear equations, consisting of these coefficients. Then, with the help of matrix algebra and computers, we can 'solve' the matrix to conform either with a target of total output or a target of final demand. In other words, given target output, or final demand, figures, input–output calculations will tell us exactly how much of the various inputs will be required all the way along the line. It thus enables the drawing up of an internally consistent set of target output figures. This is clearly a useful tool in the hands of planners. Given the target in terms of output, a plan can be drawn up which explores the full inter-sectoral implications of the target.

The whole exercise is based upon the assumption that the proportionate relations between the sectors remain fixed. This is a major limitation, for these basically technical relations are changing continuously over time. For example, new power stations with higher thermal efficiency require less coal or oil per kilowatt hour of electricity produced. As new techniques of production are introduced so input–output relations change. It is for this reason that Soviet planners have been somewhat cautious in their approach to the use of input–output analysis. They make considerable use of input–output coefficients (which are not referred to by this name but are called 'norms') in drawing up the plans for each individual sector, but make little attempt in drawing up the inter-sectoral 'material balances' to explore the full implications of the inter-sectoral relations. Their view is that it is unrealistic to plan on the basis of inflexible norms, for performance is to some extent 'pliable' in the hands of the planners, depending upon pressure applied during plan implementation. They argue that it is misleading to use past relationships to plan forward. This is perhaps not so odd a view when one remembers that under the present system the initiative for innovation stems not from the enterprise itself but from the planners. In capitalist countries, where the initiative for innovation comes from the firm itself, plans drawn up on the basis of input–output data are amended in the light of discussions on developments in production techniques with the industries concerned. (See below in chapter 3 the discussion of the use of input–output analysis in indicative planning.)

LINEAR PROGRAMMING: Linear programming is closely related to input–output analysis. Input–output analysis seeks to analyse the relationships between intermediate products and final goods, and linear programming seeks to explore the relationships between (intermediate) activities and final objectives. In each case there is the same means–end relationship. However, whereas in input–output analysis there is one unique set of intermediate output levels which is consistent with a specified pattern of final output, a programming problem considers several alternative ways of fulfilling a specified objective; the problem is to decide which of these alternative methods is best. This is a type of problem long familiar in economics. Given various possible production levels for the firm, which is the profit maximizing output level? Given various alternative production methods which is the one which minimizes costs? Here the objective is to maximize profits or to minimize costs, subject to the technical production conditions. Traditionally economics has 'solved' these problems by the application of marginal analysis. Profits are maximized when marginal cost is equal to marginal revenue; production cost is minimized when the ratio of the marginal products of the factors of production is equal to the ratio of their prices. But marginal analysis may not always be applicable. For example, when operating at high levels of output, a firm is likely to run into a series of capacity limitations – factory size, the amount of time available on different machines, warehouse space, skilled personnel. What is the 'optimal' output combination which makes the best possible use of these scarce resources? There is no simple solution; one item may make good use of machine capacity, another of warehouse space. Marginal analysis cannot cope with such problems, for it cannot handle problems where the side conditions or constraints are expressed as inequalities – for example in the form of minimum requirements that have to be met but may be overshot, or maximum capacity limitations, which may not be fully utilized. Yet in resource allocation problems both within the firm and within the economy, these are exactly the sort of side conditions which operate. Linear programming is a method of solving these problems.

The essence of a linear programme is that it combines what is called an 'objective function', which sets out the objectives of the exercise (eg to maximize profits or to minimize costs) with a series of side constraints. It is called 'linear' because both the objective function and the side constraints are expressed in linear mathematical form, that is, all the variables are to the power of one. In two dimensions this would represent a straight line on a graph, whereas where the variables are to a higher power a graph would show curved lines. Together the objective function and side conditions form a set of linear equations and/ or inequalities which, through a series of mathematical manipulations, makes possible the calculation of an 'optimal' solution, the best possible use of resources in the circumstances. As a by-product, the solution of a linear programme also produces a solution to what is called the 'dual' problem, giving a set of shadow prices appropriate to each scarce resource used, which can represent a useful starting point when decentralizing decision taking.

The linear assumption imposes a considerable limitation upon the use of the technique, for it implies that plant capacity etc requires increases in exact proportion with output; for example that the amount of warehouse space required is exactly proportionate to output. It does not allow for the existence of economies of scale. Again it assumes that input and output prices remain constant as capacity expands. Such assumptions impose limits upon the usefulness of the technique. However more advanced forms of programming have been developed which overcome many of these limitations and it is here that much interest now centres. The great advantage of programming methods, both linear and non-linear, is that they are amenable to computation and are thus able to harness the immense potential of modern computers. Calculations that were at one time considered quite impossible are now feasible. Programming and computers have developed side by side.

Programming, like input–output analysis, received a somewhat mixed reception from Soviet planners in the early 1960s. Critics were particularly concerned with the limited 'dynamic' potential of linear programming, pointing out that investment decisions and technical progress taken within the context of a plan can substantially change input coefficients, and therefore that scarcity prices derived from a programme based upon fixed production coefficients are likely to be just as misleading as the use of current prices to planners looking five or ten years ahead. Stimulated by these dissatisfactions with existing programming techniques, Soviet economists have been in the forefront of the development of dynamic programming, a technique which takes growth into account and looks to optimization over time, with changing constraints, input relationships etc. These developments seem likely to revolutionize the whole basis of Soviet planning. As yet however it is unclear how far it has impinged upon the bureaucrat of the planning hierarchy.

Although the Soviet Union is now making considerable use of these mathematical tools as aids to the planning process, this should not hide the contrast with the capitalist system where resources are, by and large, allocated in accordance with consumer wishes expressed through the medium of the market. The Soviet economy remains an economic system where resources are allocated according to instruction, the instructions being based upon the plan. The plan is the mechanism whereby resources are allocated, and the economy is a command, not a market, economy allocating resources according to instruction and not according to the forces of supply and demand in the market.

2.4 The Eastern European countries

In the early post-war period most of the Eastern European countries of the communist bloc adopted with little variation the Soviet type of economic system with its reliance upon physical planning. Some went further even than the Soviet Union. For example Czechoslovakia attempted completely to eradicate the private agricultural sector. As the period of great scarcity of the early 1950s gave way to somewhat greater affluence, and consumers began to look for wider choice and better quality, so adherence to the system presented increasing difficulties. This was particularly true of the more developed economies of the bloc, which already possessed a relatively complex industrial base but which could not hope to be self-sufficient, and depended to a greater extent upon international trade than the Soviet Union. These countries followed the Soviet Union in introducing *ad hoc* adjustments to the system to try to cope with these problems during the late 1950s. As in the Soviet Union these reforms failed either to make much imprint upon the basic system, or to introduce anything in the way of a distinctly 'national' economic system. With the publication of Liberman's article urging the use of more 'liberal' economic methods in Pravda in 1962, and in some cases before the introduction of the more far reaching reforms of 1965 in the USSR, these countries finally took the bit between their teeth and adopted reform measures which went some way to establish a more distinctly national flavour in their economic systems. It may be worth while to look in slightly more detail at the reforms introduced in one of these countries, Hungary, for reforms here have probably gone further than in any other of these countries. (Czechoslavakia's reforms, master minded by Oto Sik, might have gone some way further but were substantially dropped after the Russian invasion in the summer of 1968 and the subsequent fall of the Dubcek regime.) It is also worth while looking briefly at the economic system which has been adopted in Yugoslavia, which departs radically from the Soviet pattern and whose success has emboldened some of the other Eastern European countries in their reforms.

The 1968 reforms in Hungary[1]

The 1968 reforms in Hungary have carried much further the type of liberalization measure which was introduced in the

---

[1] See B Belassa 'The economic reforms in Hungary' *Economica* February 1970.

Soviet Union in 1965. The aim is ultimately to replace the system of administrative direction by market discipline in order to improve efficiency in the allocation of resources and to stimulate technical progress. However, it is recognized that such changes cannot take place overnight without upsetting established institutions and practices. The desire to maintain full employment and to limit the degree of price inflation has constrained the 'revolutionary' nature of the changes. The most important features of the new system are

THE DISCONTINUANCE OF PLANNING DIRECTIVES: The firm is now substantially free to decide how much it will produce, subject to price, which may well be controlled, and to the instruction to maximize profits. The old industrial ministries, which used to supervise plan directives, continue to exist, to have responsibility for appointing the manager and his deputies, and to retain ultimate responsibility for the affairs of the firm. This is an inevitable source of friction and raises the question of how far this will affect profit-seeking and risk-taking by managers. Will they not always be looking over their shoulders for approval from the ministries? The Gosnab, the materials allocations commission, has been dissolved and the firm is free to seek its supplies where it wishes. Similarly, the enterprise's current account is no longer subject to bank control and veto. The plan remains but it is now regarded as a macroeconomic exercise, and has lost its role as the nub of the resource allocation system.

GREATER FLEXIBILITY OF PRICES: Managers are now free to fix their own prices for a fair range of goods and services. The extent of their autonomy varies somewhat from sector to sector, with price control remaining predominant for agricultural goods and raw materials and for the most important consumer goods. Fear of inflation has led to more widespread control than originally envisaged; although some attempt has been made to align prices of controlled goods more closely to cost, including capital costs, the inflationary controls limit the extent to which this can be achieved in a short period. Moreover the variable turnover tax and a cumbersome system of subsidies remains. As yet therefore although greater flexibility has been introduced in the pricing mechanism, prices are far from accurately reflecting production costs.

THE USE OF PROFIT INCENTIVES: Managers, who continue to be appointed by the state, are instructed to maximize profits. There are substantial incentives to encourage this. They are paid a bonus based on profits, not as previously on the extent to which plan targets are exceeded. This bonus can amount to as much as 80 per cent of their basic salary. The other side of the coin is that, if the enterprise fails to make a profit, managers not only lose their bonus, but face actual salary reductions. Workers also receive a bonus of up to 15 per cent of their wages if profits are high, but do not risk a reduction in basic wages if there is a loss. Fear that managers might exploit monopoly positions, particularly since imports remained restricted, has led to the limitation of profits through price controls in some instances, and the continued existence of widespread price control for anti-inflationary purposes imposes a further constraint.

GREATER FREEDOM IN INVESTMENT DECISIONS: Although much investment remains subject to state control, in manufacturing industry the manager seems to have been given considerable scope for initiative on investment. However this freedom is constrained by continuing government control over large investments, including the establishment of new factories, or increases of more than 25 per cent in capacity in any branch of manufacturing. Restraint is further exerted through control over finance, since any external finance has to come either from the government itself or from the state banking system with the latter playing a more important role as time goes by. Both sources of finance are now subject to interest payments.

All this amounts to a major departure from the old 'command' system, and a move towards market socialism. It is interesting to contrast the success of the Hungarian measures, with the relative failure of the 1965 reforms in the Soviet Union. These latter were, as we saw, very much more restricted in their nature and many were rapidly rescinded in favour of the traditional controls. The success of the Hungarian reforms may be accounted for partly by their more radical nature – it was not so much an attempt to patch the system at the edges – and partly by the greater dependence of the Hungarian economy upon international trade.

Yugoslavia

After its break with the communist bloc in 1948 Yugoslavia has gone its own way both politically and economically. The distinctive feature of the Yugoslav economy has been the institution of workers' management, a form of guild socialism under which, although ownership of the enterprise is vested in the state, ultimate responsibility for management rests with the workers whose earnings come from the enterprise's net income, thus involving them directly in its success. There are also close links between the enterprise and the 'commune' in which it operates, the aim being further to increase the sense of involvement by the community in the enterprise. Another notable feature of the Yugoslav economy is that the agricultural sector has remained predominantly private, and there has been no attempt to force the peasants into collectives; rather the reverse, for peasants after 1953 were allowed to leave collectives that had already been formed.

In the Yugoslav economy enterprises are linked together through the market mechanism with, in principle, prices fluctuating according to supply and demand. However, by no means all prices are free, for the economy has run into considerable inflationary pressures, and the authorities have resorted to the widespread use of price controls to limit this. Since the mid-1960s there has been some move away from direct price control towards more general tools of macroeconomic management to control inflation, particularly fiscal policy. This has allowed for rather greater flexibility of prices, but many prices are still subject to some control. Individual enterprises compete within the market mechanism. Given a relatively small country and backward economy, the market is often too small for many enterprises to co-exist and a 'monopoly' problem arises – particularly with the workers' council anxious to raise prices in order to maximize net income. (See next paragraph.) To offset these pressures, the state has pursued an active anti-monopoly policy to prevent exploitation of consumers by firms. On occasion this too has led to price controls.

Decisions about the level of output, inputs, investment and

technology are in the hands of the executive board of the enterprise. This is an elected body chosen by the workers' council of the enterprise, which in turn consists of elected representatives of the workers. The executive board works to policy guidelines laid down by the workers' council. Detailed day to day management is in the hands of a director appointed jointly by the executive board and the local commune. There are built in incentives which encourage the enterprise to maximize net income, that is sales revenue less the cost of bought-in materials and components. The first charge on net income is tax and capital charges (interest on bank loans, and loans from other state finance institutions). After these have been met, the residue is divided between payment for the workers and management of the enterprise, and depreciation and investment. There are no wages as such, all earnings being paid from net income. The state does however guarantee a minimum level of earnings. The workers' council decides on priorities between pay and reinvestment. Clearly the higher the net income, the greater the amount to be shared out, hence the incentive written into the system to maximize net income. But investment has to be financed also from net income. Benjamin Ward has suggested that the system discriminates against the internal finance of investment, there being every incentive to workers to maximize their own earnings, to the detriment of investment.[1] The conflict between consumption and investment is a direct one. However, to the extent that saving has not come from the enterprise of its own volition, the state has stepped in and 'forced' saving through taxation channelling these funds back into investment. What is given with one hand is taken back with the other.

The inflationary trends within the Yugoslav economy reflect both these unusual pressures of the workers' councils from below, plus the willingness of Yugoslav bankers to provide short term advances. Other communist countries suffer from inflationary pressures but these are often repressed by a battery of price controls of one sort or another. In Yugoslavia, the relative freedom of prices to move in response to supply and demand has brought the inflation out into the open.

[1] See B Ward 'The Firm in Illyria: market syndicalism' *American Economic Review* 1958.

The Yugoslav economy thus presents a curious mixture of guild, market and authoritarian socialism. It is an extremely interesting and on the whole successful experiment in the organization of an economy. Compared with the Soviet style command economy, it combines a greater flexibility gained from the decentralization achieved by using the market mechanism with correspondingly less bureaucratic pressure from the authorities. Its most striking achievement has been the fast rate of growth; for the period since 1948, gross national product[1] has increased by an average of 9 per cent per annum. In judging its success it is worth noting that Yugoslavia remains a country of extreme regional disparities, with income per head in Slovenia being four times that in Montenegro. It is by no means a foregone conclusion that the same mixture would be as successful in another economic system, or for that matter one lacking communist social discipline.

2.5 Summary and conclusions

Capitalism is only one of many economic systems. This chapter has sought to show how other economic systems, based upon other premises, can be organized and work well. The Soviet economy is a command economy; resources are allocated not by the market but by instructions, these instructions in turn being incorporated within the plan, which thus becomes the nub of the resource allocation system. Outwardly, to western eyes, the system often appears cumbersome and inflexible, with little attention paid to the needs of the consumer. However it is difficult to judge the efficiency of the system, for unlike the market system of the capitalist world it does not look to consumer sovereignty, but to planners' sovereignty. The system sets out to achieve a fast rate of growth, giving high priority to investment, and deliberately pursuing growth in a series of 'lurches' from one objective to another, designed to break through one bottleneck after another. Projects and campaigns, which to our eyes seem wasteful and irrational, assume a certain rationality within this context.

The two main difficulties that such a system encounters are, first, that man's behaviour is still fundamentally governed by

[1] Like the Soviet definition of GNP, the Yugoslav figures exclude final services.

self-interest, which can effectively make a mockery of any system of targets incorporated within the plans however good the plans themselves, and, secondly, that good plans require the assembling and analysis of vast quantities of data. Soviet plans have not been successful on this latter count, and in consequence have failed to harness the resources of the state as effectively as they might have done. The tools of mathematical planning-programming and input–output analysis may go some way to help remedy the deficiency.

The more intractable problem is the first one, namely that of marrying man's basic self-interest with the command framework of the economy. This led the Soviet Union in the mid-1960s to experiment with the use of the profit motive, linking the rewards of both management and workers to the profit made by the enterprise, while at the same time allowing prices paid to the producer in some sectors to reflect demand and supply. But the experiment was very limited and has now substantially petered out, leaving the basic functioning of the Soviet economy much as before, a command economy. It is interesting to contrast this experience with that of Hungary and Yugoslavia which both successfully developed a more market oriented approach. Hungary has developed an economic system closely related to market socialism, while, in contrast, Yugoslavia which dropped the command system some 15 years earlier has developed its unique system of workers' management, a system perhaps closer to guild socialism than to market socialism.

Further reading

A NOVE *The Soviet economy – an introduction* (Minerva Series) George Allen & Unwin London 3rd edition 1968. Very much a basic text in this field.

N SPULBER *The Soviet Economy* Norton New York revised edition 1969. Another basic text, with lengthier treatment of market socialism than Nove.

G GROSSMAN *Economic systems* Foundations of modern economics series 1966 Prentice Hall Englewood Cliffs NJ. This is an intro-

ductory text which compares different types of economic systems
– capitalism and socialism, the market system, the command
economy. Chapters 6 and 7 deal with the Soviet economy and
Yugoslavia.

A NOVE *An economic history of the USSR* Allen Lane The Penguin
Press London 1969. A readable book on the economic development of the Soviet Union in the twentieth century.

ABRAM BERGSON *The economics of Soviet Planning* Yale University
Press New Haven 1964. A detailed account and analysis of
Soviet planning institutions and techniques.

B BELASSA 'The economic reforms in Hungary' *Economica* New
Series Vol XXXVII No 145 February 1970.

B WARD 'Workers' management in Yugoslavia' *Journal of
Political Economy* Vol LXV No 5 1957.

JT BOMBELLES *The development of communist Yugoslavia* Stanford
Hoover Institute of War, Revolution and Peace 1968.

3

Planning in capitalist economies

3.1 Introduction

In the two previous chapters we have tended to use the word capitalist in a generic sense, meaning an economy where the ownership of property is in private hands and where the allocation of resources is left to the forces of the market, and we contrasted this with the organization of a command economy where ownership of property is vested in the state and where the allocation of resources is effected through instructions based upon some sort of central plan. But this is a somewhat purist definition. For the rest of this book, we shall use the term 'capitalist' to describe those economic systems where the ownership of property is largely vested in private citizens and where the allocation of resources is substantially influenced by the market. Thus the term embraces not only economies such as those of the USA or Germany, which come nearest to our 'pure' capitalist form, but also the type of economic system found in the UK, Sweden, Holland, France, where the state owns a substantial amount of property and plays an active part in influencing the allocation of resources. In none of these countries however is a preponderant part of the means of production and distribution vested in the state, nor has the state superseded the market in the allocation of resources. It would therefore seem reasonable to include such economic systems as 'capitalist', although some may prefer to call them mixed economies.

Indicative planning and uncertainty

In the last chapter we saw how in a command economy the plan allocates resources. What role can planning have then in capitalist economies where by definition the allocation of resources is left substantially to market forces? Does planning replace market forces in allocating resources, or does it perform some other function?

To answer these questions it is necessary to go back to the latter part of chapter 1, to the discussion on full employment and growth as objectives of economic policy. Ideally, we should like to be able to pursue what is termed 'an equilibrium growth path' where the economy moves through time with supply and demand for all goods and services in balance at all points of time, so that there are no market fluctuations, unemployment, etc. Moreover, we should like this growth path to be efficient in a Pareto sense, so that at all points in time it is impossible to make one person better off without making someone else worse off.

If we had perfect foresight, and there were no increasing returns to scale, indivisibilities, externalities or public goods, then such an efficient, equilibrium growth path might be achieved in a perfectly competitive world, in which the market not only looked to the present but took the future into account through forward transactions. But we have not got perfect foresight. At every point we are confronted by uncertainty. We do not know how technology is going to transform production techniques, we do not know what reserves of natural resources will be discovered, we cannot predict demographic movements even over a fairly short period, let alone predict how tastes and fashions are going to change. Some of the uncertainty which we face as producers or consumers can be eliminated by information research. Thus many manufacturers spend a good deal of money on market research which helps them to keep abreast of changing consumer tastes. There still remains an irreducible minimum of uncertainty however which, following Meade, we shall term 'environmental uncertainties'.[1]

One of the features of environmental uncertainties is inter-

[1] J E Meade *The theory of indicative planning* Manchester University Press 1970.

dependence; each economic agent makes its own subjective assessment of the probabilities attached to each element of uncertainty, but in turn these assessments will be affected by the probabilities that others attach to the same eventuality. For example, I think it more likely that it will rain if you too think it is going to rain. Producers might alter their subjective assessments if they knew how consumers thought they might behave and, in turn, if consumers knew what producers were thinking, they might alter their assessments. The movement of the economy through time will crucially depend upon the inter-action of these subjective assessments. Forward markets which take account both of time and uncertainty, ie which hedge against future risks, are one method by which the market exchanges information about the different subjective assess-ments and reaches what might be described as a 'consensus' assessment of the risk involved. But forward markets exist only in a few specialized spheres, for example in foreign exchange and commodity dealing. In most markets there is no such method of signalling information between producers and con-sumers about the future; each economic agent has to rely upon his/her own subjective assessment of the probabilities attached to different environmental uncertainties. Where we lack know-ledge, we fall back upon experience. Faced with an investment decision, the entrepreneur will assess market developments on the basis of past trends and present circumstances; perhaps he will be unduly influenced by the latter, optimistic when sales are high and pessimistic when sales are low. If all entrepreneurs act likewise, far from a smooth equilibrium growth path, there will be a constant tendency to over- or under-shoot the mark, for the economy to move in fits and starts through business cycles of varying magnitude with the concomitant ups and downs in the level of employment. The existence of environmental un-certainties frustrates the objectives of full employment and efficiency, and, through the wastage of resources involved in the business cycle, means that the rate of growth achieved over time is lower than it might otherwise have been. Planning is a method of trying to limit the impact of environmental uncertainties.

Most governments today accept responsibility for maintaining full employment and attempting to stabilize the economy around a steady growth path. Indicative planning is one of their tools. The aim is to narrow down the area of uncertainty in which firms make investment decisions, to provide a set of common expectations which helps to ensure consistency of decisions and, by avoiding bottlenecks, to achieve smoother growth. Indicative planning has a role similar to that of forward markets in enabling economic agents to exchange information about likely future developments and to arrive at some kind of 'consensus' assessment of probabilities. It has not the flexibility of forward markets which adapt immediately to changing expectations. Even though indicative plans are frequently treated as rolling projections and amended in the light of new information, inevitably they cannot incorporate the immediate and automatic feedback of the forward market.

Indicative planning is sometimes described as investment planning, for it is concerned particularly to project the investment decisions of the private and public sectors, to highlight major uncertainties, and to see whether the result is likely to under- or over-heat the economy. Such a plan does not seek to allocate resources but forecasts the way in which the market is likely to allocate resources in the future. Above all each economic agent is required to recognize the plan as indicative or suggestive. It provides him with a benchmark against which to plan his own activities, but he is still required to apply his own subjective judgement to its projections. Indicative planning can therefore be regarded as a form of planning that is perfectly compatible with the capitalist system; by and large the market still allocates resources.

However, it is easy for indicative planning to develop into a rather more positive exercise. While the state can limit its role to forecasting private and public sector investment and consumption and taking appropriate policy measures to counteract under- or over-heating of the economy, it is very easy for the state to go one step further and take a view on what the appropriate rate of investment should be, which in effect means taking a view upon what the appropriate rate of growth should be. This in turn means state intervention in the 'free market' consumption/saving decision. Planning in this sense may be the vehicle used to promote the 'growth' objective, and to make an explicit trade-off between this and other objectives. It is a much more *positive* exercise than the investment planning which we were discussing in the last paragraph, which might be regarded as *negative* planning aimed at maintaining the balance of the economy. This sort of positive planning has a more direct influence upon the allocation of resources. The aim is to shift resources from one sector to another in order to promote a faster rate of growth: it goes beyond projecting the way in which the market is likely to allocate resources, and projects a 'desirable' allocation of resources.

The difference between 'positive' planning in capitalist economies and planning in a command economy is that in the former market forces are used to achieve the desired allocation of resources. In general, the most that the planning authorities can do is to effect the introduction of policy measures designed to influence the market in this or that direction. As we shall see, the authorities are seldom vested with mandatory authority and have limited power to impose sanctions if market forces fail to achieve the desired allocation.

Factors influencing the rate of growth

Most of the rest of this chapter consists of a discussion of planning exercises in certain capitalist countries. Before going on to discuss this it is necessary to elaborate in slightly greater detail what we mean by the 'rate of growth'.

When we talk about a country's rate of growth we usually mean the rate of growth of output measured in national income terms. The recorded rate of growth of output varies from year to year according to the state of the economy: in a year of recession the recorded rate of growth may be low, or even negative, because labour and capital will have become idle. Similarly in the upturn of a cycle the recorded rate of growth will reflect the increasing use of labour and capacity which had been idle. Although these year to year variations in the recorded rates of growth are interesting, what is important for our purpose is not the actual rate of growth of output from year to year but the rate of growth of capacity – the rate of growth that would be recorded if labour and capital were always fully employed. This in turn reflects two factors

The increase in the amount of labour and capital available that is
a   the rate of growth of the labour force and
b   the rate of growth of the capital stock (investment).

The increase in labour and capital productivity which increases output
per unit of input. In turn, the main sources of this increase in
productivity are

a   improvements in resource allocation – for example the
shifting of workers from low productivity occupations such as
agriculture into higher productivity occupations;
b   economies of scale – gained from the adoption of standardized mass production techniques; and
c   advances in knowledge – reflecting both the availability of
new technologies and, more particularly, the speed with which
the economy adopts new techniques – the rate of innovation.
Education, the use of better management techniques, etc, by
increasing the skill and adaptability of the labour force, are an
important influence here.

   This last element, advances in knowledge and the reduction
in the time lag involved in innovation, is sometimes referred to
as the 'residual' element in growth. While we can measure, at
least approximately, changes in the physical inputs of labour
and capital, for example changes in working hours or the
composition of the labour force, it is very much more difficult
to measure, however approximately, advances in knowledge.
Therefore changes in the rate of growth which cannot be
accounted for directly by measurable factors tend to be grouped
into this residual category, where it is presumed that these
factors, technical progress, the innovatory lag and education,
are the main influences. Denison, in his comparative study of
growth rates in western countries,[1] estimates that the residual
category contributes up to one third of overall growth rates in
some countries. In the UK it was lower than for most of the
other countries he studied, whereas in France it was particularly
high. This may be of some significance to our discussion below of
the French planning mechanism.

   [1] E F Denison assisted by J P Poullier *Why growth rates differ: postwar experience in
nine western countries* Brookings Institution 1967.

72

A government wishing to boost the rate of growth through planning will not only look to measures which increase factor inputs, for example, switching resources from consumption to investment in order to increase the stock of capital and encouraging women to participate in the labour force, but will also take measures which will boost the productivity of inputs. There will be measures which encourage the movement of labour from low productivity to high productivity jobs. Although Britain does not have the reserve of agricultural labour which is available in some continental countries, in certain regions the relative under-employment of labour in some occupations is seen to constitute a potential source of increased productivity. Similarly, there will also be measures aimed at increasing the speed of adoption of new techniques. We shall see in the next section how these various strategies form a part of the planning programmes of Sweden, France and the United Kingdom, and how in particular France and the UK have attempted to increase the 'residual' element in growth through a programme of encouraging modernization.

Let us now turn from general discussion of planning and growth, to some specific examples of planning in capitalist countries. We shall look at three examples of planning exercises; that undertaken in Sweden, which approximates to the category of negative investment planning, and the planning exercises of France and Britain, which come closer to the category of positive planning.

3.2 Planning in Sweden

Sweden has long been in the forefront in the use of fiscal instruments for contra-cyclical and stabilization policies. From 1948 onwards, partly influenced by similar moves in other European countries, Sweden has produced every five years or so a 'Long Term Report' which deals with the development of the basic sectors of the economy during the forthcoming five year period. The report is based upon detailed enquiries and discussions with private and public sector firms and organizations and involves a major exchange of information on the basis of which the planning committee draw up a set of projections for the basic sectors of the economy. Attempts are made both through discussions and by the use of input–output data to ensure consistency in these projections, or, where they reveal inconsistencies, to stimulate changes which will ultimately ensure consistency. The plans are 'rolling' projections which are amended as new information comes to hand. The projections are however no more than forecasts, and there is no attempt to establish production targets to which industries or firms are obliged to conform; indeed, they are not even, as a rule, adopted as official government policy.

These long term reports are investment planning, aimed at communicating and amplifying information about the activities of the various sectors of the economy and making this information widely available to firms and other organizations. There is no question of going back to firms or industries and negotiating a revision in their plans in the light of national economic projections. Rather, as Svennilson, the chief 'planner' in Sweden in the post-war period, has commented, 'Firms and sectors are expected to adjust to the market development that actually follows, guided by the information they receive in the published national projection... The national projection creates an "image" of economic growth that has the backing of government policy. This image will stimulate industry to plan for long term expansion and make it possible to do it more realistically. In this way national projections may contribute to create a better balanced growth.'[1]

Up to 1959, the main concern of the plans was with the stabilization and sectoral equilibrium of the economy. In general the earlier plans found that the level of investment during the plan period was likely to exceed the level of planned saving thus creating considerable inflationary pressure. The emphasis had therefore been on the restriction of private consumption in order to allow for an expansion in the proportion of GNP devoted to investment.

Since 1959, there has been more interest in the growth rate implications of the investment projections and in the share of resources devoted to education, research and development. At no time however has there been any attempt to use these projections as a method of evaluating the allocation of resources arrived at via the market mechanism, nor to use the

[1] I Svennilson *Planning in a market economy* Weltwirtschaftliches Archiv 1965.

plans as a method for allocating resources between sectors. Discussion about the allocation of resources has in general been limited to macroeconomic variables such as the ratio between consumption and investment. Sometimes recommendations have been more detailed. Thus on occasion the reports have advocated priority for investment in housing and the public services and, on another occasion, priority for the industrial and distributive sectors. There has however been no general pattern here. As one commentator put it, 'A sector discriminated against in one report has been favoured in the next report (except for private consumption which has never been favoured).'[1]

One innovation of the Swedes, which is not really part of their planning machinery but which has become an important macroeconomic tool, is the investment reserve system. Under this system firms are given the incentives to set aside a part of their profits in periods of boom to be frozen in a special reserve fund which may be used to finance investment in times of recession. The authorities control these funds and release them when the economy needs stimulus. They are also able to stipulate the use to which such funds are put, and are thus able to channel them towards specified industries and regions. First initiated in the mid 1950s, by the early 1960s the investment reserve had built up to sizeable proportions – for example the building work in the reserve was equivalent to 10 per cent of the annual value of all forms of construction – and was used with good effect to cushion the recessions of the early and late 1960s.

To summarize, planning in Sweden fits into the pattern of negative indicative planning that we were discussing earlier. It is based upon five year projections whose use is essentially one of information and policy action for stability. As we shall see it is a very much more limited exercise than that developed in either France or the United Kingdom.

3.3 Planning in France

Planning in France developed in the immediate post-war period as a result of the demands of the European Recovery Programme (the US sponsored Marshall Plan) that the monies provided

---

[1] Assar Lindbeck 'Theories and problems in Swedish economic policy in the post-war period' *American Economic Review* Supplement June 1968.

under the programme should be shown to be used to good purpose. Its continued vigour was largely due to the personality of Jean Monnet, who was set the task of developing and co-ordinating the post-war reconstruction programme in France. Since 1947–8 there have been a series of plans each of four to five years' duration. The first plans were really only projections of the development of the basic sectors of the economy, concentrating on the reconstruction of these industries, the coal, steel and electricity industries in particular, as well as the main macroeconomic variables, and it did not aim or claim to represent a total 'picture' of the development of the economy. However, since at that time most of the basic raw materials were subject to direct allocation, the plans did have a somewhat more normative significance than mere projections.

As time went on the plans became more and more elaborate and planning in France became a more positive exercise, the vehicle for the expression of the government's economic strategy and embodying within its framework decisions about income distribution, the division of income between private and public consumption, investment, defence spending and so forth. It reached its apogee in the 4th plan which covered the period 1962–5. Since then, the development of the EEC has constrained national economic policies and has made planning a more difficult and less exact exercise. The 5th plan, for the period 1966–70, was in some respects a less ambitious enter-prise than the 4th plan, and the 6th plan, for 1971–5, was still less so. Indeed it is rumoured that the 6th plan will be the last of the series. For this reason we shall be examining in more detail below the development of the 4th plan rather than the 5th or 6th plan. Moreover, it was the 4th plan which played a substantial part in influencing Britain's experiments in planning in the 1960s, and this adds further logic in examining this plan rather than its successors.

The drawing up of the 4th plan fell into four main stages.

STAGE I was the responsibility of the Commissariat du Plan, a semi-independent body responsible to the Minister of Finance but with its own staff headed by an independent Commissioner. Work on the 4th Plan began in 1959 with two general models of the economy, the first up to 1965 and the second up to 1975, which the planners used to explore the implications of a wide range of possible rates of growth in relation both to the major macroeconomic variables and to the other objectives of economic policy such as price stability and balance of payments equilibrium.

STAGE II of the exercise was the presentation of these projections and their implications to the Economic and Social Council, a high level advisory body to the government consisting of some elected members of the Chamber of Deputies as well as a large number of representatives from business, the trade unions, etc. The task of the Economic and Social Council was to consider the various projections and their implications within the broad framework of the government's social objectives, and to advise the government on the choice of the target rate of growth and overall objectives within the plan. This particular stage was developed further in the 5th and 6th plans when Parliament itself, and not just the Economic and Social Council, participated in the fixing of the *grandes options* of the plan, such as whether economic policy should concentrate on increasing wealth or leisure, and on the desirable distribution of the new wealth created. Following the work of the Council, the government issued a directive setting out the general objectives of the Plan; in the 4th plan it was decided that public consumption should be given priority and that the rate of growth with which the planners should work should be 5–5½ per cent.

STAGE III was back to the Commissariat. On the basis of the target rate of growth of 5–5½ per cent, and the general objectives outlined by the government, detailed projections were made, broken down on an input/output model into projections for the twenty main sectors of the economy. These mathematical projections were then passed onto twenty 'vertical' commissions, each representing one of the main sectors and consisting of industrialists, trade unionists, academics and civil servants concerned within that sector. In addition, there were five 'horizontal' commissions dealing with features of the economy as a whole, finance, manpower, research, productivity and regional problems. Each commission was staffed by at least one member of the Commissariat, who acted frequently as rapporteur and link-man with the Commissariat. Otherwise the

77

commissions drew widely from the 'lay' community outside the immediate government machine, and over 3,000 persons in all were drawn into the planning exercise at this stage. Each commission examined the projections made by the Commissariat for their sector, assessed their feasibility, supplemented the data available to the Commissariat and amended the estimates in the light of this data when necessary. In other words, what was happening at this stage was that the 'fixed' coefficient projections of the input–output model[1] were being amended to take account of developments in production methods, working hours etc, and in general being moulded into a more flexible pattern than would otherwise be possible. But the basic mathematical model did provide an important framework for these discussions, and ensured that some account was taken of the intricate inter-relations between all sectors of the economy. This stage was an elaborate process of exchange of information between the planners and those more closely concerned with the production base of the country.

STAGE IV After the work done by the commissions, the government with the advice of the Commissariat decided on the actual rate of growth to be incorporated into the plan, 5 per cent, and on this basis the Commissariat drew up the final Plan, which was submitted to Parliament for them to see and discuss the detailed implications of the Plan decisions. Although the Plan was the vehicle used to announce the main features of government economic strategy and to examine their implications and although it was submitted to and adopted by Parliament, the Plan did not have the force of law. Moreover, though enshrined in mystique, there was no attempt to give it the force of law. Indeed, no attempt was made to draw up plans for individual firms; the twenty main sector projections were broken down into more detailed industrial projections, but individual firms were left free to go their own way and the government had no method of forcing them to comply with planned developments.

There are two outstanding features of French planning that have received a great deal of attention. One is that it is indicative planning – that it is not concerned to plot the detailed progress of the economy within the Plan period, but seeks to

[1] See chapter 2 p 53–6 for an explanation of this.

provide a general framework into which major decisions of government economic strategy can be incorporated and which can provide the guide lines for individual decisions. In this respect it is similar to Swedish planning, concerned with macro-economic balance and the wider dissemination of information, although in both respects it goes somewhat further than the Swedish exercise.

The other notable feature of French planning is that it is consensus planning, the idea of the *economée concertée* in which a large number of people are drawn into the planning discussions. This, it is felt, enables it to act as a spur to modernization, since discussion of what is feasible will bring those participating to consider new techniques available, and stimulate them, not only to adopt new techniques themselves, but also to put pressure on others to adopt new techniques. The idea here is that, if they see what they might be able to achieve, competitive and patriotic instincts will together spur them towards such achievement. Another advantage seen in this type of consensus planning is that, since a large number of people are concerned with the development of the sectoral projections, many have an interest in seeing the projections achieved. This consensus element takes French planning considerably beyond Swedish planning. It is aimed at achieving a faster rate of growth of the residual element, first by stimulating the adoption of new techniques, and secondly by raising people's sights as to possible achievement. This latter effect has variously been called the 'expectations' and the 'propaganda' effect, and it is based on the view that human effort depends to some extent on the aspiration level set, and that a gentle raising of the aspiration level can stimulate greater effort.[1] While this has been found to be true both of school children and of business managers, we are still some way from accepting it as a general proposition. However, as we shall see, it has played a considerable part in influencing British planning exercise.

Although a much more positive exercise in planning than the Swedish example, French planning is still within the framework

[1] See below the discussion of managerial aspirations on pp. 94-9 chapter 4. The setting of target rates of return for the British nationalized industries (see chapter 6) is based upon a similar philosophy.

of capitalist planning. As we noted above, there is no attempt to draw up plans for the individual units or to force units to comply with the plan framework. In one respect however, French planning may go beyond the bounds of capitalist planning as defined early in this chapter. This is because the French government, which has a more *dirigiste* tradition than many other western capitalist countries, has at its disposal a number of instruments which can be used to bring pressure upon firms to conform with the guidelines laid down in the Plan. For example, the government controls access to the capital market and the discount market for industrial bills and is therefore in a position to influence access to long and medium term credit facilities. Again, the tax system can be used deliberately to discriminate in favour of those firms who toe the line. Discrimination can be exercised in the administration of price controls and even such things as granting access to officials can be used to bring some pressure to bear upon recalcitrant firms and to encourage those who follow the lines suggested by the plan.[1] These sanctions can be used to effect fairly substantial changes in the market allocation of resources or rather to push the market allocation of resources into line with the planned allocation of resources. Because of this some commentators have argued that French planning goes beyond the strict confines of 'capitalist' planning,[2] which they associate with the investment or negative planning model of Sweden. This would seem something of a semantic quibble; the fact remains that whatever French officials have done to try to bring the allocation of resources into line with the Plan the overall allocation of resources in France remains substantially market dominated and the planning exercise takes place within a capitalist environment.

[1] See A Shonfield *Modern capitalism* Oxford University Press 1965 pp 148–50, 165–71.
[2] The French civil service is interventionist by nature and training, and has no qualms about using interventionist techniques to gain their objectives, indeed they deliberately worked through the larger and more go-ahead firms in order to bring pressure to bear upon others. The type of discriminatory treatment towards individual persons and firms used by the French authorities is wholly antipathetic to the British civil service tradition of equality of treatment to all-comers. Such a tool for enforcing plan guidelines was not therefore at the disposal of British planners. See A Shonfield *op cit* chapters VII and VIII.

3.4 Planning in Britain

After a limited exercise in stability planning in 1947–48, which was very similar to Swedish practice in that period, Britain dropped economic planning until 1962–3, when the authorities turned to planning as an attempt to escape from the stop–go cycle which had been such a feature of the British economy in the 1950s. Indeed, rather oddly, it was a Conservative and not a Labour government which made the first planning initiatives, although the planning machinery which they established was taken over and expanded by the Labour government of 1964.

There are a considerable number of factors which explain why the Conservative government turned to planning at this time. One was the mood of desperation in trying to break away from the traditional fiscal and monetary instruments of economic policy, which had done little to help, indeed in the eyes of some commentators had exacerbated, the stop–go cycles of the previous decade.[1] Another influence was the Plowden Report on Public Expenditure[2] which had belatedly introduced longer term thinking and objectives into public expenditure decisions, and led to five year forward planning on the public expenditure front, planning which required to be slotted into a wider economic framework. The third influence was French planning experience at that time, when the preparation of the 4th plan was in its final stages and the French economy was benefiting from the drastic devaluations of 1957–8 and emerging triumphantly from the period of austerity which had immediately succeeded the devaluations. The French seemed to have achieved precisely what the British wanted to achieve. In spite of the successive political and economic crises of the 1950s, they seemed to have built up a sound basic economic structure which was now enabling them to break away from the vicious stop–go circle into an export-led boom and to face their Common Market partners from a position of strength. To British eyes this strength seemed to stem, in part at least, from French

[1] See for example J C R Dow *The management of the British economy* Cambridge University Press 1964 part IV.
[2] *The control of public expenditure* Cmnd No 1432 HMSO London 1960.

planning which had kept the French economy fixed on long term sights through short term squalls.

In some ways, French planning undoubtedly did help to give France a sound, modern economic base. But, unlike the British economy, the French economy was until the early 1960s substantially insulated by high tariff walls and quotas from the international market; and the franc was not a major international reserve currency. This meant that France had been able to put the strengthening of productive capacity above the balance of payments and had devalued when necessary. The development of the EEC in the 1960s has meant that France has become subject to much greater international pressures, partly because it has greatly diminished trade restrictions but largely because the complications of devaluations within the Common Market framework have made this a less accessible resort. It is now less easy than before for France to set its sights on the long term objective and to try to get there by the straightest possible route, and the whole planning exercise has become more difficult. As we have seen, this has reflected itself in more generalized planning and the move away from specific plan targets. Britain, in contrast, has always been exposed to the international economy. With the pound a reserve currency, we could not do as the French had done and devalue whenever the Plan came into conflict with the balance of payments constraint – which is why planning à la française never really worked in Britain.

British planning was indeed planning à la française. In 1962 our Commissariat, the National Economic Development Office (NEDO), was set up as the organ for drafting the plan. Its staff were not all civil servants; many were seconded from industry, banking and the universities, and the office was set aside from the Treasury and the main Whitehall machine. In this respect it had greater autonomy, but arguably less power, than the Commissariat. Over NEDO sat the National Economic Development Council (NEDC), chaired by the Chancellor of the Exchequer and with representatives in equal numbers from business and the trade unions, with, in addition, two lay members. Under NEDC were the Economic Development Committees (the little Neddies), modernization commissions responsible for different sectors of industry. Under the Labour government of 1964 the Department of Economic Affairs took over from NEDO the role of drafting the Plan, and the Prime Minister took over the Chairmanship of NEDC, but otherwise things really did not change very much.

One element however that was markedly different from the French models were the plans themselves, which were rather hastily drawn up within a matter of months, in contrast to the $3\frac{1}{2}$ years it had taken to draft the 4th French Plan; in the case both of the Plan of 1962–3[1] and that of 1964–5[2] there was considerable political pressure for the production of a Plan as quickly as possible. No-one claimed that these plans were the last word in planning. They were intended to provide, and indeed did provide, a set of guide lines for the future development of the economy and suggested a set of policies which would oil the wheels of the economy and help to achieve the plan targets. Another respect in which British planning exercises differed from the French was in the way Parliament was denied any say in their formulation; they were presented to Parliament as a *fait accompli*. They provided the subject for a debate upon economic affairs, but there was no attempt to bring Parliament directly into their formulation.

THE NEDC PLAN OF 1963: The first planning exercise to emerge from these arrangements took the form of two reports produced by the NEDC after about a year of deliberations and consultations. 'Growth of the United Kingdom economy to 1966'[1] was the main report, published in March 1963, with a subsidiary report 'Conditions favourable to faster growth'[3] appearing a month later. These reports comprised a fairly detailed feasibility study of a 4 per cent rate of growth for the period 1962–6. They represented little more than the first stage of the French planning process, limited to considering the implications of only one possible rate of growth rather than a range of possible rates of growth. They did include something of the French stage III in so far as the implications of a 4 per cent growth rate had been considered in relation to some seventeen major industrial sectors and some discussion with interested

---

[1] National Economic Development Council *Growth of the UK economy to 1966* HMSO London 1963.
[2] *The National Plan* Cmnd No 2764 HMSO London 1965.
[3] NEDC *Conditions favourable to faster growth* HMSO London 1963.

trade associations and large firms had taken place. But there was no attempt to see how far industry's own projections for the future anticipated a 4 per cent rate of growth. The questions put to industry were, 'Assuming that GNP grows at 4 per cent per annum, what does this imply in terms of, first, demand for factor supplies for your industries, secondly, demand for the product of your industry, thirdly, do you anticipate that such supplies will be forthcoming?' Some attempt then was made at reconciliation between sectoral demand and supply (though little use at any stage was made of input/output analysis to help secure consistency), and obvious bottle-necks were pin-pointed and remedies suggested, this being the relevance of the second document, 'Conditions favourable to faster growth'. From this exercise it was concluded that a 4 per cent rate of growth was feasible, in spite of the fact that this was some 1 per cent above that achieved in the past. This made the whole exercise something of an act of faith for little suggestion was made as to how the movement from feasibility to reality should be made. Like the French we hoped that the 'propaganda' effect would be sufficient to raise expectations – that, having been told to assume a 4 per cent rate of growth, businessmen would then believe and plan for expansion on this basis. Unfortunately, the only people who actually did this were the nationalized electricity industry, who thus created for themselves, on paper,[1] considerable excess capacity by the end of the decade! Most other businessmen waited to see whether the projected increase in demand would be forthcoming before committing themselves to new capacity. And it might have been forthcoming, and the whole confidence trick might have worked, if the massive deficit on the balance of payments had not forced the new Labour government of October 1964 to limit severely the rate of growth of demand.[2]

[1] In fact delays in the construction of power stations combined with considerable difficulties in the commissioning of the new 500 MW sets meant that there was very little margin of spare capacity in the early 1970s – but if all had gone according to plan there would have been considerable excess capacity.

[2] 'The first and indispensable condition for successful economic planning in the context of modern capitalism is confidence on the part of the business community in the seriousness of the Government's intentions as stated in the plan. Once it is thought that the public authorities may, after all, not be in earnest, that their production targets are little more than maximized hopes, which will be readily forgone as soon as circumstances demonstrate that there is going to be some

THE NATIONAL PLAN OF 1965: Although a more elaborate
exercise, the second attempt at planning which culminated in
the National Plan of 1965 was built on very similar foundations.
Like its predecessor this started with the establishment of a target
rate of growth. This time a slightly less ambitious target was
chosen, 25 per cent over the six year period 1964–70 or 3·8 per
cent per annum. In arriving at this target, there seems to have
been very little detailed consideration of alternatives as in stage
1 of the French planning process. Since the rate of growth of
the labour force was projected to be 0·4 per cent per annum
this implied an 'underlying rate of growth' (the combined
effect of capital expansion and the increase in capital and
labour productivity) of 3·4 per cent. Now the 'underlying rate
of growth' had in fact increased in Britain since the early 1950s
from about 2 per cent to 2·8 per cent, but it was again a considerable act of faith to believe that it could be raised during the
plan period from 2·8 to 3·4 per cent, and again implied a
belief on the part of those concerned that expectations could be
turned into reality and that the rate of growth could be pulled
up by its own bootstraps. Just as in the previous planning
exercise, firms were then asked in a detailed industrial questionnaire, on the assumption that GNP would grow by 3·8 per cent
and exports by $5\frac{1}{4}$ per cent, to make estimates of output,
demand at home and abroad, input requirements and invest-
ment. The rate of $5\frac{1}{4}$ per cent was considered to be the necessary
rate of growth of exports if GNP was to be able to grow at 3·8 per
cent, without running into severe balance of payments trouble,
and compared with a rate of growth of exports of only 3 per
cent per annum in the early 1960s. The results of this industrial
inquiry were then put side by side with projections made on the
basis of an input/output model of the UK economy, and the
two 'reconciled' by discussions with the industries concerned
under the auspices, where they existed, of the little Neddies.[1]

difficulty in achieving them, businessmen will hold back. They will refuse to risk
their own capital on Plan projects, which they will come to regard more and more
as unhedged bets. Scepticism is corrosive to the whole exercise.' A Shonfield
Modern capitalism p 134.
[1] By no means all were covered by little Neddies (Economic Development
Committees). The first of these was not appointed until spring 1964 and many
industries had no such machinery. In such cases discussions proceeded through
trade associations, employers' organizations, trade unions and similar groups.

This process of discussion and reconciliation was very similar to stage III of the French 4th Plan. The National Plan was then drawn up on the basis of these discussions, establishing the target rate of growth of 3·8 per cent.

The Plan makes the distinction between a target, a projection and a forecast. A projection is defined as being the extrapolation of existing trends; a forecast takes into account likely changes in trend; while a target goes further than this and calls frequently for expansion beyond the forecast totals. For example, a projection of the previous rate of growth of exports would indicate a rate of growth of 3 per cent per annum; taking credit for likely improvements in the UK export performance would establish a forecast rate of 4 per cent per annum; but the expansion of exports required to meet other aspects of the plan is $5\frac{1}{4}$ per cent, and it is this rate which becomes the target and planned rate of growth of exports. Similarly, the forecast underlying rate of growth revealed by the industrial inquiry was only 3·2 per cent, whereas the target underlying rate of growth was established as 3·4 per cent; if this were not met and if the rate of growth was only 3·2 per cent, an extra 400,000 workers would be required by 1970. Thus the National Plan lent just as heavily as the first NEDC plan on the 'expectations' aspect of planning, and again it might have succeeded if the whole had not come unstuck so rapidly on the balance of payments. But the British government at that stage refused to give the rate of growth of output priority over the balance of payments, and scepticism rapidly set in.

To do them justice the planners recognized the 'leap of faith' required in jumping from forecast to target, and a section of the 1965 National Plan set out a list of policies which would help the economy to make such a jump. This amounted to a list of policies necessary to ease the bottle-necks that appeared as the plan was being drawn up; policies of import-saving, rationalization in industry, regional development to bring into use the unused resources of the less prosperous regions; policies for a more purposeful use of government expenditure and so on. In addition the plan also contained projections as to the use that should be made of the new resources which would become available. For example it was suggested that personal consumption over the six year period should grow rather less rapidly than GNP, by 21 per cent compared with the growth target in GNP of 25 per cent, while public expenditure was projected to grow at a rate of 27 per cent. Thus, as with the French Plans, the National Plan was the vehicle which the government used to state their main objectives on the future distribution between the major macroeconomic categories.

The National Plan was published in September 1965. Within a few months of publication it became obvious that the balance of payments assumptions in the plan were hopelessly optimistic, granted the exclusion of devaluation as a policy instrument, and within ten months all pretence of following the 'Plan' was abandoned in the severe deflationary measures of July 1966, which aimed to restore equilibrium on the balance of payments front.

'THE TASK AHEAD' – THE 1969 PLAN: This was not however the end of indicative planning in the United Kingdom. In March 1969, the Department of Economic Affairs published a new planning document in the form of a green paper.[1] This was a much more modest document than the National Plan, its stated purpose being to set out the assumptions lying behind government economic strategy up to 1972. Rather than a single, arbitrary, chosen growth rate for this period it gave a range within which the growth rate was likely to fall, the range being between 3 and 4 per cent, and similarly a range estimate was given for the other macroeconomic variables, the spread being from less to more optimistic assumptions. There was little attempt to work out the implications of such growth rates for the microeconomic sectors, although some breakdown was given for the major sectors, chemicals, agriculture, motor vehicles etc, and here, rather than a range, a single growth rate of $3\frac{1}{4}$ per cent was assumed. The detailed work on the sectoral implications of the assumptions was regarded however as the next stage in the planning process, involving consultations with the industries concerned. For some industries these took place after the publication of the green paper; a further planning document

---

[1] Department of Economic Affairs *The task ahead* HMSO London 1969. Whereas a white paper sets out government policy, a green paper is a consultative document setting out suggested policy developments.

setting out the sectoral implications in more detail was projected but never appeared.

'The Task Ahead' was a much less ambitious plan than the National Plan, consisting of no more than a series of forecasts (in the National Plan sense, ie projections of trend plus likely changes in trend) which represented the basic assumptions underlying government economic strategy and provided both a long term framework for stabilization policies and guidelines for the individual firm making investment decisions. This third planning exercise in Britain was therefore much closer to the Swedish model than to the French model. Admittedly the publication of the detailed sectoral 'follow-up' plans would have brought it closer to the French model, but the whole exercise was a much more modest 'negative' exercise than the brazen and positive approach of earlier exercises. Above all the 'expectations' element had been dropped. It was an exercise in feasibility rather than in propaganda.

3.5 Summary and conclusions

We have looked at three different attempts at planning within a capitalist system, the 'negative' investment planning of Sweden, the more 'positive' planning of the French, and Britain's attempts at planning, which have been substantially influenced by the French model. The main feature of these exercises in capitalist planning, as distinct from planning in the command economy, is that the plans are not used to allocate resources and thus to replace the market mechanism as a method of resource allocation. Planning in capitalist countries can be seen primarily as a tool of macro-management, not micro-management; it is concerned with forecasting the way in which the market mechanism will be allocating resources over the next few years and, although it may suggest measures which will influence this allocation, at no stage are targets set for individual firms and little in the way of sanctions are imposed upon firms or organizations which flout planning decisions.

It is possible to distinguish three aspects of this type of planning

a it attempts to narrow down the area of uncertainty surrounding the future both at the macro- and at the microeconomic level; at the macroeconomic level it examines the long term implications of policy decisions; at the microeconomic level, it provides a uniform and consistent framework within which investment decisions may be made;

b it is concerned with the stability of the economy and attempts to use policy instruments to forestall and eliminate bottlenecks which might throw the economy 'off course'; and

c it is concerned to eliminate the wastage of resources, by helping firms to arrive at decisions which are sectorally consistent.

The hope has been that planning of this kind will itself improve the rate of growth. In the French and British case there has additionally been the more positive belief that the process of confrontation and discussion in the planning exercise would serve generally to raise expectations and that these rising expectations would pull the growth rate up behind them.

It is difficult to judge whether planning lives up to these aspirations. Of those who look to it essentially as a method of achieving stability and consistency, who look to a 'negative' sort of planning, few deny its utility. Above all, given the importance of the public sector in most western capitalist countries, the government needs a framework within which to plan public spending, a framework that inevitably involves forecasting the short and medium term trends within the economy as a whole, and it does not really matter for this purpose whether this forecasting is dressed up into a fully fledged planning exercise; it can be conducted wholly as an internal exercise within the government machine as is currently (1972) the case in the UK.

As a more positive exercise in attempting to increase the rate of growth of the economy, planning requires a major leap of faith, both to endorse its aspirations and to believe that they will be translated into reality. This type of planning has a good deal in common with the 'campaignology' of the Soviet five year plans. Many economists are highly sceptical about its application to a capitalist economy, and Britain certainly seems to have gained little from it. Yet sceptical though one may be at this attempt to pull off a 'confidence trick', there is no denying that the 'residual' rate of growth of the French economy

– growth stemming from advances in knowledge and changes in the average lag of putting new techniques into practice – has been higher than that of any other western European country, and that there is no obvious explanation other than that France had a good deal of leeway to make up why this should have been so. While there is certainly no necessary relationship between the existence of planning and the growth achieved, there are those who see in this some limited vindication of this more positive type of capitalist planning.

Further reading

JE MEADE *The theory of indicative planning* Manchester University Press 1970. A non-mathematical exposition of some of the basic theory of indicative planning.

A SHONFIELD *Modern capitalism* Oxford University Press London 1965. Part 2. Very readable: compares and contrasts the development of planning institutions and techniques in France, UK and Sweden.

G GROSSMAN *Economic systems* Foundations of modern economics series Prentice Hall Englewood Cliffs 1967 chapter 5 'Planning and control in capitalist market economics'. A simple introduction to some of the concepts of capitalist planning.

J TINBERGAN *Central planning* Yale University Press New Haven 1964. A brief treatment of some of the more formal aspects of planning.

I SVENNILSON *Planning in a market economy* Weltwirtschaftliches Archiv 1965. A brief description of Swedish planning techniques.

J & AM HACKETT *Economic planning in France* George Allen & Unwin London 1963. A detailed description of the institutional aspects of French planning.

PEP (Political & Economic Planning) 'Economic Planning in France' *Planning* Vol XXVII No 454 August 1961. A brief but useful survey of the drawing up of the 4th French Plan.

UK The National Plan Command No 2764 HMSO London 1965

A RUBNER *Three sacred cows of economics* McGibbon & Kee London 1970. An anti-planning essay which makes interesting, if polemical, reading.

4

Corporate objectives, market structure and market behaviour

4.1. Introduction

At the beginning of the last chapter we defined capitalism as a form of economic system where the ownership of property is largely vested in the hands of private individuals and where the allocation of resources is substantially influenced by the market mechanism. This definition, we noted, embraces the mixed economic system of many major industrial countries. In the next two chapters we shall be looking in more detail at the workings of the market mechanism within capitalist countries. Since we are concerned not merely with the question 'How does the market mechanism work?' but also with the question 'How well does it work?', we shall find ourselves returning to some of the issues raised in the first chapter when we were discussing what criteria we could use for assessing the performance of the economy. Particular themes which we shall be coming back to are

a whether some element of monopoly is inevitable because the technically efficient firm is bound to be sufficiently large that it exerts some influence in the markets where it buys and sells;

b how public policy adapts itself to the 'second best' world; and

c whether there is conflict between the static resource allocation objective and the other objectives of the economic system, particularly in relation to income distribution and growth.

For the moment however while keeping these themes in mind, let us return to the way in which the market works within the capitalist system.

Within the capitalist system, it is the production unit which actually allocates resources and decides how much labour shall be employed in the production process, whether production shall be expanded, and so forth. The most important type of production unit is the firm. Resources are allocated by decisions taken within the firm; decisions on price/output levels, investment expenditure, advertising expenditure, product characteristics, etc. These decisions are, in themselves, a response to consumer preferences expressed through the market and they fall under the group heading of 'market conduct' or 'market behaviour'. We are interested in how sensitive producer responses are to 'signals' about consumer preferences sent through the market. We must therefore look further at market conduct.

Market conduct is itself the product of two further influences; one, whether the objective of the firm is to maximize profits or to look to some other goal or goals; the other, the environment in which a firm operates. Take the example of the firm in perfect competition. Given the perfectly competitive environment and the objective of profit maximization, its price/output behaviour is determinate; it will produce that output at which price is equal to marginal cost. In this case the environment dominates all. The firm has no freedom of choice on price, and, with no product differentiation, there is no question of choice over product quality or characteristics; no advertising expenditure for nothing is to be gained by advertising. Even the firm's objectives are determined by the environment; unless it seeks to maximize profits, it will be driven out of the market. At the opposite extreme, the pure monopolist has considerable freedom of action or discretion, for he has freedom to determine his aims. He does not have to maximize profits but may opt for different ends. His behaviour in the product and factor markets will similarly depend upon these aims; when we know them we can predict his behaviour. If he is a profit maximizer, he will equate marginal cost with marginal revenue to derive his optimal price/output combination; similarly, his advertising and quality decisions will be guided by profit considerations.

93

But given different objectives, his behaviour will differ.

Pure competition and pure monopoly may be thought of as being the two polar extremes of market structure. Between them lies a spectrum of structures, ranging from atomistic competition, with many small buyers and sellers, through varying shades of imperfect and oligopolistic markets to duopoly and monopoly.

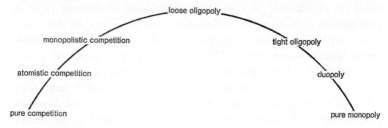

loose oligopoly

monopolistic competition

tight oligopoly

atomistic competition

duopoly

pure competition

pure monopoly

Figure 5. The spectrum of market structures.

Within this spectrum, as we shall see, we lose the neat determinacy of the two polar positions, and our predictions become hedged by uncertainty. Nevertheless, in a general sense the market behaviour of firms can still be seen as the product of objectives and environment. Since ultimately the economist is interested in the market conduct of the firm, for it is this which affects resource allocation and income, it seems logical to begin by looking in more detail at these two factors. This we shall do in the next two sections of this chapter. In the final section we shall return to market conduct.

4.2 Objectives

We suggested that the entrepreneur in an environment of perfect competition is perforce a profit maximizer, for otherwise he would be driven out of business by profit maximizing competitors. Is this a reasonable assumption to make about the large corporate firm, with its hierarchy of managers, its thousands of employees and shareholders?

We can distinguish two separate influences which together may lead the modern firm away from profit maximization. First, it is frequently large in relation to its market which means that, unlike the Victorian family firm, it does not operate in an environment of atomistic competition, but wields some monopoly power. This market power gives it the option of pursuing a 'quieter life' if it so wishes. It will not be driven from the market if it does not exert itself to maximize profits, but will continue in existence, albeit yielding a lower rate of return on its assets than potentially obtainable. (As we shall see below, the threat of takeover may provide some stimulus towards profit maximization.) The second influence which may lead the firm away from profit maximization is the separation of power between the management and the ownership of the enterprise, the so-called 'managerial revolution' of the twentieth century. It is this institutional change, combined with the increased 'discretion' to opt for a quieter life, that has led many commentators to question whether we can any longer confidently assume that firms are profit maximizers.

Let us look at the typical set-up within the modern firm. Ultimate responsibility for decisions lies with the board of directors who are elected by shareholders and who might therefore be assumed to look primarily to the shareholders' interests, that is to maximizing the return on the capital assets of the enterprise. For most modern corporations however shareholders are too numerous to be more than an impersonal force and a passive impersonal force at that, content so long as their dividends are satisfactory. The real force in the enterprise is the managers who control day to day affairs. Top managers become directors, because they are experts in the company's affairs. They are seen in many instances to have created themselves into a self-sustaining oligarchy in the board of directors, which becomes in turn dominated not by shareholder but by management interests. To quote Galbraith, 'The annual meeting of the large modern corporation is perhaps, our most elaborate exercise in popular illusion.'[1]

In such circumstances it is not surprising that many commentators should have shown incredulity at the assumption of profit maximization. Since profits go to shareholders and managers do not represent the majority of shareholders, why should managers seek to maximize profits? Rather they may be expected to pursue ends which contribute to their own satisfaction and prestige – to maximize their own profits, or equivalent, rather than profits which will accrue to shareholders. Interest

[1] JK Galbraith *The new industrial state* Hamish Hamilton London 1967 Penguin 1969 p 93.

has therefore centred on the ends pursued by managers – if not profits, then what is it that they seek?

Suggestions are not lacking. Observation reveals that managers' salaries and status are more closely related to the size of the enterprise than to its profitability. Managers, it is suggested, are therefore interested in maximizing sales. They set prices at a level which covers costs and yields a sufficient dividend to keep shareholders quiet, but then try to maximize sales.[2] This hypothesis accords well with other investigations revealing the widespread use by management of 'rule of thumb', mark-up methods of setting prices and making investment decisions.

Other economists look to the firm as a dynamic unit and suggest that, rather than trying to maximize sales at a particular date, managers seek to maximize the rate of growth of the enterprise.[2] Since growth needs to be financed, and finance comes either from internal sources, undistributed profits, or from external sources, the capital market (which provides funds the more cheaply if current and future profit prospects are good), maximizing the rate of growth of the firm and maximizing profits can be seen to be complementary to each other, the one a dynamic extension of the other. However, the 'growth maximizers' go further than this. They place considerable emphasis on the firm as a group institution, developing through time and establishing its own momentum. The firm is not the impersonal 'chemical' reagent as it appears in price theory, but a group of individuals with human aspirations and human failings, and possessing a group dynamism.

This 'group behaviour' aspect of the theory of the firm has been developed by another school of economists.[3] They see the firm as a 'coalition' of diverse interests – the management, workers, shareholders, customers, etc who are represented directly or indirectly in the top decision-making group of the firm. The decisions deriving from this group may be seen, not as an attempt to meet a single objective such as profit maximiza-

[1] WJ Baumol *Business behaviour, value and growth* The Macmillan Co New York 1959 chapters 6–8.

[2] R Marris *The economic theory of managerial capitalism* Macmillan London 1964.

[3] R M Cyert and J G March *A behavioural theory of the firm* Prentice Hall Englewood Cliffs NJ 1964.

tion, but as an attempt to meet a complex of objectives representing a complex of interest groups. The sales director will seek to maximize sales and to increase the market share held by the firm; the production director will be interested in long and stable production runs. Profits feature among these objectives. Shareholders must be kept happy with dividend payments, funds are needed to finance investment, and top management needs a success indicator. The group decisions are compromise or coalition decisions reflecting relative pressures from the different interest groups; sacrifices in one instance may be offset by gains in another. The firm has not the simple, single objective of profit maximization, or indeed any other *single* objective such as sales maximization, but a complex of objectives, the weighting between which will change over time reflecting the shifting power structure within the decision making group. Major changes in policy, frequently associated with new faces in the boardroom, are similarly associated with external shocks to this power structure.

The behavioural theory has introduced a new vocabulary into the discussion of the theory of the firm. Objectives are expressed, for operational purposes, as absolute levels. Thus in the current financial year, there may be a production goal of, say, 10 million units; a profit of say £4m. These goals represent *aspiration levels*, the setting of which in themselves is seen to stimulate management to their attainment (thus, *management by objectives*). Similarly, the process of compromise involves side payments to different members of the coalition. For example, the sales director may be persuaded to back a certain policy decision only on condition that he gets an increased advertising budget. Such side payments, which are not strictly necessary to the functioning of the firm, are paid from *organizational slack*. Organizational slack stems from the existence of market power. Monopoly profits provide the necessary element of 'slack' which can be used in this way and if they are not going to be distributed to shareholders they can be used to oil the wheels of compromise. When times are hard, and competition increases, organizational slack is squeezed; when times are easy, and competition lessens, organizational slack expands. Thus organizational slack provides something of a cushion, within the firm, against the ups and downs of the market.

The behavioural theory of the firm is particularly useful because it is amenable to computer simulation. Predictions from such simulated models have shown themselves to provide a convincing likeness to the business behaviour of large corporations. Yet how far are these behavioural theories an alternative to profit maximization? The answer is that they do not really provide such an alternative for they do not provide us with a generalized model of firm behaviour which could be substituted for the profit maximization model within price theory. They are tailored to the individual firm and concentrate upon the internal decision making processes of the firm, an area ignored by the traditional price theory, which looked upon the firm as a passive agent, dominated by market forces. In this respect these theories are complementary to the profit maximization hypothesis. They are a particularly useful complement because they deal with decision taking in the large corporate enterprise where, as we suggested earlier, competitive forces may be muted and where there is discretion in the hands of the decision takers to opt for goals other than profits. But unless we can establish that a good deal of discretion resides with the managers of the individual firm, it would be dangerous to suggest that such a model represents the generality of firms.

The relevant question here is how much discretion the managers of such enterprises do in fact exercise. So far we have spoken of competition as being only competition in the product market. Yet there is also competition in the capital market. A firm can be seen as a collection of resources. Where these resources are being inefficiently used there is potential gain to another management group which may take over the firm, work the resources more effectively and make bigger profits. While shareholders may be passive, other management groups are not, and passive shareholders may have little loyalty to existing management. Fear of takeover limits the extent to which managers can afford to ignore profits and pursue their own objectives and therefore the discretionary power exercised by managers. Thus this discretion may not be as great as some suppose. We noted above that profit constraint is written into the behavioural model. How far does the minimum level of profit which is consistent with managers retaining control differ from profit maximization? There will be some leeway, for the market in 'managerial control'[1] is not a perfect one; there is lack of information and there are costs involved in using the market. Moreover, official control over mergers in both the US and the UK, whose purpose is to curb mergers which increase market power in the product market (see below chapter 5), further inhibits the effectiveness of the takeover market. This gives managers some discretion, some chance to pursue their own interests; but the existence of the potential takeover bid prevents them from pursuing paths which deviate too far from profit maximization.[2] In this context it is interesting to note that in the nationalized industries in Britain, which are free from the threat of takeover, the government have found it necessary to impose upon managers certain constraints, including target rates of return, aspiration levels, which prevent them from following their own paths too far. (See below chapter 6.)

What conclusions can be drawn from this discussion of objectives? Primarily, that it is necessary to distinguish between the scope for discretionary behaviour (ie the extent to which the firm is able to look to objectives other than profit maximization) and the exercise of discretionary power. As we have indicated, the scope for discretionary behaviour will depend upon both the power exercised by the firm in the product market and upon its immunity from takeover bids. Even where the firm has considerable power in the product market, it may be constrained in its actions by fear of takeover bids; indeed, this is likely to be a powerful force within monopoly and oligopoly markets which constrains the firm from neglecting the objective of profit maximization. Where the firm is left with some discretion, perhaps because the takeover market does not work perfectly, it would appear that a model on the lines of the behavioural model can best explain the way in which decisions are taken.

[1] The term derives from HG Manne 'Mergers and the market for corporate control' *Journal of Political Economy* April 1965.
[2] Even where competitive forces within the product market are weak, a further constraint is provided by the possibility of entry of another competitor into the product market. Within an oligopolistic framework, entry by a diversifier can be particularly important. We discuss these constraints at greater length in the section below on market structure.

4.3 Market structure

If market conduct can be seen as the product of market objectives and market structure, then market structure, the economic environment in which the firm operates, is the dominant influence, since it affects the degree of 'discretion' which the firm has to opt for objectives other than profit maximization. In this section we shall examine some of the more important features of market structure.

The definition of an industry

Before proceeding, we ought to be clear in our minds what we mean by the market and the industry. The market is essentially a microeconomic concept – the buyers and sellers of a particular commodity or factor. It is easiest to envisage where products are homogeneous, for example wheat or rice. Where products are differentiated, there is in a sense a separate market for each product, for example, for each different brand of motor car, or even each brand of cigarette. But while products are not homogeneous in the sense of being complete substitutes, nevertheless they can usefully be grouped into categories of near substitutes. While one may regard some own-brand cornflakes as inferior to Kellogg's, they are substitutes and compete directly with each other. Similarly, other types of breakfast cereal compete with Kellogg's cornflakes, but are a less close substitute than other brands of cornflakes. It may be best to think of a market not as a grouping of buyers and sellers of a homogeneous product but as a looser grouping of products that are close substitutes, some closer than others. Buyers and sellers in these product groupings form the market and the producers form the industry.

This concept of an industry is analogous to a constellation, the products being the stars within the constellation. Within each grouping products are to a lesser or greater extent substitutes, and cross elasticities are high. Between groupings there is little substitution and cross elasticities are much lower.[1]

---

[1] Strictly, even if we had homogeneous products, high cross elasticities (between say rice and potatoes, butter and margarine) complicate the definition of a market or industry.

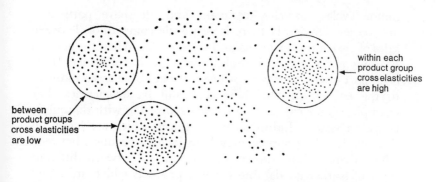

Figure 6. Industries as constellations. Few industries contain firms producing precisely the same products; rather an industry can be thought of as a group of firms producing a range of products which are close substitutes for each other, and relatively less good substitutes for goods produced in other industry groupings. When products are close substitutes, cross elasticities of demand are high.

Each grouping bears an industry label, for example chocolate and confectionery, breakfast cereals, children's clothing, steel, cars, etc. Inevitably there are some products which do not fall happily into any grouping – the stars that are found between constellations. Manufacturers of small vans, for example, can be grouped into the commercial vehicle industry or the car industry.

The concept of the market or the industry in a world of product differentiation is not therefore tightly knit, but blurred at the edges. Studying market structure means studying the structure of these different groupings.

From what has been said above, it is clear that the economist would like the statistical data which are used to study individual industries to be grouped so as to define industries to cover products having high cross elasticities of demand. Unfortunately, such data are not usually available. The industrial data most frequently used in studying industrial structure come from the Census of Production in the UK and the Census of Manufactures in the US. The definition of industries in these publications is frequently based on technical proximity rather than the economist's concept of substitutability – a supply side grouping rather than a demand side one. For example, the motor vehicle heading of the Standard Industrial Classification used in the UK covers cars, commercial vehicles, tractors, motor cycles, bicycles, caravans and all spare parts and accessories. Obviously there is very little competition between sales of agricultural tractors and sales of cars. When the general heading motor vehicles is broken down into its constituent parts each part often forms what is more recognizable as an industry to the economist. But there may still be deficiencies. For example, motor cars can be seen as competing with the public transport system. Industries in the census which are based on this supply-side grouping may both include products between which there is little direct competition (eg between different types of leather goods) and exclude products which are really close substitutes for the industry's output (eg leather goods and plastic goods).

Market concentration

We suggested at the beginning of this chapter that market structure can be thought of as a spectrum extending between pure competition and monopoly. If we think of this as a continuum in which the degree of monopoly is increasing, then our problem in classifying market structures is one of attempting to quantify the 'degree of monopoly' within an industry. An obvious start is to collect statistics about the number of firms in the industry and the relative size distribution of firms. Detailed information based on employment size groupings is available in the Census of Production which is conducted of business firms in the UK at regular intervals. This detailed information for each industry is relatively unmanageable and does not lend itself easily to comparisons between industries. For this reason, economists frequently attempt to summarize this information in some measure of concentration, which, as its name implies, is a measure of how far production is 'concentrated' in the hands of a few firms. There are various methods of measuring concentration but the most commonly used is the concentration ratio, which gives the proportion of total industry sales contributed by the 'x' largest firms in the industry. The number of firms to which it applies is arbitrary and varies from country to country. In the US the ratio is published in the Census of Manufactures relating to the largest four, eight and twenty firms in the industry. The UK used to publish concentration data relating to the largest three firms in the industry, but in the early 1960s switched to disclosing information only about the largest five firms.[1] The following table gives the five-firm concentration ratios for a selection of UK industries.

Table 1

Concentration ratios in some UK industries – 1963

man-made fibres (largest 7)	100
mineral oil refining	98–100
sugar	98·6
cigarettes	99·7
margarine	92·8
bread	71·4
beer	50·5
soap and detergents	81–85
television sets	81·6
cars	91·5
woven cotton cloth	19·3
women's and girls' outerwear	17
bricks	51·9
furniture	16
published books	33·9

Source: Census of industrial production UK 1963 summary Table 5.

Given the fairly narrow industry definition now adopted (which has the advantage of coming closer to the economist's concept of an industry), rather more than three-quarters of the industry groupings show a concentration of over 50 per cent, a figure that is often taken to show relatively high concentration with the four-firm concentration ratio commonly used in the US. In making comparisons between the US and the UK it is necessary to take account both of the different numbers of firms covered by the concentration ratio (although in fact studies have shown that the ranking order is not much affected by whether the

---

[1] This is partly explained by the fact that the industry breakdowns to which these figures relate are narrower than before. It therefore relates to fewer firms, and publishing statistics about fewer firms makes it easier to breach the basis of confidentiality on which the statistics are provided. Hence the move from three to five.

concentration ratio is based on a 3, 4 or 5 firm figure), and of the fact that the UK market is very considerably smaller than the US market. This would lead one to expect a higher level of concentration in the UK.

The concentration ratio is a continuous measure up to 100. As such it accords well with the concept of a spectrum of market structures. Industries can be ranked on the spectrum according to concentration ratios, the lowest being associated with the more competitive structures and the highest with the more monopolistic. It would be rash however to take the concentration ratios as a measure of the 'degree of monopoly' within an industry. Not only is it a one-dimensional measure, when we need to think in several dimensions when looking at market structure, but also in itself it is a limited measure. Its limitations stem partly from the 'supply' oriented industry definitions used by the census authorities (we are frequently not considering a group of products which compete with each other) and partly from the limited nature of the concept itself. The concentration ratio is no more than a statistic telling us the proportion of industry sales contributed by the 'x' largest firms. It tells us nothing about how many firms there are in the industry or what sort of size they are. It makes no allowance for such things as the geographical fragmentation of the market – products like beer and cement, for example, being produced mainly for regional markets – nor for competition from imports. Indeed, it has so many shortcomings that it is surprising that it is used so frequently as a starting point for studies of industrial structure.[1] Yet it has one substantial virtue, namely that it is a statistic readily available from official sources, and as a simple summary measure provides a ready means of comparing industries. We can use it as a starting point in the knowledge that, by and large, the fewer firms there are within an industry the more likely they are to wield market power; but in the knowledge too that a good deal more information needs to be gathered before we can begin to draw any conclusions.

[1] For a detailed discussion of the limitations of the concentration ratio as a proxy for monopoly power, see R Evely and I M D Little *Concentration in British industry* Cambridge University Press Cambridge 1960.

Market concentration in British industry

The most detailed study of concentration in Britain is that based upon the 1951 Census of Production by Evely and Little.[1] This gives us a starting point from which to gain some idea of concentration in British industry. Using a three firm concentration ratio, and defining high concentration as ratios over 67 per cent, medium concentration as ratios 34–66 per cent and low as 0–33 per cent, their finding in relation to the 220 trades which they analysed was as follows

Table 2
concentration in British industry 1951

	trades number	employment per cent
high (67 per cent and over)	50	10
medium (34 to 66 per cent)	69	24
low (33 per cent and under)	101	66
	220	100

Source: Evely & Little *op cit* p 51.

The surprising feature of this table is that in 1951 two thirds of employment covered in this sample was in trades with low concentration and only 10 per cent in trades with high concentration ratios. Some of the trades with high concentration ratios were relatively insignificant; others, such as cotton thread and cement, were more important. Within each concentration group, there were substantial variations in the size of industries, and in the number of firms per industry. No definite pattern emerged, but in general capital intensive industries, such as chemicals, oil refining, electrical engineering, vehicles and iron and steel appeared, as one would expect, amongst the more highly concentrated trades, and sectors which one associates with smaller firms, clothing and footwear, furniture, building and contracting, amongst the low categories.

[1] Evely and Little *op cit*. For a summary of their findings see the general introduction which precedes the book.

Evely and Little supplemented the concentration data with data on the number of firms in each trade and the size ratio (the average size of the three largest firms in an industry in relation to the average size of the remainder) which gives some idea of the equality in the size distribution of firms in the industry, whether it is dominated by a few large firms with a 'halo' of small firms or whether all the firms are of roughly equal size. This enabled a much more comprehensive picture of industrial structure to be gained. This data is used by Utton[1] to group the trades into three structural categories as follows:

Table 3
market structure in 1951

		trades number	employment per cent
group I	*monopoly and concentrated oligopoly*		
	High or medium concentration combined with *either* many firms with large size ratios, *or* few firms with small size ratios	90	30
group II	*unconcentrated oligopoly*		
	Medium concentration with many firms and small size ratios *or* low concentration with many firms and large size ratios	69	49
group III	*competitive*		
	Low concentration, many firms and small size ratios	60	21
		219	100

Source: MA Utton *op cit* p 79 table 7.

This more detailed analysis of industrial structure shows a much greater prevalence towards oligopoly – domination of an industry by a few firms – than revealed by the concentration figures alone. Group III, the competitive sector, accounted for

[1] See MA Utton *Industrial concentration* Penguin Modern Economics Texts 1970.

only one fifth of total employment, compared with two thirds of employment in the low concentration category. A somewhat similar conclusion was reached by Kaysen and Turner in their analysis of the US market: 62 per cent of total sales were made by industries of an oligopolistic type, and only 39 per cent by industries of a competitive type.[1]

Comparisons of concentration over time are tricky because census authorities redefine from time to time the definition and scope of industries. Even where there are no problems of definition, an unchanged concentration ratio may mask considerable changes in ranking within the industry because the concentration data tells us nothing of the dynamics of change within the industry. Evely and Little made an attempt to compare concentration in 1935 and 1951 in the UK and came to the conclusion that there was relatively little change. Comparison between 1951 and 1958 is bedevilled by the adoption, in the 1958 Census, of the Standard Industrial Classification. One study[2] found that only for 63 out of a total of over 200 industries were the definitions comparable between 1951 and 1958. Of these, thirty six showed some increase in concentration, sixteen a decrease and two industries showed no change. Industries particularly affected by increases in concentration were textiles and food.

It seems likely that concentration in the UK has increased markedly since 1958, although there is as yet no detailed analysis of later Census of Production figures, nor any published data yet from the 1968 Census. One reason for suspecting that concentration has increased is the volume of merger activity, particularly in the years 1966–9, mergers which often involved some of the largest firms in industries – for example the British Leyland merger of 1968, and the GEC–AEI merger in 1967. Another is that the Census for 1963 shows a definite tendency for concentration to increase. Of the total of 216 trades covered by the Census for which comparable data was available, 150 showed an increase in concentration, 65 a decrease and 1 no change. Given these changes in concentration, it seems likely

[1] C Kaysen and DF Turner *Anti-trust policy* Harvard University Press 1959 chapter 2.
[2] A Armstrong and A Silberston 'Size of plant size of enterprise and concentration in British manufacturing industry 1935–58' *Journal of Royal Statistical Society* vol 128 Series A pt 3 pp 395–420.

that the structure of industry in the UK has become more oligopolistic since 1951.

Economies of scale

Economies of scale are one of the most important influences on the level of concentration found within any industry. It is therefore worth looking in more detail at the sources and extent of economies of scale.

THE SOURCES OF ECONOMIES OF SCALE: Economies of scale stem from many sources. In a book of this nature, there is no sense in attempting to provide a detailed list and description of these sources.[1] Here we mention only the most important and general sources of such economies. They can usefully be divided between economies of the large scale plant, which are substantially technical in origin and affect the minimum efficient size of the factory or establishment, and economies of the large scale organization which apply to the large scale firm, which may be a multiplant unit.

ECONOMIES OF THE LARGE SCALE PLANT: There are three major sources of cost reduction to the large scale plant.

a Specialization Large scale output encourages specialization of labour and management and the use of flow rather than batch techniques of production.[2] It also enables the use of specialized machinery which may be more efficient than general purpose machinery. Moreover large scale machinery normally costs less per unit of capacity than smaller scale machinery. This is especially so where volume or capacity is an

---

[1] H Townsend *Scale, innovation, merger and monopoly* Pergamon Press Oxford 1968 provides a comprehensive and simple introduction.

For a detailed description see EAG Robinson *The structure of competitive industry* Nisbet 1959 chapters 2–5. A more detailed description of the sources and extent of economies of scale is to be found in CF Pratten *Economies of scale in manufacturing industry* Department of Applied Economics Cambridge Occasional Paper No 28 Cambridge University Press 1972.

[2] The specialization of labour is a source of two different types of economy. On the one hand, the saving of time, energy etc involved in changing tools, resetting jigs, etc; on the other, the increased efficiency gained from the repetition of a process – sometimes called the 'learning effect'. The latter economy derives not from a large output *per se*, but from the cumulative nature of large output totals – large output over time.

important feature, as for example in plant or machinery incorporating storage tanks, for, while volume increases by the cube of size, the surface area to which construction costs are related increases only by the square.

b Indivisibilities The appropriate machine for performing some process may be large in relation to the output of a firm, which may therefore operate the machine below capacity. Expanding output enables the fixed costs of such machinery to be spread over more units of production. Moreover the machine may itself operate more efficiently at capacity level than at below capacity. This effect may be exaggerated when a machine forms part of a production line and has to be combined with other machines whose optimum capacity varies. Thus to combine a machine with optimum capacity output of 300 units with another with optimum capacity of 400 units requires a production line with an output of 1,200 units, combining 4 optimally sized units of the one type of machine and 3 of the other. An output of less than this level would mean that one machine was working below capacity levels. Besides machinery, such things as research and development, advertising, initial tooling costs – any input which requires a minimum 'threshold' level of expenditure to be effective – can be considered as an indivisibility whose cost can be spread over more units as output expands.

c Economies of massed resources As a plant gets larger, savings may result from the fact that stocks of raw materials, spare parts, reserve capacity maintained in case of breakdown, etc, do not need to be increased in proportion to output. Thus an electricity grid system linking a number of generating plants needs a smaller percentage of reserve capacity than a generating plant which alone supplies the needs of an area, for the risk of simultaneous breakdown in a number of plants is considerably lower than the risk of breakdown in one plant.

ECONOMIES OF THE LARGE SCALE ORGANIZATION: Here we list four major sources of economy to the large scale organization. As we shall see, although we are able to identify these possible sources of economy to the large scale organization, empirical evidence indicates that they may not be a major source of cost saving.

a Further specialization of management The large organization provides scope for able management and can pay to attract it. Moreover, its size enables it to use specialists in the different fields of management to their full capacity. For example, employing a specialist sales manager represents something of an indivisibility. But the use of specialists may lead to cost reductions. An accurate sales forecast means a smoother production flow and lower stock costs. Working with specialist and able managers, plus organized training schemes which a large scale organization can undertake, in turn attracts talented recruits, themselves providing a pool of management talent for future use.

b Promotional and research costs This is an extension of the indivisibilities factor of the large scale plant. Promotional and research costs are both seen to have 'minimum effective' expenditure levels. Advertising, for example, has been shown to be more effective if conducted at a national level, through national newspapers and television networks, and at a saturation rate. Similarly in some industries firms face a high minimum or threshold level of annual expenditure on research and development which they judge necessary in order to remain competitive. The computer industry is an example of such an industry, for here the pace of technical progress is such that any firm which fails to keep abreast of the giants is rapidly lost by the wayside.[1] In the case of both advertising and research and development the threshold level of expenditure is an absolute (indivisible) one. Clearly in such cases the larger the level of output/sales, the lower the advertising or research costs per unit of output.

c Diversification and spreading risks Diversification can be viewed from two angles. On the one hand it is a method of spreading fixed costs because it enables fuller use to be made of specialist knowledge acquired and used by the firm in its primary product market – for diversification is usually into a field where the firm has some experience on the technical, production or marketing front. A similar spreading of overheads could be achieved through the expansion of the firm in its primary product market, but diversification may replace this

[1] See for example the article by C Freeman 'Research and development in electronic capital goods' *National Institute Economic Review* November 1965.

when it is difficult, for anti-trust reasons, or costly, for oligo-poly reasons, to expand in its primary market. In the second place, diversification may be looked upon as a method of spreading risks – the firm is putting its eggs in several baskets. Such a spreading of risk is often of importance in science-based industries where the cost of innovation is substantial and where failure in one product line could cripple a firm if the cost were not to be carried by profits on other lines.

d *Finance* The large well-known firm can raise capital more easily and more cheaply than the small firm.

The extent of economies of scale

ECONOMIES OF THE LARGE SCALE PLANT: The importance of economies of large scale plant varies from industry to industry according to the extent to which production processes lend themselves to mass production techniques, to the size of the market and to the extent to which consumers are prepared to accept a standardized product. These inter-industry variations are well illustrated by a recent study by CF Pratten of the importance of economics of large scale plant in UK manufactur-ing industry.[1] Here we quote the findings on three of the industries studied, oil refining, cars, and footwear, which in turn can be regarded as representative of the three main categories of industry distinguished in the study, the process industries concerned with processing raw materials, engineering industries and the textile and clothing industries.

Table 4
economies of large scale production in three UK industries

oil refineries

crude refinery capacity (m tons)	1	2	5	10	20
refinery costs (1m tons capacity = 100)	100	75	56	44	40

table 4.2 CF Pratten *op cit*

footwear

output in pairs per day	300	600	1200	2400	4800
production costs (300 pairs per day = 100)	100	97	95·5	94	93

[1] See CF Pratten *op cit*.

MARKET STRUCTURE AND MARKET BEHAVIOUR

(Table 3.0 in the interim report for the Pratten study – CF Pratten and RM Dean *The economies of large scale production in British industry: An introduction* Cambridge University Press 1965)

cars
(Illustrative estimates of costs for a range of models including 3 basic bodies and 5 basic engines)

output (000s per year)	100	250	500	1000	2000
index of average costs	100	83	74	70	66

(table 14.4 CF Pratten *op cit*)

From the table it can be seen that a tenfold increase in the output of shoes cuts production costs by slightly over six per cent, whereas a tenfold increase in refinery capacity cuts costs by over 50 per cent. Generally speaking, the processing of bulk raw materials lends itself to large scale production and economies are derived from increased dimensions, large machines and the spreading of initial costs. But for many engineering industries too there are substantial economies to be gained from the spreading of initial costs of developing new products, through learning and through more efficient techniques for longer runs and higher rates of output (particularly in terms of specialization in one product rather than a range of products). For the textile and clothing industries the scope for achieving economies of large scale plant was much less, although there were some economies to be gained from long runs in these industries.

ECONOMIES OF THE LARGE SCALE FIRM: The existence of important economies associated with the multi-plant firm is more doubtful. Moreover they are particularly difficult to measure. It is one thing to make estimates of the necessary expenditure on plant, labour and raw material inputs for different sizes of plant, but quite another to assess the necessary managerial inputs, risk factors and so forth associated with the different sizes of firm and any attempt to do so must inevitably be somewhat subjective. Where such attempts have been made, the general conclusion is that multi-plant economies are not important relative to the economies to be gained from large scale plant. Bain for example, in a study of twenty manufacturing industries in the US,[1] arrived at estimates of the importance of multi-plant economies for twelve of the twenty industries. In only three of the twelve did multi-plant economies of any significance appear to be present and in all cases they led only to small reductions in cost. Bain's conclusion was that multi-plant economies did not increase the size of the efficient firm significantly above the size required to reap plant economies.

DISECONOMIES OF THE LARGE SCALE FIRM: A more contentious issue is whether there exist diseconomies of large scale firms. The existence of economies of large scale plant means that there is a *minimum efficient size* of firm – the minimum size at which the firm is able to take full advantage of all the economies of large scale plant and below which the firm is failing to reap full advantage from such economies. Is there similarly some upper limit to the size of the firm? Is there any reason why, as output expands beyond a certain point, unit production and distribution costs should begin to rise? Since the firm can always expand by duplicating the minimum efficient size of plant there is no reason why actual production costs should rise. There may however be costs associated with the larger scale of organization which will tend to push up overall unit costs as the size of the firm increases. It is often suggested that the more bureaucratic structure of large firms inevitably involves some 'control loss' on the part of management both in terms of the receipt of information and in the execution of decisions.[2] (Just as a message whispered from person to person around a room becomes distorted so, it is contended, information and commands become distorted as they are passed up and down the bureaucratic hierarchy.) Such diseconomies, it is argued, may well offset any gains to the larger firm from the availability of more able and more expert management and thus lead eventually to rising unit costs. Moreover, when increasing size (in output terms) means that the firm moves from being a small peripheral unit within the industry group to being one of the major producers, the firm may move from an environment where it

[1] JS Bain *Barriers to new competition* Cambridge Harvard University Press 1956 pp 83–93.
[2] OE Williamson 'Hierarchical control and optimum firm size' *Journal of Political Economy* April 1967.

could operate with a fair degree of independence to one of interdependence and this too may bring with it increasing unit costs, for the firm will now be faced by greater uncertainty. To combat this greater uncertainty the firm will be involved in the cost of gathering and organizing information necessary for decision taking, an exercise which itself will be subject to 'control loss'. On the selling side too, costs will tend to rise as it tries to penetrate further into an oligopolistic market against rivals who, though relatively unconcerned about its activities when it was a small firm at the periphery of the industry, may be determined now to prevent any further growth and to counter any sales initiative. Both these items may mean that costs for the larger firm may be disproportionately greater than for the smaller firm.

If diseconomies of scale are present we would expect to find the firm facing the traditional 'U' shaped long run average cost curve, with unit costs falling as economies of scale are exploited and then rising as diseconomies set in. The lowest point on the 'U' shaped cost curve then tells us the most efficient (in the sense of producing at lowest unit cost) or optimal size of firm. Where there are no diseconomies of scale, then once economies of scale are exhausted we would expect to find the long run average cost curve flattening out to create an 'L' shaped cost curve, where there is not one, single, optimal size of firm, but only a minimum optimal size (firms above this size being no less and no more efficient in a cost sense than a firm of the minimum optimal size). This is illustrated in figure 7 below.

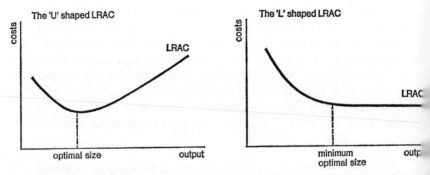

Figure 7. The optimal size of the firm with the 'U' shaped and the 'L' shaped long run average cost curve.

There is a good deal of controversy over the shape of the long run average cost curve faced by the firm, and a large number of attempts have been made to 'measure' it in one way or another – to assess whether the firm (as distinct from the plant) really does encounter economies or diseconomies of scale. Such studies run into considerable practical and conceptual problems, but it is probably fair to say that on balance the empirical data comes down in favour of the 'L' shaped cost curve, supporting the view that if diseconomies occur they do so at larger output levels than achieved in practice by most firms.[1] This in turn would imply that, for most industries, rather than one optimal size of firm, there is only a minimum optimal size – the size when all scale economies are exhausted – and that above that size a firm need be no less (and no more) efficient than the smaller unit.

DYNAMIC EFFICIENCY: However, the concept of efficiency embodied in attempts to measure economies of scale is essentially a static one, for the cost curve itself is a static concept. Given best available technology at any given moment of time it is concerned with how unit costs vary with the different levels of output. As important, if not more important, than static efficiency is the question of whether the management is alert and responsive to change, whether it seeks to find out about and use least cost methods of production, whether it seeks to exploit potential economies of scale – whether it is generally 'on its toes'. This concept of efficiency is sometimes referred to as dynamic or 'X' efficiency after the name given to it by Professor Liebenstein.[2] Managerial economies and diseconomies fall, in part, within this notion, looking as they do to the group responsiveness of the large organization, and this is one reason why attempts to go beyond the measurement of the significance of economies scale to the plant and to try to assess their importance to the firm run into difficulties. For example the idea lying

---

[1] For example Bain (JS Bain *op cit* chapter 3), although finding little evidence to support the existence of significant economies to the multi-plant firm, did find concentration in manufacturing industries well above levels explained by plant economies. He concluded from this that firms were able to operate several plants of optimum size without significantly increasing their average total costs. See also J Johnston *Statistical cost functions* McGraw Hill New York 1960.

[2] H Liebenstein 'Allocative efficiency versus "X" efficiency' *American Economic Review* June 1966.

behind the name 'managerial diseconomies' is that large organizations become slow and bureaucratic, with a tendency to opt for the least troublesome solution, an idea that falls within the dynamic rather than the static concept of efficiency. Note too that we are back here to the notion that the firm may opt for a quiet life rather than to maximize profits.

However, while conceptually we may be able to separate the notions of dynamic and static efficiency, we have no method of satisfactorily quantifying dynamic efficiency – it has proved far too nebulous a concept. Yet without such quantification we have only a partial, static idea of optimal size, such as the attempts mentioned above to measure long run average cost curves. One method which tries to overcome the static nature of measurement and to arrive at some notion of overall efficiency (static and dynamic) and its relation to firm size is what is called the 'survivor technique'. The idea behind this is the simple Darwinian one of the survival of the fittest. If there is a clear tendency over time for firms in an industry to cluster towards one size group, this suggests that this size of firm may be more efficient than others. Using this technique, Stigler[1] found a tendency, in a majority of the industry groups studied, for firms to group themselves in the size category below the largest, which suggested that the largest firms were not the most efficient and that diseconomies of scale might be a more important factor than suggested by earlier evidence. However, the survivor technique is only of use where competitive forces are strong and where there are large numbers of firms in the industries under consideration. It can only give an indication of the efficient size of firm for the 'competitive' category of industries, that is those with low concentration, a large number of firms, or low size ratios between largest and smallest firms, but not for the large, modern, oligopolitics corporation.

This leaves us in a most unsatisfactory position. From the public policy point of view what is required is a clear indication of whether large size is likely to be associated with increasing efficiency in its full dynamic sense. Size is clearly positively associated with market power and we are anxious to know whether increasing market power is, in these circumstances,

[1] GJ Stigler 'The economies of scale' *Journal of Law and Economics* Vol 1 1958.

counterbalanced by gains in efficiency. The empirical evidence here is quite inconclusive. The existence of, in some cases substantial, economies of large scale plant is not in dispute, but it would be dangerous to go beyond this and to conclude from the evidence available that there are substantial advantages or disadvantages to the large scale organizations. Generalizations are impossible: one is thrown back on a case-by-case study.

CONCENTRATION AND ECONOMIES OF SCALE: The minimum efficient size of firm will clearly influence the number of firms one is likely to find in an industry. The larger the minimum efficient size of firm in relation to total industry output, the smaller the number of firms one would expect to find in the industry and the higher the concentration ratio.

For the UK the Pratten studies provide data on minimum efficient plant size.

Table 5

output of efficient plants as percentage of UK industry output

	1969
oil refining	10
dyes	100
beer	3
bread	1 (33 per cent city market)
cement	10 (40 per cent regional market)
steel (rolled products)	80
cars (range of models)	50
domestic electrical equipment	20
knitting	Less than 3 per cent UK installed capacity
footwear	0·2
plastic products	Less than 1 per cent

Source: CF Pratten *op cit* table 30.1.

Note The Pratten definition of minimum efficient size differs somewhat from the Bain definition which has been used here. The Pratten definition is as follows: The MES is the minimum scale above which *any* possible subsequent doubling of scale would reduce *total* average unit costs by less than 5 per cent and above which *any* possible subsequent doubling in scale would reduce value added per unit of output by less than 10 per cent. (CF Pratten *op cit* p 26)

The importance of economies of scale does not depend only upon the size of the minimum efficient size of firm, but also on the extent to which firms below the minimum size are at a disadvantage compared with firms of a larger size. In many cases the disadvantage is not great, and the cost curve does not rise steeply at output levels below minimum efficient size. This explains why, although for over half the twenty industries Bain studied the minimum optimal size of plant/firm was at least 10 per cent of national industry capacity, he ranks economies of scale to be very important in only two of them, typewriters and automobiles, with the cement, steel, farm machinery, tractor, rayon, soap and shoe industries exhibiting 'moderately important' scale economies.[1] Similar conclusions emerge from the Pratten study of uk manufacturing industries.[2]

When considering these findings in relation to smaller countries such as the uk, allowance has to be made for the smaller size of the market. For example, the market for cars in the uk is one fifth that of the us and if the minimum efficient size of a car firm in the us is 10 per cent of its market, the minimum efficient size of firm in the uk would be at least 50 per cent of the uk market. But such adjustment is somewhat crude.[3] Factor price differences between the two countries – labour costs are substantially lower in the uk – mean that the most efficient production methods may vary considerably between countries with resulting differences in the minimum efficient size of plant. Moreover, it quite neglects the possibility of a major export market.

The presence of economies of scale can go a good way towards 'explaining' the levels of concentration which are found in different industries. One would expect to find high concentration levels in, for example, the car industry, the steel industry, the cement industry and the oil industry, because the

[1] JS Bain *op cit* chapter 3 pp 90–2.
[2] CF Pratten *op cit*. See in particular table 30.1, final two columns.
[3] JS Bain has in fact attempted to make some international comparisons of efficiency of plant size and its relationship to comparative levels of concentration in his *International differences in industrial structure* Yale University Press New Haven and London 1966 see pp 57–66.

minimum efficient firm is large in relation to the national market, just as one would not expect to find (and does not find) high concentration in the clothing industry and the book publishing industry.

Other aspects of market structure

An appreciation of economies of scale is therefore important to an understanding of market structure. But it does not carry us the whole way. There are other aspects of market structure which both help to explain concentration levels and supplement the concentration data. We shall look at only two of them here, product differentiation and barriers to entry.

PRODUCT DIFFERENTIATION: We saw earlier when discussing the concept of the industry that some industries come much closer to the idea of a homogeneous product than others. Thus each of the basic agricultural and raw material industries, such as wheat, rice, bananas, iron ore, copper, bauxite, and alumina, may be considered to produce a homogeneous product. Admittedly for all of them there are different grades and types, and prices vary according to grade, but this is not what is meant by production differentiation; within the same grade one farmer's wheat is no different from another's and he cannot obtain a higher price for it. This is not so in manufacturing industries. For example in the car industry, where cars might be grouped into 'grades' by engine size, not only do producers attempt to make their models as distinct as possible from those produced by their rivals but they even differentiate between variants of their own model – British Leyland produce many variations on the basic Mini model. Product differentiation is particularly important when the buyer lacks the knowledge to distinguish between different brands. Households do not generally have such knowledge, particularly of the more complicated consumer durable goods. Moreover, personal preferences differ – some prefer red to blue; some like a lot of salt, some a little; some like square lines, some rounded curves. It is to the manufacturer's advantage to play upon these preferences and to exaggerate physical and psychical differences in their products. Thus most of the manufactured products sold to the household, from toothpaste to motor cars, carry a brand label and are in some degree differentiated from rival products.

Product differentiation is relevant to market structure in four ways.

a It helps the producer to isolate himself from competitors
Where the product is differentiated the producer is able to some extent to isolate himself from the market and thus to act independently of competitors. He is trying to limit the extent to which his product has substitutes; to reduce the degree of cross elasticity between his product and others in the same industry grouping. To return to the constellation analogy which we used earlier, the producer is trying to move away from the other 'stars' in his industry group. If he is successful he ultimately forms his own industry in which he is a 'little monopolist'. Defining market power as the extent to which a producer can act independently of competitors, then it is clear that, when product differentiation is of importance in an industry, the concentration data can understate the degree of market power exercised by individual firms.

b It limits the exploitation of economies of scale
Product differentiation may prevent the full exploitation of economies of scale. When consumers have been encouraged to indulge their diversity of tastes, some economies of scale may remain unexploited. It is suggested for example that the UK car industry produces too many models, catering for too great a diversity of tastes, and that other UK industries too exhibit too great a degree of product differentiation.[1] But much differentiation is introduced in the last stages of production and the loss involved may not be very great. Moreover, it should not be forgotten that while standardization may bring lower costs it also entails some loss in consumer satisfaction.

c It stimulates competition in product characteristics
Where the product is differentiated, competition spills over from price into product characteristics. It is extended, on the one hand to physical characteristics and packaging, which

---

[1] See R E Caves (ed) *Britain's economic prospects* chapter VII The Brookings Institution Washington George Allen & Unwin London 1968.

help the consumer visibly to distinguish one product from another, and, on the other to advertising which is used both to inform the consumer of physical differences and to create psychical differences – the secret ingredient that makes your washing whiter, your car's performance better, etc.

d It creates a barrier to entry

Product differentiation creates a barrier to entry, since it means that a newcomer to the industry has to establish his 'brand' on the market by widescale advertising among retailers and consumers. This may be very costly. But it may also facilitate entry, since it is easier for a new entrant to make his presence in the market known. Advertising provides a ready channel for information in the market.

BARRIERS TO ENTRY: Built into the competitive process is the automatic erosion of excess profits by new entrants attracted into the industry. This is the dynamic aspect of the competitive process. If however there is some factor, or group of factors, which inhibits new entry, then this dynamic process fails. In terms of industrial structure, the *status quo* is preserved; a degree of concentration, once established, will remain over time. Moreover the whole rationale of the market mechanism is impaired, for resources will not automatically be shifted into industries where demand is growing and away from industries where it is declining.

Barriers to entry are thus an important feature of the economic environment. Their existence in turn is likely to affect behaviour. Take the example of the monopolist. If his position is fully protected from possible entrants by, for example, control over all known sources of raw material, then he is able to charge whatever price will maximize his profits confident that his position will not be eroded. If, on the other hand, he is aware that raising his price above a level that yields him normal profits will attract a large number of competitors into the industry, then he may prefer to opt for a quieter life in the longer run rather than attempt to reap maximum profits in the short run. In such a case he might set his price at a lower level, earning lower profits, in order to preserve his monopoly position in the long run. From this stems the idea that it is possible to gauge the extent to which barriers to entry exist in an industry from the difference between the price levels actually prevalent in the industry and the 'competitive' price level based on minimum unit costs of production and distribution (the lowest point on the long run average cost curve). The greater is the extent to which the firm can raise its prices above 'competitive' levels without attracting entry, the greater the presumed barrier to entry. Bain, for example, defined high barriers to entry as existing when industries were able to set prices 10 per cent or more above minimum average costs without attracting entry, moderate barriers as existing when prices could be raised 5–8 per cent above minimum average cost, and low barriers at below 5 per cent.[1]

Three main sources of barrier to entry are usually distinguished.

a Economies of scale Where economies of scale are substantial, new entrants may face a choice of either entering the industry at the minimum efficient scale level, thus increasing total industry output substantially and depressing market prices[2] or of entering the industry at below the minimum efficient scale and incurring the cost disadvantage that this would entail. The extent of this disadvantage will depend upon the shape of the long run cost curve: if the curve is steeply sloped, then those operating at below minimum efficient scale levels are at a considerable disadvantage, but if the slope is gentle, then the disadvantage may not be very great. As we saw above, JS Bain in his study of economies of scale found that, although economies of scale were significant in half the industries he studied, their importance was in most cases limited by the fact that firms operating below the minimum optimal size were at little cost disadvantage.[3]

b Product differentiation When an industry has a high degree of brand loyalty the new entrant has to embark upon a major sales promotion campaign in order to penetrate the market and overcome preferences for the products of established producers. This involves him in heavy sales promotion expenditure which

[1] JS Bain *op cit* chapter 6.
[2] Or, if market prices are held, the new entrant will have the problem of penetrating the markets of established firms – itself an expensive process.
[3] JS Bain *op cit* chapter 3.

raises his unit costs above those of his established producers. In turn, this gives established producers a chance to raise prices without attracting entry.[1]

c *Absolute cost barriers* This is a category of cost disadvantage that the new entrant sometimes meets where access to raw materials, patents and technical knowhow is controlled by established firms, and where the new entrant has to pay dearly to secure them. This shifts his whole cost curve above that of established firms. A rather special case of this absolute cost disadvantage is that of capital. The small firm may be at a disadvantage *vis-à-vis* the larger firm in access to the capital market and in the cost of raising capital. Where scale economies are important, this can create a significant barrier for the small firm, for the initial capital requirement will be large. It poses a lesser barrier however for the large firm diversifying into a new industry, for example Shell Chemicals moving into the agricultural fertilizer industry. Such diversification has been the source of a good deal of new competition in both UK and US industries in recent years.

In addition to these three structural barriers to entry, there are often legal barriers to entry deliberately created to protect certain categories of firm. For example, patent legislation gives the inventor monopoly rights over the exploitation of an invention for a certain period of years – in the UK it is for 15 years. Again licensing laws have limited the number of public houses and help to preserve the tied-house system in the brewing industry; planning laws have limited the development of the hypermarket in the UK.

As a feature of industrial structure, barriers to entry are not always readily apparent but require detailed industry-by-industry study. Of the twenty he studied, Bain[2] found five industries – tractors, distilled liquor, cigarettes, automobiles and quality fountain pens – to exhibit high barriers to entry

---

[1] This may not however pose such a major constraint on entry. In the first place brand names and advertising provide a ready means of informing the market of the existence of a new entrant. Secondly, in order to establish brand preferences, established firms must at some time in the past have had to finance advertising costs etc. The main difference is that the new firm has to face them immediately upon entry, and therefore requires the capital resources to finance such expenditures. Product differentiation may therefore create more of a 'capital' barrier to entry more than any other form of barrier.

[2] JS Bain *op cit* chapter 6.

(prices 10 per cent or more above minimum average cost), and another four – steel, copper, oil refining, and soap – to have moderate barriers (5–8 per cent above minimum average cost). Perhaps his most interesting finding was that the prime source of high barriers to entry was product differentiation. Economies of scale, although a frequent source of low or moderate entry barriers, were not a source of high entry barriers. Absolute cost barriers in some cases explained relatively high entry barriers. In the UK there is no study as broad or systematic as Bain's, although some of the reports of the Monopolies Commission have highlighted barriers to entry in certain industries. Its study of the detergent industry,[1] for example, criticized the high level of selling costs in the industry as providing a very significant barrier to entry. Again, in its report on petroleum distribution,[2] the practice of the major refiners of buying up key sites for prestige development of service stations was criticized for pushing up the capital required for entry.

Conclusions on market structure

We have attempted in this section to outline some of the more important features which the economist looks for in analysing market structure – concentration, economies of scale, product differentiation and barriers to entry. This is not claimed to be an exhaustive list. There are a great many features of structure, such as interlocking directorships, the rate of growth of demand, the instability of market shares and ranks, countervailing power amongst buyers and sellers, the geographical fragmentation of the market, which we have not attempted to look at. What it is hoped that this survey has achieved is to give the reader some comprehension of the complexity of environmental influences which operate upon the firm. We began by talking about the 'spectrum' of market structures, and the 'degree of monopoly'. This gives a too simplified, one-dimensional, picture. Both concepts are multi-dimensional. We may start with a single

---

[1] Monopolies Commission *Report on the supply of household detergents* HMSO London 1966.
[2] Monopolies Commission *Report on the supply of petrol to retailers in the United Kingdom* HMSO London 1965.

dimension, such as concentration data, but this has to be qualified and supplemented with a great deal of other material before
a comprehensive picture is obtained.

4.4 From market structure to market behaviour

Market behaviour refers to a firm's behaviour in its product
market – primarily its policies towards prices and outputs, but
also policies towards product differentiation, advertising and
sales. We saw earlier in this chapter (see table 3 and accompany-
ing text p 106) that British industry in 1951 could be characterized by concentrated or unconcentrated oligopoly structures
and that if anything there had been a tendency for concentration to increase since 1951. The same picture holds true of the
US, except that the evidence would indicate that concentration
has changed little in US industry since the early 1950s. This
oligopolistic structure derives from the presence of economies
of scale, economies of scale, even at the plant level, of sufficient
importance that the market can only support a limited number
of firms; and it is preserved, indeed extended, by two other
prevalent features of market structure, product differentiation
and barriers to entry. This section seeks to explain how these
features influence market behaviour.

Interdependence and oligopoly

The most important structural feature of the oligopolistic world
is the existence of sufficiently few firms for the actions of one
to affect the others. Where this is so, the actions of firms in
the market are dependent upon the reactions of others to the
decisions that they take, or rather upon the reaction that the
firm thinks will come from its competitors. This interdependence is not limited to price/output policies. As we saw earlier,
product differentiation adds an extra dimension to market
conduct, for the firm is able to compete in terms of product
policies, and the degree of interdependence is carried along the
line; the reactions of rivals to the introduction of new physical
characteristics in a product, to a new advertising campaign or
to a new sales gimmick are just as important to the success of a
policy as their reactions to a price change. Similarly, a firm

which fails to react to a change in product policies by a rival may find itself losing out, just as if it does not follow a price cut it may lose its customers. Thus much advertising expenditure, sales gimmickry, and so forth can be seen as defensive rather than aggressive behaviour on the part of firms.

Pricing policies in oligopoly

Let us for a moment neglect product policies and concentrate upon pricing policies.

For the industry as a whole, maximum profits could be obtained if the firms were to act together as a monopolist. Such outright collusion is difficult for two reasons. First, in most countries there are legal constraints on the most explicit forms of collusive behaviour. Firms are therefore forced back into the looser forms of collusion such as price leadership, where one firm becomes the acknowledged initiator of price changes and the other firms follow suit, or information agreements, where firms exchange information about prices and other product features but without any formal agreement to adhere to a particular pricing structure. (One has to bear in mind here that frequently one is dealing with not a single product but a range of differentiated products with its associated range of prices.) In the second place, while firms may agree on price collusion, it is less easy to reach agreement over the division of the spoils. If a firm is able to increase its share of the market at the going price its own profits will be increased at the expense of its competitors. A price cut by the individual firm might be worthwhile as a means of increasing both market share and profits, but only where price is above the firm's marginal cost and where it can keep the cut to itself for long enough for it to be able to secure some profit from the move. Hence the incentive to secret price cutting, the phenomenon of discounts below list price etc. The longer such moves can be kept from rivals, the more profitable it is for the firm in question. Eventually, price cutting is bound to come to light, if only because competitors will find customers slipping away from them. Such a discovery may well spark off a price war amongst oligopolists.

A price war in this context is a situation when all prices are in a state of flux with established differentials destroyed. There may well be no outright winner of such a price war. Sometimes a new price leader will emerge, but more often than not the new range of prices which will emerge in the long run represents a sort of stalemate position among the firms, a price war being the explicit acknowledgement that existing differentials have become unworkable. A firm may initiate a price cut when it feels that it will gain in the long run from such a move, for example when it achieves some technological breakthrough which cuts its costs *vis-à-vis* its rivals and thus puts it in a strong position in relation to its rivals. Alternatively, the move may reflect changes on the demand side. For example, excess capacity puts a good deal of pressure on capital-intensive firms to seek additional markets to help keep down unit overhead costs. In such a case, the first price cuts will probably be 'secret', but they will be made in the knowledge that secrecy cannot be maintained for any length of time.

Product policies

When a firm is unwilling to take the initiative to cut prices, it may well look to other methods of increasing its share of the market. Implicit collusion may hold prices relatively stable for a while, but it does not divide up the market between competitors. It is therefore open to a firm to use other methods to try to increase its market share at prevailing prices. This is where product policies play a part for they are designed both to enhance the attractiveness of the product in the eyes of the customer and the retailer, and to differentiate the product from its rivals. There are three main types of product policy.

POLICIES DESIGNED TO ENHANCE THE ATTRACTIVENESS OF THE PRODUCT TO CUSTOMERS: These involve policies aimed to give the product physical and metaphysical properties (through advertising etc) found through market research to be sought after by the public. Thus advertising which stresses the value of 'whiteness' in the different brands of detergent, masculinity in sports cars or in the different brands of petrol, sophistication associated with cigarettes or drink, and so forth. Such policies combine selling with product differentiation. Policies aimed more directly at 'selling' a product are free gifts, discount coupons, etc, the hope being that some customers, attracted from other products by these gimmicks, will subsequently stay loyal to the product.

POLICIES DESIGNED TO ENHANCE THE ATTRACTIVENESS OF THE PRODUCT TO RETAILERS: For some products the customer, while having certain loyalties, will place the convenience factor higher than loyalty and will buy the brand that is stocked by the retailer. Sweets and chocolates, many foodstuffs, ball point pens are examples here. In these cases it is important to secure the loyalty of the retailer as well as the customer, and a good deal of advertising and other selling features will be aimed at securing retailer loyalty. The extreme is the tied garage or public house, where the retailer becomes an exclusive outlet for one brand or product, total loyalty being gained in return for favours, discounts, etc. Resale price maintenance was another method of gaining retailer loyalty, the retailer being offered an assured margin on sales and no competition on price from other retailers.

POLICIES DESIGNED TO DIFFERENTIATE THE PRODUCT FROM ITS RIVALS: Some products are naturally differentiable. For example, furniture, cars, washing machines and television sets may be differentiated by design, and the designer will aim to produce a design that both pleases and differs from those of rivals. Sometimes, where a rival introduces a new feature that catches on and becomes popular, such as enzyme 'biological' detergents the oligopolist cannot afford to ignore the fashion and is forced to introduce a similar feature in his own product. Where a product cannot be differentiated physically – examples here are petrol, detergents, garden fertilizers – emphasis is put on packaging and advertising. The oligopolist is in an environment which encourages product innovation in its broadest sense of developing new types of product and new characteristics in existing products, and new uses for existing products. Indeed, the system may encourage a degree of product differentiation which is greater than the customer really wants.

It is worth remembering that the indeterminacy of oligopoly applies as much to product policies as to price policies. Just as, when collusion disintegrates, it is impossible to predict with any certainty how prices will be fixed, so it is not possible to say with certainty how a firm will employ the various product policies open to him. The interdependence applies on all fronts; product policies may be 'stalemated' by the reactions of a rival just as much as price policies. Price and product policies are the weapons of the oligopolistic cold war; they are employed in conjunction and used for both aggressive and defensive reasons.

Behaviour designed to change market structure

So far we have assumed that market structure is in some way 'given', and that the firm can do little to change the environment in which it finds itself. This is not so. There are various ways in which a firm can change its environment and the oligopolist has an incentive to do so. First, because increasing market power can mean higher profits. If a firm can manoeuvre itself into a dominant position in its industry then it can ignore its competitors and set prices at their profit maximizing level. Secondly, because increased market power means a quieter life for the firm is able to act to a substantial degree independently of others.

PRODUCT DIFFERENTIATION AND INCREASING THE DEGREE OF MONOPOLY: Product differentiation is one method of trying to obtain these advantages. Through product differentiation the firm seeks to create a brand image and a brand loyalty which makes the demand curve it faces less elastic. Where there is brand loyalty, if prices are raised, few customers are lost; similarly, a drop in price does not attract as many as in an undifferentiated market, but neither, for this reason, do rivals feel obliged to follow suit. Ultimately, where successful, the product differentiator creates for himself a little monopoly with no close substitutes for his product, and in such a situation he is able to act independently of his rivals. Thus he will have succeeded in escaping from the struggle implicit in oligopoly. It may not be so easy to do so, for moves towards product differentiation may be countered by rivals, who, while anxious to isolate themselves from the market, may also be anxious not to lose part of their market to others. Product differentiation may not be wholly successful, therefore, in keeping rivals at bay; but it does have another useful function in helping to keep potential rivals out of the market by creating a barrier to entry, thus enabling existing producers to raise price above average cost without attracting entry. The creation of such a barrier to entry where none existed before may therefore enable the established firms in the industry to change the economic environment in which they find themselves – to make it more monopolistic and slightly cosier for themselves.

MORE AGGRESSIVE METHODS OF INCREASING THE DEGREE OF MONOPOLY: Product differentiation is a relatively passive and not necessarily very effective method of increasing market power. Some firms may adopt more 'aggressive' tactics aimed at eliminating existing rivals from the market and keeping potential rivals at bay. There are various different methods that may be used.

Merger and takeover within the industry group This is sometimes called a horizontal merger. The aim is to increase profits, or net worth. In some cases this may be achieved by cutting costs, for example by exploiting economies of scale or improving managerial efficiency of the enterprise. In other cases the aim may be to obtain monopoly profits through exploiting increased market power. The two in fact frequently go together. For this reason both in the US and the UK the anti-trust authorities keep a firm watch on mergers between large companies. Particularly suspect are 'trust' or 'holding company' mergers, where there is no intention of merging physical assets, but which are merely amalgamations of financial assets and financial control. The aim may be to improve managerial efficiency and keep management on their toes, but it may also be aimed, as with many of the giant trusts formed in the US in the 1890s, to use market domination to secure excessive monopoly profits.

The use of price discrimination to weaken rivals Straightforward merger or takeover can be a relatively expensive method of acquiring market power, since the companies have to be bought at their stock exchange valuation. It may be cheaper to adopt tactics in the product market which will force a rival into liquidation or enable it to be bought up relatively cheaply. A favourite method is that of selective price cutting. A firm with substantial assets behind it – its strength stemming either from lower costs, greater financial reserves accumulated from past profits or from diversification – may eliminate competitors by cutting prices below profitable levels. Having done this it then exploits its market position and raises prices. This practice is easier where the market is geographically fragmented; for example, Standard Oil of New Jersey was able to manipulate itself into a dominant position in the eastern US in the 1890s by eliminating one competitor after another in regional markets in this way. Here too lies the power of the conglomerate, a large firm which has diversified into many industries. While its size and financial strength enable it to overcome barriers to entry, which would inhibit another entrant, so too these factors enable it to increase its market share within any one field by temporarily undercutting its rivals, the losses being borne by profits on other lines of production. Another variant of selective price cutting for a firm with market power at one stage of production is to integrate backwards or forwards into other stages of production and extend its monopoly position at the other stage by 'squeezing' rivals out of the market through price discrimination which favours its own subsidiaries.

Creating barriers to entry   The creation of barriers to entry will, as we have seen, inhibit potential competitors from entering the industry and thus help to preserve a monopoly position once created. We discussed above the use of product differentiation to create a barrier to entry. Vertical integration can create another barrier to entry. A dominant firm which integrates forward into retail outlets may make it difficult for a potential entrant to enter separately at either stage, necessitating entry at both stages and thus raising the capital requirements for entry. A similar effect can be achieved by 'tying' arrangements between manufacturers and retailers, which means that the new entrant has to woo retailers away from existing suppliers or enter simultaneously at the retail stage. In the UK such arrangements are commonly found in petrol distribution and the brewing industry, and have been subjected to the scrutiny of the Monopolies Commission.[1] Another type of barrier to

[1] Petrol: *A report on the supply of petrol to retailers in the UK* 1964 House of Commons Paper 264 HMSO London 1964–65. Beer: *A report on the supply of beer* 1969 House of Commons Paper 216 HMSO London 1968–69.

entry that a dominant firm can create is through control over machinery supplies. For example, the British Match Corporation, through an agreement with the Swedish Match Corporation, effectively controlled the supply of match-making machinery to the UK[1] which made sure that if 'outsiders' attempted to enter the industry they could only obtain machinery on relatively unfavourable terms. Again, the United Shoe Machinery Company, which had a monopoly of many kinds of machinery employed in the boot and shoe industry, used only to lease the machines to manufacturers on the condition that they did not use certain types of machinery available from other suppliers.[2]

CARTELS AND BARRIERS TO ENTRY: The formation of a cartel (a collusive agreement amongst buyers and/or sellers of some product) can be seen as an alternative way of achieving monopoly profits and a quieter life. Unlike mergers, firms within a cartel keep their identity and there will be no gains from economies of scale or increased managerial efficiency.[3] An effective cartel will represent all the firms in the industry, and such a cartel will not therefore usually indulge in the sort of discriminatory pricing practices which might be used by the dominant firm to extend its market power. Rather the cartel's aim will be to preserve the market power of the group; to prevent newcomers from destroying the cosy circle. Thus agreements fixing prices or market shares are frequently accompanied by exclusive dealing arrangements whereby members of the group will supply only those distributors who refuse to stock competitors' products. When distributors are covered by this sort of agreement then it is difficult for a potential entrant to the market; it provides an effective barrier to entry, as well as an effective sanction against dissident members, producers or retailers, who break the agreement. As we shall see in the next chapter, collective discrimination and exclusive dealing arrangements of this type have been amongst

[1] See Monopolies and Restrictive Practices Commission: *Report on the supply and export of matches and the supply of match-making machinery* pp 35 and 38 HMSO London 1954.

[2] Board of Trade Working Party *Boots and shoes* HMSO London 1947.

[3] Some cartels claim to promote the public interest by, for example, maintaining minimum safety or health standards. See discussion of the Restrictive Practices Act in chapter 5 below.

the first targets of policies aimed at controlling restrictive practices.

4.5 Summary and conclusions

This chapter has described some of the forces at work within the modern capitalist economy. We looked first at the aims and objectives of the firm. Modern group behaviour theory suggests that, rather than seeking to maximize profits, the managerial group may look to other objectives, including that of increasing their own salaries, status and responsibilities, decisions emanating from the group being compromises between the varying objectives of different members of the group. Two questions arise about such models. First, whether they can be generalized sufficiently to provide a general theory of firms' objectives, and secondly, how far decision makers are constrained by the knowledge that if they pursue their own interests too far and neglect profits, they will expose themselves to takeover by another management group. We suggested that the possibility of takeover was an important force encouraging profit maximization, but that nevertheless the behavioural theories, concentrating as they do upon the internal decision making processes of the firm, provided a useful extension to traditional theory.

The second section of the chapter looks at market structure. Market structure can be thought of as a spectrum which stretches between the polar positions of monopoly and pure competition. In trying to assess market structure, we are searching for some measure of the 'degree of monopoly' within the industry. A first approximation to this comes from data on the number and size distribution of firms in the industry, summarized in concentration data. But this data needs to be supplemented. On the one hand by data on economies of scale, for this goes a long way towards explaining the differing levels of concentration found amongst industries – higher concentration levels being found among those industries where economies of scale are substantial in relation to market size. On the other hand, it needs to be supplemented by information about factors affecting competition within the industry group – such things as product differentiation and barriers to entry which help to maintain and extend concentration levels within the industry.

Market behaviour emerges as the product of objectives and environment. Where there are many firms in the industry, little product differentiation and low entry barriers, the competitive model provides accurate predictions of market behaviour. Where there is one dominant firm in the market, then the monopoly model is relevant. Within manufacturing industry in the UK and US the more prevalent structure is oligopolistic, sometimes with a fairly large number of firms, but dominated by relatively few big firms, and sometimes with relatively few firms, but usually accompanied by product differentiation and some form of barrier to entry. The main feature of the oligopoly world is inter-dependence, the decisions taken by one firm immediately affecting its rivals. This inter-dependence and the uncertainty associated with it does not make for an easy life, and there is therefore a tendency for firms to seek to escape from it. This can be achieved through collusive agreements (which tend to be unstable being difficult to police and facing legal constraints), or through seeking isolation from the industry group through product differentiation. The world of oligopoly is a world of games. The general strategy of each firm can be taken as that of establishing greater independence for itself from the market, but since actions taken to achieve this end will be countered by its rivals, day to day tactics will depend on estimates of actions to be taken by its rivals in the market. On some occasions the firm may attempt to buy out its rivals, or undermine their position by price discrimination or other 'unfair' practices.

This chapter is closely linked to the next chapter which describes the development of public policy towards monopolies and restrictive practices. Is there anything which emerges from our survey which suggests that there is need for public control over market structure or market behaviour? Two features stand out. First, whether we like it or not, that firm size is an important feature of industrial structure. Secondly, that there are both gains and losses from size. The gains stem from economies of scale. Empirical studies have established that economies of large scale plant stemming from technical relationships underlying production processes are to be found in nearly all industries, but that their importance varies immensely from industry to industry, being on the whole most important in raw material processing industries. The evidence relating to large scale firms, as distinct from plants, is less conclusive. Empirical studies have failed so far to establish clearly the existence of either economies or diseconomies in the large scale firm – whether the larger size management unit with the advantages of specialization etc is likely to be more efficient or less efficient than the smaller unit – although it is here that public policy interest centres, for it is the amalgamation of plants into large scale management units, which possess considerable power both within the market group and in the economy as a whole, that causes concern. The concern arises for three reasons. First, because it affects the allocation of resources. We have to be rather careful here, for within a second best world we cannot glibly say that the further price diverges from marginal cost the worse the allocation of resources. But where the 'degree of monopoly' is increasing; particularly when associated with the creation of barriers to entry which prevent factors from moving into expanding industries, there is a presumption that it has an adverse effect upon the allocation of resources. In the second place, increasing market power may be associated with dynamic inefficiency; large firms may not be interested in minimizing costs and maximizing profits. Lastly, increasing market power affects the distribution of income, tending to redistribute income towards management and shareholders in large enterprises. Public policy has to weigh the advantages of size against these disadvantages. This creates a very real issue of policy as we shall see in the next chapter, but one where the lack of any conclusive evidence on either side leads to caution and pragmatism.

Further reading

RE CAVES *American industry structure and performance* Foundations of modern economics series Prentice Hall Englewood Cliffs New Jersey 2nd edition 1967. A concise and readable introduction.

H TOWNSEND *Scale innovation merger and monopoly* Pergamon Press Oxford 1968. A short introductory work with emphasis upon economies of scale and firm size.

KD GEORGE *Industrial structure and industrial organization* George Allen & Unwin London 1971. A lengthier, but more complete, introductory text.

GC ARCHIBALD (ed) *The theory of the firm* Penguin modern economics parts 1, 3, 5 and 6 Penguin Books Harmondsworth 1971. A useful follow up to some of the issues discussed in this chapter.

D NEEDHAM *Economic analysis and industrial structure* Holt, Rinehart & Winston 1970. A more advanced textbook dealing with industrial structure and the economic rationale of public policies affecting industrial structure.

5

Anti-trust[1] – the policy framework

5.1 Introduction

At the end of the last chapter we suggested that there were three main reasons for concern at the existence of monopoly power within the economic system. These were that it may adversely affect the allocation of resources, the dynamic efficiency and the distribution of income within the economy. If this is so, then the existence of monopoly power wielded by individual firms within the economic system, and *a fortiori*, any increase in the 'degree of monopoly', vitally affects the three main objectives which, in the first chapter of this book, we suggested characterized our economic system – namely objectives relating to allocative efficiency, growth and the distribution of income. Let us look at these in more detail.

Monopoly, allocative efficiency and the world of second best

One of the salient findings of the last chapter was that the prevalence of monopolistic/oligopolistic structures can be explained at least in part by the presence of economies of scale. While there seems little evidence to support the creation of mammoth organizations, nevertheless economies of scale are of sufficient importance in many industries to make remote the

[1] The term 'anti-trust' is used here in its generic sense of policies aimed at controlling monopolies and restrictive practices. As we shall see, such policies were first brought to bear against the trusts, combines and holding companies which sprang up in the US in the 1880s and 1890s. Hence the name 'anti-trust'.

practical possibility of a perfectly competitive economy and thus to cast us irredeemably into the 'second best' world. This is important, for, as we saw in the first chapter, once we have fallen from the grace of the first best world, the rules of that world are no longer appropriate. Within the second best world no generalized set of rules is applicable; the only way we can judge whether a particular policy is likely to lead to a better or worse allocation of resources is to consider each case on its own merits. In this situation, unless we are prepared to condemn all monopoly, root and branch (which would mean denying ourselves the benefits of economies of scale), we cannot condemn monopoly structures out of hand as leading to a mis-allocation of resources, nor, *a priori*, can we claim that the establishment of a more competitive market structure would be likely to lead to a 'better' allocation of resources. On allocative efficiency grounds, therefore, we have no *a priori* case for condemning the existence of monopoly. But we have no grounds either to condone it, and in particular should look with caution upon developments and practices which *increase* the degree of monopoly within an industry.

Monopoly and dynamic efficiency

The competitive process should not be thought of in static terms, but as a dynamic process where new cost reducing techniques are being continuously introduced, replacing older, more expensive methods of production. Our concern is thus as much with the development and introduction of new produc-tion techniques which will minimize costs over time (dynamic efficiency) as with short run cost minimization (static efficiency). The fear here is that without the stimulus provided by the competitive environment the firm will not attempt to keep costs down to a minimum but will go for a quieter, easier life. This amounts to the contention that given the 'discretion' which goes with the acquisition of monopoly power, the firm will not seek to maximize profits, and minimize costs, but will opt for other goals.[1] In contrast to this view there are some economists,

---

[1] See section 2 of chapter 4 where we discussed this issue and argued that the takeover bid provides some constraint on the ability of firms to pursue objectives other than profit maximization.

foremost amongst whom is Schumpeter,[1] who argue that, far from inhibiting innovation, a monopolistic/oligopolistic environment is more conducive to innovation than the 'riskier' environment of the competitive world. Dynamic efficiency, they argue, is thus more likely to be achieved within a monopolistic than a competitive environment.

There are three separate strands of thought behind the Schumpeterian hypothesis:

a that the greater profitability of the monopolistic environment provides a source of finance necessary to pay for innovation which, because of the risk attached, can only attract funds from the capital market at high interest rates;
b that the higher and more secure returns associated with a monopolistic environment are necessary to induce the 'riskier' innovative investment;
c that the lack of price competition under oligopoly leads to competition on process manufacture and product improvement which in turn stimulates innovation.

Here are two opposing hypotheses both of which, *a priori*, seem reasonable enough. To decide between them though, we should look, not to *a priori* 'reasonableness', but to their ability to stand up to empirical testing. The main difficulty that empirical work here has encountered has been in attempts to find suitable measures of innovation. Some studies have used expenditure on research and development (R & D), the 'input' into innovation; others have tried to develop some measure of innovatory output based upon patent statistics. Neither of these measures has been entirely satisfactory. Another difficulty is that major variations in inter-industry innovation records may reflect not differences in industrial structure but differences in the technological opportunities to develop new products and processes by R & D – for example the pace of innovation has been high in the chemical and electrical engineering industries where the underlying rate of technical progress is fast, whereas

---

[1] Schumpeter is regarded as the 'originator' of this school of thought. See his *Capitalism, socialism and democracy* Harper New York 2nd edition 1947 chapter VII and VIII. For a general comment on views variously ascribed to Schumpeter and Schumpeterians see JW Markham 'Market structure, business conduct and innovation' *American Economic Review* papers and proceedings May 1965.

innovation has been low in the food and textile industries where technical progress is slow. Some studies allow for such inter-industry differences in the underlying rate of technical progress.[1]

The weight of the evidence seems to be against the Schumpeterian hypothesis. Assuming that the larger firms tend to exercise greater market power, which seems a fair assumption to make, then, if the Schumpeterians are correct, one might expect to find more innovative activity on the part of large firms than small. Generally, it has been found that the larger the firm the greater the expenditure on R&D, but the larger firm has not been found to spend more *proportionately* than the smaller firm, and, when allowance is made for size, the record of the larger firms is no better than that of the smaller firms – indeed in some industries, such as steel and pharmaceuticals, small firms have performed relatively better than large ones. Some studies have sought to measure directly the relationship between concentration and innovative activity, and these too lend little support to the Schumpeterian hypothesis. One author has found a 'positive but weak' relationship to exist[2], another a negative relationship.[3] There is some evidence to suggest concentration and innovation may be associated in the 'middle range' of concentration (for a 4 firm concentration ratio of, say, 10 per cent up to 50–55 per cent) but that the relationship does not exist for either very low or very high levels of concentration.[4] Overall, this amounts to very little support from these empirical studies for the Schumpeterian hypothesis of a positive relationship between monopoly power and innovation. Nor, on the other hand, is there support for the view that the more competitive the environment the greater the level of innovation. The main conclusion to be drawn from these studies is that we cannot conveniently link innovation or 'progressiveness' with a particular form of market structure and we really have to judge each case on its own merits.

[1] FM Scherer 'Firm size, market structure, opportunity and the output of patented inventions' *American Economic review* vol XLVII 1965.

[2] FM Scherer *op cit American Economic Review* 1965 and also his 'Market structure and the employment of scientists and engineers' *American Economic Review* 1967.

[3] OE Williamson 'Innovation and market structure' *Journal of Political Economy* 1965.

[4] See FM Scherer *op cit* and WS Comanor 'Market structure, product differentiation and industrial research' *Quarterly Journal of Economics* Vol LXXXI 1967.

Income distribution

Where there is monopoly there is output restriction, price above production costs, and monopoly profits. Other things being equal, the greater the degree of monopoly the greater the share of income going to profits, ultimately to be distributed to rentiers, the owners of capital. This is what might be described as the grassroots objection to monopoly. To the average man in the street, monopoly means that he is being exploited either as a consumer, in the prices he pays for his purchases, or as a producer, in the prices he receives for his products; and the people to benefit from this 'exploitation' are the capitalists – the rich. 'To them who hath shall it be given.' This he thinks, with some justification, is unfair. Other things are not however equal; in a modern economy governments can and do use the tax/benefit system to redistribute income and it is in their power, if they so wish, to tax away excess profits and redistribute them back to the 'man in the street' in one form or another. We need not, in these circumstances, be too much concerned about the fact that an increasing degree of monopoly will change the distribution of income in favour of the owners of capital, for, within limits, we can use the tax/benefit system to redistribute income. (See the discussion in chapter 8 about redistribution.) But the grassroots tradition dies hard, and we shall find in it much of the popular clamour for controlling monopoly.

Workable competition

None of these three considerations, resource allocation, dynamic efficiency or income distribution provide an overriding case against monopoly. Does this mean that the economist's traditional bias against monopoly disappears? By no means. What emerges is the need for pragmatism, for treating each case on its merits.

There is a 'set of rules' which economists have evolved which is based not upon logic but upon pragmatism. It is called 'workable competition'. Underlying it is still a basic faith in the goodness of competition for, it is argued, as long as we look to the market as the main method of allocating resources, the market needs to function reasonably well. An industry or firm is judged by its responsiveness to market pressures. Does excess demand lead to an expansion of capacity? Is inefficiency eliminated by the market process? Do factors of production move freely from declining to expanding industries? There remains the presumption that where the firm is subject to competitive pressures, it is likely to be more responsive to market pressures. Stress is therefore put on the extent to which the firm meets competition from rivals within the product group, or from countervailing pressures from buyers or sellers with whom it deals, and on the extent to which it is cushioned from competition by barriers to entry or collusive agreements with other firms. Again dynamic efficiency is important, and the firm's record on innovation and cost consciousness.

Workable competition, more than any other standard suggested by economists has influenced the development of policies towards monopolies and restrictive practices. If anything, it has probably had a greater influence in the US, where the underlying philosophy that competition is a good thing is more readily accepted than in the UK where the authorities, while adopting a general pro-competition stance, have been prepared to be rather more pragmatic with emphasis on the case-by-case approach.

Let us now consider the development of public policy towards monopoly and restrictive practices. We shall look first at the US, and then at the UK.

5.2 Anti-trust policy in the US

The US was the first country to attempt to control monopoly and monopolistic practices and has since remained the most doctrinaire in its approach. To understand the evolution of US anti-trust policy it is necessary to go back to the major merger movements which developed in US industry in the late nineteenth century, which transformed industries previously characterized by small and medium sized firms into groups dominated by one or a few large firms, and created the basis of present day industrial structure in the US. This merger movement affected, amongst other industries, both the transport and the food processing industries, but left agriculture and retailing more or less untouched so that the small man, the farmer and the retailer, was faced by powerful buyers and dealers. The political pressure from these small men (who counted for many more votes than the major industrial giants) for legislation which would provide some protection against these monopoly elements goes further towards explaining the evolution of anti-trust policy in the US than any fancy economic theories being developed simultaneously in Europe. It also helps to explain the subsequent interpretation placed upon anti-trust legislation, the attitude, for example, towards resale price maintenance, and the evolution of agricultural marketing legislation, which, on the face of it, might seem openly to flout the pro-competition ethos in the US.

The first major landmark in US anti-trust legislation was the Sherman Act of 1890. This declared illegal, under section 1, 'contracts, combinations or conspiracies in restraint of trade' (ie restrictive practices) and, under section 2, the act of 'monopolizing' or attempting to 'monopolize'. The Sherman Act was extended and strengthened in 1914 by two further measures. First, the Clayton Act, which outlawed certain types of business practice which 'substantially lessen competition or tend to create a monopoly'. Its most important sections were section 2 which bans price discrimination – charging one buyer a different price from another for the same thing[1] – section 3 which restricts exclusive dealing arrangements and tying contracts, and section 7 which forbids mergers which would 'substantially lessen competition'. In contrast to section 1 of the Sherman Act, the Clayton Act was concerned with policies pursued by individual firms rather than with agreements between rivals. Section 3, the exclusive dealing clause, and section 7, on mergers, were both concerned with aggressive tactics threatening competition – section 3 with arrangements which could create a barrier to entry, for example, by forcing new entrants to establish their own retail outlets, and section 7 with amalgamations which would increase concentration and lessen

[1] The Clayton Act was specifically aimed at predatory price discrimination (see chapter 4). The Robinson–Patman Act of 1956 aimed at protecting the small shop-keeper from the chain-store and supermarket, extended the ban to cover other forms of price discrimination even where the price differential reflects a differential in delivery costs, etc. This has the effect of limiting competition rather than promoting it and is another example of how US anti-trust gets soft when it applies to the 'small man'.

competition.[1] The other Act of 1914 was the Federal Trade Commission Act which established a commission with wide powers to investigate business practices, and to outlaw 'unfair methods of competition in commerce'. The responsibilities of the Federal Trade Commission overlapped considerably with those of the Anti-Trust Division of the Department of Justice, which had been established to deal with litigation under the Sherman Act, and the division of powers between the two bodies has remained obscure ever since.

As with all legislation, it is not so much the acts themselves but the interpretation placed on them by the legal authorities which counts. Section 1 of the Sherman Act, as subsequently strengthened by the Clayton and Federal Trade Commission Acts, was fairly straightforward in application. It prohibited *per se* all collusive agreements among buyers and sellers, agreements to fix or maintain prices, to limit output or productive capacity, to share markets, to share profits and so forth. The *existence* of such collusion has only to be proved for the practice to be condemned outright – no other considerations were relevant. The main difficulty that arises is in relation to implicit rather than explicit collusion, for evidence of overt collusion is not necessarily required by the courts, which apply a doctrine of 'implied conspiracy'. This doctrine creates particular difficulties for oligopolies for, as we saw in the last chapter, the border line between oligopoly pricing practices and collusion is a hazy one, and this haziness has reflected itself in judgements in the courts on this issue. Does the exchange of information among firms through trade associations amount to collusion? Does price leadership constitute collusion? One commentator has remarked that many of the decisions are close and it is tempting to regard the different results from rather similar sets of facts as reflecting inconsistency and vacillation on the part of the courts. He continues however by saying that such an interpretation would be unwise. 'The job seems on the whole to be done with realism and good sense. The cases show that collusive price fixing, like any other violation of the law, may be estab-

[1] In fact section 7 of the Clayton Act originally applied only to the acquisition of shares in another company and left open the possibility of merger through the acquisition of physical assets. This loop-hole was closed by the Keller–Kefauver Act of 1950, since when action against merger has been the most active part of US anti-trust activities.

lished by circumstantial evidence: direct evidence of an express agreement is not needed.'[1] The fact that some people in the US feel that the courts are too easily persuaded of collusion, while others feel that it is too easy to get away with tacit collusion, would seem to bear witness to the fairness of the interpretation.

A bigger question mark hangs over the interpretation of section 2 of the Sherman Act, for the very language in which it is couched is ambiguous. What is meant by the phrase 'to monopolize'? The legal interpretation of this has varied. Two famous cases in 1911, the Standard Oil and American Tobacco cases, established what was known as the *rule of reason*. Both these companies had, by predatory practices of one sort or another (see chapter 4), manoeuvred themselves into positions of considerable market power. The judgement was that they were guilty of monopolizing, not because of their size in relation to the market, but on account of the unfair methods of competition which they had used to get themselves into such a position. In other words, 'to monopolize' was regarded as a question of *market conduct* rather than of market structure. Size as such was no offence, and a large dominant firm which had not indulged in predatory practices was not guilty of monopolizing. This 'rule of reason' interpretation of section 2 of the Sherman Act survived until 1945 when it was reversed by the Alcoa judgement. Here the court took the view that the large market share held by Alcoa, which had controlled 90 per cent of production in the aluminium industry, in itself constituted a violation of section 2 of the Sherman Act. In other words, *market structure* was taken to constitute an offence, not market conduct.

The Alcoa judgement was not quite the *volte-face* against the rule of reason which it appears at first sight. Alcoa had reached its dominant position through tactics which, though perfectly legal and above board, had nevertheless effectively prevented potential competitors from entering the market. The decision nevertheless marked a major shift of emphasis on the part of the courts. No longer was intent to 'monopolize' seen only in open tactics of weakening and taming competitors but could be

---

[1] AD Neale *The anti-trust laws of the USA: A study of competition enforced by law* Cambridge University Press 2nd edition 1970 pp 46–7.

read into other tactics which more insidiously enabled the firm to gain and maintain a monopoly position. As we saw in chapter 4, monopoly positions can be established and maintained through product differentiation and the creation of barriers to entry without resort to openly aggressive tactics. This shift in emphasis mirrors the development under section 1 of the Sherman Act (dealing with restrictive practices), of the doctrine of 'implied conspiracy' in relation to oligopolistic collusion. Tacit methods of establishing monopoly positions were now taken into account.

It was fair enough to extend the interpretation of the legislation in this way, but the real problem is what can be done about it. Just as price leadership is very much a natural way of life within an oligopoly environment, so frequently a dominant position in the market comes not from merger or takeover but from internal growth which presumably only takes place where there are cost advantages, perhaps arising from economies of scale, to be gained. In these circumstances, dissolution of the constituent parts of the company, the solution used in the case of monopolies like Standard Oil and American Tobacco in the early part of the twentieth century, is clearly inappropriate. The consequence is that, in spite of the seemingly tougher line towards monopolies since the Alcoa judgement, there has in fact been a considerable reluctance on the part of the courts to disturb the corporate giants.

This helps to explain the tendency on the part of the anti-trust authorities to concentrate on restrictive practices and mergers. The former can be dealt with by 'cease and desist' orders; the latter, currently the most active area of anti-trust in the US, enables the authorities to nip monopoly neatly in the bud. On the merger front there is little question that market, structure and firm size are the predominant criteria. Even mergers giving the combined firms only a relatively small share of the national market, or a moderate share of a regional market, have been blocked, irrespective of arguments based on economies of scale, rationalization and so forth. Again, the courts have tended to block mergers which involve vertical integration, backwards or forwards in the stages of production, where there is a danger of the larger firm 'squeezing' out smaller firms. Similarly the anti-trust authorities have taken a firm line on conglomerate mergers, in which they have seen little good but much potential evil, and, in the eyes of some commentators, have effectively killed them.[1]

On the face of it therefore, with its *per se* condemnation of restrictive practices and the reversal of the rule of reason on the monopoly front, the US appears to adopt a tough uncompromising attitude towards monopoly – an attitude which can really be attributed, not so much to the influence of economists in high places as to the continuing political pressure of the small man in a society whose ideas retain a substantial element of rugged individualism. We have seen that, in spite of the apparent simplicity of this tough attitude, there are difficulties both in interpretation and in follow-up action. Moreover, it has a 'soft spot' when it comes to considering fields where the small man predominates, agriculture and retailing. With this important exception it remains true that emphasis in American anti-trust policy has been on structure; more competition being unquestioningly taken to be a 'good thing' and less competition a 'bad thing', with little attention being paid to the actual performance of the firm or the industry. We shall see that by contrast, UK policies, particularly towards the dominant firm, put considerable emphasis on performance.

5.3 Anti-trust policy in the UK

It is interesting to reflect that in the less egalitarian society of the UK legislation to control monopolies and restrictive practices was introduced half a century after the Sherman Act in the US, although our industrial revolution preceded that of the US by about half a century. Admittedly in the UK there existed common law rights against conspiracy and restraints on trade, and it has been argued that these rights might have formed the basis of legal control over monopolies and restrictive practices had not the courts carefully withdrawn themselves from consideration of such questions as part of a general retreat in the late nineteenth century from issues of public law and policy.[2]

Nor, in the early twentieth century, was there much pressure

---

[1] See J Roeber 'How they killed the conglomerates' *The Times* Sept 30 1970.
[2] For an interesting discussion of this issue see R B Stevens and B Yamey *The restrictive practices court* Weidenfeld & Nicolson London 1965 chapter 2.

for the introduction of legislation to control monopoly or monopolistic practices. This lack of interest can be explained, in part, by the fact that the UK did not experience at any time a merger movement equivalent to that experienced by the US in the late nineteenth century. Merger movements did take place, both in the last two decades of the nineteenth century and in the 1920s, but they were not of the intensity of the US merger movement of 1890–1900, and the small man did not suddenly feel squeezed by the giants. Moreover, free trade limited the power exercised by the larger companies. The lack of interest in this field of policy can in part too be explained by the priority given after the 1914–18 war to the problem of unemployment and economic depression; opinion was sympathetic to measures which helped to keep firms in business, and antipathetic to measures which aimed to weed out the inefficient. Indeed the 1930s in the UK, as in the US, saw the establishment of many government sponsored restrictive practices introduced as measures to overcome the unemployment problem.

It needed the commitment to a full-employment policy in the 1940s to bring the first moves towards positive control over monopoly and restrictive practices. It was recognized that the adoption of Keynesian measures to promote full employment might be frustrated by the existence of widespread monopoly, which might divert attempts to stimulate a higher level of activity into price increases. Thus the 1944 White Paper on employment policy,[1] which accepted a commitment on the government to pursue policies which would promote full employment, stipulated that surveillance over monopolies and restrictive practices would be a necessary part of such a policy. This statement of intent was followed by the 1948 Monopolies and Restrictive Practices Act, which established an administrative body, the Monopolies and Restrictive Practices Commission, to review on a case-by-case basis the monopoly position of and practices pursued by any firm or group of firms controlling at least one third of the market. The Commission itself was given very little power. Cases were to be referred to it by the government department concerned, the Board of Trade, and action on its recommendations lay also with the Board of Trade. Its field of reference expressly excluded the service

[1] *White Paper on employment policy* Cmd No 6527 1944.

industries, the professions, trade unions and the nationalized industries. The job of the Commission was to find out the facts, for which purpose it had a small official staff attached to it, and to consider in the light of the factual evidence whether the situation disclosed and the 'things done' by the firm or firms concerned operated against the public interest. No specific definition of 'the public interest' was given in the Act. Section 14 stated that 'all matters which appear in particular circumstances to be relevant shall be taken into account' and that 'particular regard shall be had to

a the production, treatment and distribution by the most efficient and economical means of goods of such types and qualities, in such volume and at such prices as will best meet the requirements of the home and overseas markets;
b the organization of industry and trade in such a way that their efficiency is progressively increased and new enterprise is encouraged;
c the fullest and best distribution of men, materials and industrial capacity in the UK; and
d the development of technical improvements and the expansion of existing markets, and the opening up of new markets.'

This definition is, as GC Allen, later one of the members of the Commission, comments, 'a string of platitudes which the Commission found valueless', leaving them 'to reach their own conclusions by reference to assumptions, principles or prejudices which their training and experience caused them to apply to public affairs'.[1] Nevertheless, the pragmatism was intentional; there was no assumption written into the Act that monopolies or restrictive practices were 'bad'; judgement was to be on a caseby-case basis.

Since 1948, the development of 'anti-trust' policy in the UK can be divided into three distinct phases, first the period 1948 to 1956 covering the early reports of the Monopolies and Restrictive Practices Commission; secondly the period 1956 to 1963 when the Restrictive Practices Court was making the running and an emasculated Monopolies Commission was substantially dormant; and lastly the period 1963 to the early

[1] GC Allen *Monopoly and restrictive practices* George Allen & Unwin London 1968 p 66.

1970s which saw, on the one hand, renewed interest in anti-trust with considerable strengthening of both the Monopolies Commission and the Restrictive Practices Court, and on the other, the evolution of a number of other institutions concerned with promoting efficiency in private industry. We shall look at each of them in turn.

1948–56 The Monopolies and Restrictive Practices Commission

In the period 1948–56 the Monopolies and Restrictive Practices Commission produced 20 reports on subjects ranging from dental goods to tea, from insulin to electrical machinery. Some of the industries covered contained a large number of relatively small firms (such as the London building industry), some were almost complete monopolies (the British Oxygen Company having an almost complete monopoly of industrial and medical gases), while the majority fell in between these two extremes, but tended towards oligopoly. Fifteen of the 20 reports were concerned not with the behaviour of one dominant firm, but with restrictive practices on the part of a group of firms. These restrictive practices ranged through the usual gamut of 'practices in restraint of trade', which in one way or another protected manufacturers and/or retailers from competition or potential competition – exclusive dealing arrangements between manufacturers and distributors, resale price maintenance both individually and collectively, price fixing agreements, price discrimination, market sharing arrangements, and agreements to fix tender prices, to restrict access of outside firms to machinery or materials, to restrict imports and to discriminate over patents or technical knowledge. By and large the commission condemned all these restrictive practices. It did not, however, condemn individual resale price maintenance but it did condemn the collective enforcement of resale price maintenance. Its stand on price fixing arrangements was also somewhat equivocal. It did not condemn price fixing arrangements which it saw as necessary to preserve technical or research co-operation, nor where it felt the industry to be faced by the countervailing pressures of a monopoly buyer, the Ministry of Health in the case of insulin, and the Post Office and the nationalized electricity industry in the case of the cable manufacturers. In these latter cases it did however recommend that those buyers should have access to production cost information in their price negotiations. In so far as any general principles underlay its approach, they were the principles of workable competition. Emphasis was put on freedom of entry, mobility of capital and labour amongst producers and perhaps above all on capacity to innovate and experiment. By and large it saw the competitive environment as the best means of achieving those ends and therefore usually recommended the abandonment of an agreement, but, as we saw above, it also put some emphasis on the use of countervailing power and was prepared to condone a practice which it considered to have promoted technical experiment and innovation.

The work of the Monopolies Commission during this phase of its life culminated in a general report on Collective Discrimination,[1] in which it attempted to draw together general conclusions from its work on specific cases. The question was really whether, given its generally hostile attitude towards most of the restrictive practices it had investigated, the commission could recommend a move in the direction of condemnation *per se* of such restrictive practices, a move from the essentially pragmatic, case-by-case consideration which it had adopted, towards the more dogmatic line of the US legislation. In the event the Commission found itself divided. A majority favoured the declaration of all such restrictive practices illegal, with provision for certain exceptions where there seemed 'public interest' arguments in favour of retention, while a minority felt that wholesale condemnation was going too far and recommended instead a system of registration of all such agreements followed by a case-by-case examination; agreements which, upon examination, were found to be contrary to the public interest should then be prohibited.

At the same time there developed considerable pressure from business interests for the reform of the Monopolies Commission. Although its reports had only skimmed the surface of the iceberg[2] they had received considerable publicity. Business

[1] Monopolies Commission *Report on collective discrimination* HMSO London 1955.

[2] Restrictive practices at that time were very much a way of life to British business. The protectionist attitude of the 1930s combined with the controlled economy of wartime (controls which had in many cases been administered for the government by the relevant trade association, and which had been removed only

complained that the Commission acted both as prosecutor and judge, and that, while it was given good opportunity at an early stage to comment on factual evidence and to argue its case before the Commission, it did not know and therefore could not reply to the prosecution case until the report was published. In fact, of course, action on the recommendations of the reports lay not with the Commission but with the President of the Board of Trade, and business interests made sure that he knew their case before any action was taken. They felt however that, by that stage, criticism embodied in the reports had already made its impact on public opinion and the damage had been done. Let us, they argued, separate the functions of prosecutor and judge.

1956–63 The Restrictive Practices Court

The passing of the Restrictive Practices Act in 1956 can be seen as the interaction of these two strands of thought. A compromise solution between the majority and minority reports on collective discrimination established a system of registration of all restrictive agreements, introduced a general presumption that restrictive practices were contrary to the public interest and provided for the exemption from this general presumption of those practices which might be deemed to be in the public interest by provision of the seven 'gateways' set out in section 21 of the Act. The Act established a Registrar of Restrictive Practices who was to be responsible for ensuring registration and for the preparation of the 'prosecution case' against the particular practice to be argued before the Restrictive Practices Court. This was an entirely new judicial body constituted to try restrictive practice cases and including, for the first time, laymen on its bench.

Following the presumption that restrictive practices were contrary to the public interest, the onus lay upon the defendants to argue before the court that their practices passed through

slowly in the post-war period) had led to an acceptance of 'co-operation' between business firms as a way of life both by business interests and by consumers. Moreover, unlike the US, business in this country had not suffered an early post-war period of substantial recession which had served to 'shake out' such practices. The trade unions were in a very similar position – restrictive practices were much more prevalent in the UK than in the US.

one of the seven gateways; where the Court was satisfied on this score, it had then to decide whether the benefits derived from the practice outweighed the 'detriment' it imposed on society. Until it had been given the opportunity to argue its case before the Court, no agreement was banned. The approach was therefore case-by-case and the procedure judicial, in contrast to the 'administrative' procedures of the Monopolies Commission: in the presumption that these practices were contrary to the public interest, the UK had moved some way towards the *per se* condemnation of the US system, but the provision of the gateways meant that a considerably more pragmatic position was still retained.

One would expect an Act which looked to the judiciary for its execution to have included a more specific definition of the public interest than the earlier Monopolies and Restrictive Practices Act. On the whole it did. The first two gateways of section 21 are concerned with situations where particular restraint on competition may promote the interests of consumers, gateway *a* on health or safety grounds, and gateway *b* 'where it confers on the public as purchasers, consumers or users specific and substantial benefits'; gateways *c* and *d* are concerned with situations where a restriction is necessary to neutralize monopoly elements in other sectors of industry; gateways *e* and *f* acknowledge that there are other objectives for economic policy besides the promotion of competition and are concerned with the promotion of employment in 'depressed regions' and with the promotion of exports. The final gateway *g* is not unlike gateways *c* and *d*, in so far as it protects restrictions which are required in order to maintain restrictions that have been held by the court to be in the public interest.

Yet, in fact, these seven gateways give the Court little more guidance of where the public interest lies than the 1948 Monopolies and Restrictive Practices Act, for much hinges on the interpretation to be placed on such phrases 'reasonably necessary', 'specific and substantial benefit', and 'fair terms'. The 'tailpiece' to section 21 leaves most of all to subjective judgement. It requires the Court, where it considers a restriction to pass through one of the gateways, to weigh up whether the overall benefit gained is greater than the cost imposed on society. Whereas the Monopolies Commission in the 1948 Act was asked only to judge whether the 'things done' in the past by the firm or group of firms were contrary to the public interest, the Court is asked to predict what the likely effect in the future of the retention, or removal, of the agreement would be.

These difficulties over the definition of the public interest led to two major criticisms of this attempt in the UK to establish a judicial framework to assess restrictive practices. The first relates to the justiciability of section 21.[1] Is the court really competent to make judgements about the public interest or is the judiciary being asked to make decisions which are really the province of the legislators? What happens when there is a conflict of policy objectives as, for example, arose in the Yarn Spinners case[2] when the advantage of the extra jobs preserved through the agreement had to be offset against the loss to consumers of a price fixing arrangement? Who can decide what is 'the public interest' but the body that represents the nation, namely Parliament? Whereas with the monopolies legislation action lay with the Minister who was answerable for it in Parliament, with the restrictive practices legislation it is the Court which has to make decisions on matters of public interest. Parliament cannot overthrow the decision of the Court.[3] The most it could do, if it felt that the Court had misinterpreted the public interest, would be to amend the legislation.

The second criticism of the Restrictive Practices Act was that the court was not well fitted to make judgements involving predictions about the likely behaviour of firms and markets; this was more a matter for economists than lawyers. Admittedly each side could, and did, call expert witnesses to support their case. But was the court in a position to judge between the arguments of the academic witnesses? Surely, it was argued, an administrative body of the Monopolies Commission type, which had amongst its members academic economists and could call upon expert advice when needed, was more appropriate than a court of law where, although including lay members, the lawyers predominated and which could not call for evidence other than that presented to it by the respective sides?

[1] See RB Stevens and B Yamey *op cit* chapter 3 'The justiciability of section 21'.
[2] *Re Yarn Spinners Agreement* 1959 LR1RP 118.
[3] Appeal can be made to the House of Lords, but only on points of law.

In these circumstances, it is perhaps not surprising that critics of the workings of the Restrictive Practices Court believe both that some of its judgements have been inconsistent and generally that it has relied upon doubtful reasoning.[1] For example, in the Black Nuts and Bolts case[2] the Court accepted the argument that price fixing saved the costs of 'shopping around' amongst competitors, an argument that was rejected by the Court on several later occasions. In the Cement case[3], the Court accepted the agreement on the grounds that the existence of a pricing agreement cut the degree of risk faced by the industry and led to the price of cement being 'substantially lower than it would under free competition', without explaining why the risk would have been greater under circumstances of competition or why the rate of return on capital in the cement industry was above the average for British industry as a whole. In this case, and the Permanent Magnets case[4], the fact that a cartelized industry earned only what the Court considered to be a 'reasonable' rate of profit was regarded as a major factor favouring the agreement, irrespective of whether it led, in some firms at least, to an unduly high level of costs. In the Net Book Agreement case,[5] the Court argued that price cutting by retailers was likely to be occasional and sporadic, and yet argued that such price cutting was likely to have major and widespread repercussions on the bookselling trade.

The criticisms that the Act is not justiciable and that the Court's judgements are questionable in respect of many of the major restrictions that have been accepted led these commentators to argue that we should have adopted the *per se* condemnation of all such restrictive practices on American lines. This would both have made the Court's role more straightforward and have saved the costs of litigation, costs which Sutherland maintains are not offset by benefits stemming from the restrictions which were upheld.

However, for all that economists might quibble with the

---

[1] See RB Stevens and B Yamey *op cit* chapter 4 'The economics of section 21'; and A Sutherland *Economics in the Restrictive Practices Court* Oxford Economic Papers 1965.
[2] *Re Black Bolt and Nut Association Agreement* LR 2 RP 50 1960.
[3] *Re Cement Makers' Federation Agreement* LR 2 RP 241 1960.
[4] *Re Permanent Magnet Association's Agreement* LR 2 RP 241 1960.
[5] *Re Net Book Agreement* LR 3 RP 246 1962.

Court's findings, most would agree with the Court's main aim of limiting the prevalence of collusion and restriction in the UK economy, and new procedures had gone some way to meet these immediate aims. By 1966 a total of 2,550 agreements had been registered, of which 1,875 had been voluntarily abandoned. Of the 29 major agreements brought before the Court, 19 had been declared illegal and only 10 had been approved. Moreover, a large number of agreements were modified in order to avoid registration.

Abolition, abandonment or modification is not however everything. What is important is that the restrictive agreement should not be replaced by another looser form of agreement that amounts to the same thing. Some economists argue that the effect of the Act had in practice been minimal since the abandonment of formal agreements either stimulated the firms concerned into outright merger or encouraged them to substitute looser agreements, such as the exchanging of price lists and other information, or some form of price leadership.[1] (The possibility of establishing information agreements was recognized as a loophole in the Act and in 1968 legislation extended its scope to cover these.) Others pointed to evidence to show that in less concentrated trades, where it was difficult to police looser types of agreement, the Restrictive Practices Act has led to a more competitive environment and lower prices.[2] That restrictive practices were pervasive throughout the British economy in the 1950s is evident from the number of agreements that were registered under the new legislation. The relatively tough line taken towards such agreements by the Court had certainly resulted in something of a shake out, even if that shake out has not been as extensive as some would have wished.

1963–70 The Industrial Reorganization Corporation and all that

The years 1963 to 1970 were a period of somewhat paradoxical developments towards anti-trust in the UK. In general it seems fair to say that it was a period in which there was increasing interest in the effects of the economic environment upon

[1] GC Allen *op cit* pp 97–101.
[2] JB Heath 'Restrictive Practices legislation. Some economic consequences' *Econ. Journal* Sept 1960.

industrial performance. But there were two somewhat contra-
dictory schools of thought, both influential.

The first favoured the creation of a more competitive environment. Examples of its achievements are

a the passing of the Resale Price Maintenance Act of 1964,
which extended the scope of the Restrictive Practices Court to
cover resale price maintenance, again with the presumption
that this practice was contrary to the public interest, and with
gateways or escape clauses as in the earlier Restrictive Practices
Act (but somewhat more specific);

b the 1965 Mergers and Monopolies Act which extended the
scope of the Monopolies Commission to cover services trades
and, more important, gave to it the role of vetting major
mergers. (The Monopolies Commission could still investigate
only cases referred by the department concerned (at this time
the Board of Trade), who had the important role of sifting
possible references and deciding whether it would ask the
Monopolies Commission to investigate);

c the extension in 1968 of the Restrictive Practices Act to
cover information agreements.

The second school of thought looked to greater efficiency
springing from the exploitation of potential economies of scale,
from innovation and from injecting lively management into
slumbering firms. Examples of its achievements are

a the establishment of the 'little Neddies', the Economic
Development Committees for various industries, whose job it
was on the one hand to 'co-ordinate' investment plans of the
different sectors for the purpose of the national planning exercise (see chapter 3 p 82 above) and on the other, to stimulate
maximum growth particularly export growth in industry, by
making firms aware of new techniques and processes. Both
functions were complementary for the process of discussion of
investment plans helped to disseminate information about new
techniques.

b the setting up of the Industrial Reorganization Corporation[1]
(IRC), whose function it was to promote 'reorganization'
(mergers, takeovers etc), where there were substantial gains to
be made in terms of economies of scale and/or management.

[1] Cmd No 2889 *Industrial Reorganization Corporation* HMSO London 1966.

The IRC was behind two of the largest mergers we have seen in this country, the GEC–AEI merger in the electrical engineering industry, and the BMC–Leyland merger in the motor industry. This interventionist spirit was encouraged and fostered by the establishment and growth of the Ministry of Technology, whose prevailing philosophy was to intervene, if necessarily discriminatorily, in order to promote practices it considered good and to discourage those it considered bad. This contrasted directly with the traditional liberal, non-discriminatory philosophy of the Board of Trade.

c   the establishment in 1964 of the National Board of Prices and Incomes (NBPI) to whom many wage and price increases were referred. It interpreted its terms of reference widely and, rather than limiting its reports to the narrow justification for a price or wage increase, used them as an excuse to delve more deeply into the economic position of the firms and industries concerned. Its reports frequently read like reports from management consultants, full of suggestions as to how productivity might be increased. Unlike the IRC it could only make recommendations, and action on its recommendations depended mainly upon the firms concerned. But, in spirit if not in deed, it was interventionist.

These two movements are not totally in conflict. On the one hand, as we have seen, British industry had been cushioned by collusive agreements of one sort or another and the fairly tough line on restrictive practices had helped to shake out some of these. This very process had stimulated mergers and strengthened price leadership; therefore it was important that our legislation on monopolies and dominant firms should be effective. Side by side with this is the fact that many British industries were inefficient either because of a failure to exploit potential economies of scale[1], or because of a tendency to pursue an excessive degree of product differentiation,[2] or

---

[1] See CF Pratten *op cit* particularly chapter 35.

[2] RE Caves in his chapter 7 'Market organization, performance and public policy' in *Britain's Economic Prospects* RE Caves ed Brookings Institution 1968 George Allen & Unwin London concludes as follows: 'The available data do not support the view that UK industrial production suffers unduly from production units too small to reap the available benefits of scale economies, although small scale, high product differentiation and low capital intensity probably interact in a package of forces that contributes to explaining low productivity' p 295.

because their equipment was out of date and their managements content to let things ride.[1] If the state is stepping in to encourage what perhaps in the long run the market forces would achieve, it is necessary to have some continuing sanction which can limit the abuse of this state created market power. Clearly the dividing line is a narrow one, and there are some who were concerned to point out how ridiculous it was on the one hand to have the little Neddies manufacturing agreements amongst firms to share research information and on the other the Restrictive Practices Court unscrambling agreements as hard as possible;[2] again, to have the IRC fostering mergers on grounds of management efficiency and the Monopolies Commission rejecting mergers where the management of one firm was clearly more 'efficient' than the management of the other.[3] However as Crosland, then President of the Board of Trade, was at pains to point out in 1969, in most instances the conflict was more apparent than real and there was a place in government policy both for what might be called 'strategic' generalized controls over monopoly and restrictive practices and for interventionist procedures.[4]

Government blessing to rationalization may have helped to stimulate the merger movement which the UK experienced in the latter half of the 1960s, and which reached a crescendo in the merger-fever year of 1968. It seems probable that this merger movement has resulted in an increase in concentration in a fair number of industries. It should be remembered that quite a number of these mergers were not horizontal but conglomerate, that is between firms with wide ranging industrial interests, and such mergers do not add to concentration within individual industries. Conglomerates may not however be without market influence because their substantial financial resources give them the ability to withstand competitive pressures in individual markets (see above, chapter 4, p 131).

[1] See RE Caves *op cit* pp 300–6.
[2] The conflict was sufficiently real that the 1968 Restrictive Practices Act included a clause which specifically excluded agreements which had been sponsored as being 'in the national interest' from the scope of the restrictive practices legislation.
[3] See for example Robert Jones's article in *The Times* Sept 27 1967 on the Burton United Drapery Stores merger.
[4] See *The Times* 1st August 1969.

1963–70 The Monopolies Commission

The period 1963–70 was a very active one for the Monopolies Commission. Having been substantially dormant for the period 1956–63 (largely through lack of references), it re-emerged in the early 1960s with a spate of references and reports and was rewarded for its endeavours by being given, under the 1965 Monopolies and Mergers Act, the important role of vetting mergers.

THE PROBLEM OF OLIGOPOLY: Some of the reports that the Commission produced during this period were concerned primarily with the single, dominant firm; (for example the reports on Lucas, the car equipment firm; Pilkington's, the glass firm; and Courtaulds, in relation to the manufacture of cellulosic fibre); while other reports were primarily about tightly knit oligopoly situations where often there were only two or three firms sharing the market between them; (for example the reports on detergents, colour film, petroleum distribution, cinema films).[1] The Commission came up against the same problem as the US authorities – namely what effective action can be recommended against these firms? Most had achieved their dominant position through internal growth, and dismemberment is therefore no answer. The Monopolies Commission has taken a rather more flexible attitude towards size than the US authorities. As in its early days, it tended to look to a workable competition model but it has consistently put more emphasis on the market performance of the firm, or firms, under consideration, and in particular more emphasis on the record in innovation and research. On these grounds Pilkington's, the glass manufacturers, escaped from its investigation with a completely clean bill of health, although it is doubtful whether it would have emerged with a similarly clean

[1] See the following reports from the Monopolies Commission HMSO London.
The supply of electrical equipment for mechanically propelled land vehicles 1963.
Petrol (supply to retailers) 1965.
Films: supply for exhibition 1966.
Household detergents 1966.
Colour film 1966.
The supply of flat glass 1968.
The supply of man-made cellulosic fibre 1968.

bill from an investigation by the US authorities. Indeed this verdict surprised some British critics as well[1]

With this more flexible attitude, one might have expected the Monopolies Commission to be able to deal more effectively than the US authorities with the dominant firm. This is not so. The Monopolies Commission has had little difficulty in identifying those practices which constitute abuse of market power enjoyed by the firm or firms under consideration – for example, in the detergents report it identified the high selling costs inherent in the tight oligopoly structure of the industry as creating a major barrier to entry, and enabling the firms to make excessive profits; in colour film, the tying of processing to the sale of film and the refusal to supply film to any but accredited retailers had a similar exclusive effect and again enabled the firms concerned to make excess profits; in cellulosic fibres, Courtaulds vertical integration into the textile fabricating industry put it in a position where it could discriminate in favour of its subsidiaries and 'squeeze' other fabricators. And so on. The Commission's difficulty comes in finding effective remedies. The detergent manufacturers could be told to cut prices and selling costs, but this would weaken Unilever, the weaker of the two rival firms and probably increase the market power of Procter and Gamble, the market leaders; with colour film, a price reduction would similarly tend to strengthen Kodak's position *vis-à-vis* the weaker Ilford; a reduction in tariffs is difficult when the balance of payments is weak. Sometimes a straightforward remedy is available; Courtaulds was restricted from participating in further vertical mergers; Kodak and the two big cinema film distributors, Rank and ABC, were told to discontinue their tying and exclusive dealing arrangements; but this is rare. The Monopolies Commission is further hampered by the fact that it has to operate by making recommendations to the Board of Trade (now the Department of Trade and Industry), and has no method of enforcing its recommendations nor a continuing responsibility to see that they are adhered to, in spirit as well as in word. Sutherland, for example, argues that Kodak obeyed the letter but not the spirit

[1] A Sutherland *The Monopolies Commission in action* Cambridge University Press 1970.

of the Monopolies Commission recommendations.[1] He suggests that the emphasis upon performance means that the Commission ignores structural changes as possible remedies – for example the dismantling of Courtaulds empire.[2] Whether such remedies are feasible is a moot point. We saw in relation to the us that authorities there, who have no similar bias in favour of performance rather than structure, have been loath to dismantle large organizations and have preferred to stick to the 'cease and desist' orders which relate to specific practices. Like its American counterparts, the Monopolies Commission has found no easy solution to the problem of oligopoly.

MERGERS: The other field in which the Monopolies Commission was active during this period is that of mergers. As in the us, concern with mergers arose, in part at least, from the realization that it is very difficult to deal effectively with a monopoly once it has been established, and it is preferable therefore to nip it in the bud. But the Commission's role is no easy one, for its job is to assess what the likely effects of the merger will be. The argument here centres on the costs and benefits of proposed mergers (although the Commission has never attempted to quantify its arguments in a full cost-benefit analysis). Since in most cases the merger involves not the physical merging of plant but the merging of managements, it is really a question of whether such a merger will result in cost savings which could offset the costs to society of the increased market power enjoyed by the combined firms; the vexed question of economies to be gained by the multi-plant firm on which, as we saw in the last chapter, there is no clear evidence to guide policy makers. There are those who argue that the Monopolies Commission is ill-equipped for this exercise, indeed that the whole exercise is unnecessary since the merger would never have been proposed if there were not profits to be made from cost savings. Such critics either prefer to ignore the possibility that increased profits could come from increased market power in which the public has an interest, or implicitly assume that the effect of this would be negligible.[3] On the other

---

[1] A Sutherland *op cit* pp 71–2.
[2] A Sutherland *op cit* pp 74–5.
[3] See R Jones and P Jacobson *The Times* 27 and 28 September 1967

ANTI-TRUST – THE POLICY FRAMEWORK

side of the fence are those who, arguing similarly that Whitehall does not always know best, attack the IRC/Ministry of Technology policy of promoting mergers.[1] If there are gains to be reaped from merger then the market will promote it; if the market does not promote it, then there are likely to be no substantial gains and there is no case for government intervention. If in these circumstances the government does intervene and force merger, then the result may be the creation of a chronically weak management, or what is often termed a 'lame duck'. Intervention by the government in promoting mergers can only be justified if there is imperfect information available to the market and better information available to the government. This may on occasions be so, and this is the case for an 'interventionist' body like the IRC which aims not so much to promote mergers which the market would not have backed as to speed up the market process. On the whole the marriage broking of the later 1960s was circumspect.

Monopoly policy in the UK after the 1970

In 1969 the Labour government proposed the merger of the Prices and Incomes Board (NBPI) and the Monopolies Commission into a Commission for Industry and Manpower. The novel feature of the plan was that the Commission's terms of reference should be widened to cover all companies with assets over £10m, which would mean the 400 or so largest companies in the UK; they were also to inherit the NBPI's job of making 'efficiency audits' on the nationalized industries. With the defeat of the Labour government in 1970, these plans disappeared. The Conservative government axed the interventionist institutions of the Labour era – the Ministry of Technology, the IRC, the NBPI all disappeared; only the little Neddies, which were in any case originally a Conservative creation, remained. The Conservative government have announced their intention to replace the Monopolies Commission by a commission which would have similar but rather wider powers, involving it in looking into the affairs of small as well as large firms and a general surveillance of nationalized industries – a combination not unlike the one proposed by the

[1] B Hindley *Industrial merger and public policy* Institute of Economic Affairs London 1970.

previous government, but in which the dominant flavour comes from the Monopolies Commission rather than the NBPI.[1] The interventionist element in policy seems however as this book went to press to be refusing to lie down. In 1972 a new Industry Bill was presented to Parliament which gave promise of a continuation into the mid-1970s of the dichotomy between different elements of policy which had been so much a feature of the late 1960s. This bill gives the government wide and generous powers of intervention in the affairs of private industry.

Policy in the future in this field as in others will have to take account of the UK entry into the EEC. In general the countries of the EEC have been less tough in their treatment of large firms and cartels than the UK and the US, although practice varies considerably from country to country. The Treaty of Rome itself is worded in tough terms, though of course it only applies to practices which affect trade between member states: article 85 of the Treaty prohibits arrangements and practices which prevent, restrict or disturb competition within the common market (ie restrictive practices such as price fixing, market sharing, etc), and article 86 prohibits the pursuit of unfair or improper practices by a dominant firm if these impair trade among member states. Interpretation of these articles is left to the Court of Justice and policing to the Commission in Brussels. The Commission has been busy deciding which restrictive practices fall within the ambit of article 85, establishing a register of agreements and those party to them, and

[1] The Fair Trading Bill which sets out the new competition policy was published in November 1972 when this book was in process of publication. It contains a number of interesting features. First, is the clear association of the public interest with consumer interests and the emphasis upon competition as the most effective way of safeguarding consumers' interests: the workable competition ethos is as strong as ever. Second, is the redefinition of the 'official' monopoly which in future will embrace firms and mergers controlling 25 per cent of the market, as compared with the 33 per cent share stipulated at present. This will increase the scope of the Monopolies Commission, though not as much as under the Labour party proposals which put forward the £10m capital asset limit. The last is the creation of the new super-post of Director General of Fair Trading, who will take over from the Registrar of Restrictive Trading Agreements, but with extended oversight over the whole field of monopolies, restrictive practices and consumer affairs. The Monopolies Commission will come under his general supervision, but references both for monopoly and merger are still to come from ministers and action on its recommendations remains with ministers.

granting block exemption to some forms of agreement – a procedure which borrows from the UK restrictive practice and resale price maintenance legislation. In general it would appear that UK practice has been rather tougher than anything we will encounter in the EEC and we shall have little difficulty in fitting in with their arrangements.

5.4 Summary and conclusions

This chapter has traced the development of policy towards monopolies and restrictive practices in the UK and the US. Although in origin they owe little to the theories of economists, the development of both sets of policies, particularly in the post-war period, has lent towards the workable competition model, with belief in the virtues of competition being rather stronger in the US.

In its origin, anti-trust policy in the US owes much to pressure from the small man for protection from the large combines which developed in late nineteenth century, and this helps to explain the juxtaposition of the competitive ethos of anti-trust with the protectionism of legislation dealing with agriculture and retailing. The competitive ethos of the anti-trust policy shows itself in the *per se* condemnation of restrictive practices, in Court decisions under section 1 of the Sherman Act, and, in relation to the dominant firm, in the increased emphasis since the Alcoa judgement of 1945 on structural features, such as market shares and the potential ability of the firm to abuse its market position.

Anti-trust policy in the UK dates from as recently as 1948. From the start the line adopted has been rather more pragmatic than in the US. Since 1956 restrictive practices have been dealt with by a judicial procedure and there has been the presumption that restrictive practices are contrary to the public interest, which takes the UK part of the way towards the *per se* condemnation of the US. However the policy has remained pragmatic, the escape clauses requiring that consideration be on a case-by-case basis. Dominant firms have continued to be dealt with by the Monopolies Commission, an administrative rather than judicial body, where investigation is on a case-by-case basis. Although like the US authorities the Monopolies

ANTI-TRUST – THE POLICY FRAMEWORK

Commission has adopted an approach that approximates to the workable competition model, it has consistently put emphasis upon market performance – indeed consideration of the 'things done' by the firm was written into the legislation. The Monopolies Commission has also tended to put more emphasis on dynamic efficiency, innovation and R & D, than their US counterparts.

Both authorities have encountered most difficulty in dealing with oligopoly situations. Although the simplicity of the *per se* condemnation of the US system is appealing when contrasted with the legal niceties of judgements under the escape clauses of UK restrictive practice legislation, it cannot cope effectively with the grey world of oligopoly, where matching price changes are a part of life. In the UK oligopolies tend to fall within the ambit of the Monopolies Commission, and, although its flexible approach might seem more appropriate to these situations, it too has failed to find an effective way of dealing with problems posed by closely knit oligopolies. This goes far to explain the shift of emphasis in both countries in recent years towards the control of mergers. If monopolies cannot effectively be 'controlled' by legislation, let us, the argument runs, at least prevent their emergence.

Further reading

A HUNTER (ed) *Monopoly and competition: selected readings* Penguin Books Harmondsworth 1969. This is a general selection of readings on the topics covered in this chapter. See particularly readings 3, 4, 9, 10, 11, 13 and 14.

GC ALLEN *Monopoly and restrictive practices* George Allen & Unwin London 1968. A concise description of the development of UK policy, with a chapter on the US and the EEC.

R B STEVENS and B YAMEY *The Restrictive Practices Court* Weidenfeld & Nicolson London 1965. A fairly detailed analysis of the development and workings of policy towards restrictive practices in the UK. See particularly parts 1 and 2.

RE CAVES (ed) *Britain's economic prospects* Brookings Institution Washington 1968 George Allen & Unwin London. Chapter VII 'Market organization: performance and public policy' pp 306–23. A good description of some of the more recent developments on the monopoly policy front.

6

Economic aspects of nationalized industries

6.1 Introduction: Public control or public enterprise

In the last chapter we were looking at attempts to control monopolistic aspects of industrial structure and behaviour. One of the most intractable problems that arises in this type of control is that presented by what is termed 'natural monopoly'. This arises when an industry operates under conditions of increasing returns to scale, for in such a situation the larger firm is able to undercut smaller rivals and eventually to drive them from the market. Many public utilities are natural monopolies; they are characterized by highly capital intensive techniques with major indivisibilities, so that marginal cost and average variable cost are, except when capacity is exhausted, well below average total cost, a situation in which competition is well nigh impossible. For this reason, many of the public utility industries, railways, electricity, gas and water, have for long been subject to public control which involved not merely the general constraints on monopolistic behaviour of the anti-trust programme, but detailed regulation of prices and services provided. Frequently, as a *quid pro quo* for this detailed regulation, the public utility companies were granted statutory monopoly rights in the provision of the service in question.

An alternative to attempting to control private enterprise in this manner, is to bring the whole enterprise under state control to nationalize it, and for the state to operate it in a manner which seems best to promote social welfare. Indeed, as we saw in chapter 2, some economists have despaired of the ability of a private enterprise economy, however controlled, to promote social welfare, and have advocated the wholesale nationalism by the state of the means of production and distribution. By and large, however, it is accepted that public enterprise in capitalist countries is an alternative to public control of private industries and that public and private enterprise can co-exist amicably. There is no consensus as to which type of public intervention is the more efficient method of promoting social welfare. On the one hand, the advocates of nationalization argue that it creates a more pliable instrument which can be used for the pursuit of social ends; on the other, it is argued that if we expect these industries to operate within a market environment it is important not to remove them from the constraints of the market, and that within the public sector these industries become flabby and bureaucratic. But practice is never perfect and comparisons between the two types of organization, for example between the controlled, but privately owned, public utilities of the United States and the nationalized utilities in the UK, leave many questions unanswered; there are a great many other factors affecting such comparisons than methods of control. The two can be seen as alternatives, but there is no objectively 'right' choice between them. The actual solution arrived at, the mix of private and public enterprise, control and intervention, is a political rather than an economic choice.

6.2 The statutory framework

Once it has been decided to nationalize an industry, a host of interesting issues arise. What form shall the organization take? Shall it be a civil service department or an independent organization? If the latter, to whom and by what means shall it be accountable? What instructions should be given to its managers? Should it be instructed to maximize profits, or should it be required to look at some wider 'public interest'?

In the UK the nationalized industries were created as semi-independent public corporations, rather than either as departments of state or as totally autonomous units. The main characteristic of these public corporations was that, although a minister of the government and through him Parliament, was given certain powers of oversight and control, responsibility for the running of the enterprise rested squarely with its Board, which was an independent legal entity, whose finances were entirely separate from those of the public Exchequer, and whose employees were not civil servants but could be hired and fired on terms laid down by the organization itself. Such a form of organization arose not so much from any positive vision on the part of its creators[1] but from a negative desire that the organization should not be hamstrung by the cumbersome, bureaucratic civil service tradition, that its finances should be independent of Treasury control and that it should not be subject to detailed Parliamentary enquiry through the medium of the Parliamentary question. The Post Office had been since the mid-nineteenth century a civil service department and it was felt by many that it had suffered on this account.[2]

The industries therefore are in large part independent, but they are nevertheless public corporations, owned by the state and ultimately accountable to the state. The general public may be considered the shareholder and the enterprise is accountable to its shareholders through Parliament. As we have seen however there is no direct accountability to Parliament as with a civil service department; accountability is indirect. For each public corporation a government minister, amongst his other duties, is vested with responsibilities *vis-à-vis* the industries and powers of oversight and control for which he is accountable to Parliament. Three of these deserve mention here; the responsibilities for the appointment of Board members, for the approval of the general investment programme and for the borrowing power of the industry. In addition, the minister has the power to issue the Board of the nationalized industry 'directions of a general character as to the exercise and per-

---

[1] It might be argued that Lord Reith's pre-war creation of the BBC, one of the precursors of the public corporations established in the post-war period, was a 'positive vision'. The BBC was in fact given substantially greater autonomy than the post-war public corporations.

[2] Why this should be is difficult to know, since the Post Office had established a system of postal services in the UK which was probably the most efficient in the world, and while the telephone services did undoubtedly suffer during the 1950s and early 1960s from too low a rate of capital expenditure, this was by no means apparent in 1945 when the telephone service, given the inevitable run down of capital during the war years, compared reasonably with that of the US, and was far better than in most European countries.

formance by the Board of their functions in relation to matters which appear to him to affect the public interest'. In the desire to achieve the happy mean between independence and accountability for the nationalized industries, ministers are placed somewhat at arm's length. It is agreed that they may have a general say in long term policy, but the running of day to day affairs is firmly the responsibility of the Board.

The responsibilities of the Boards of the different nationalized industries are laid down in the various statutes. Each Board has a 'general duty'[1] which is couched in broad (and some would say meaningless) terms, such as to provide the service, or make the goods, in question 'with due regard to efficiency, economy and safety'. One notable feature of the statutes is that no industry is specifically required to operate 'in the public interest'. In some instances industries are asked to make more or less comprehensive provision to consumers, but even here the requirement is heavily qualified. For example, the electricity boards are required to provide electricity in rural areas 'where practicable'; London Transport was required to provide 'an adequate and properly co-ordinated system of passenger transport'. Even the main financial duty, to 'break-even taking one year with another', although more specific, still gives no clear guidance without definition of what 'one year with another' really means.[2]

It might be argued that this statutory framework has been highly unsatisfactory. Far from achieving a 'happy mean' between independence and accountability, the relationship between minister and Board has been a constant source of friction, with ministers exceeding their legal duties and frequently intervening in the day to day affairs of industry. The interventions stemmed from two sources. The first was the desire on the part of ministers to stimulate the industries to greater efficiency, intervention which reflected the inadequacy of the break-even financial requirement. Secondly ministers intervened in order to make sure that the Board operated in a manner which they (the ministers) felt to be consistent with

[1] With one exception; the British Airways Board established under the 1971 Civil Aviation Act has no general duty.
[2] The industries which are permitted access to government funds on 'equity' terms are subject to the more specific duty of achieving a given return on net assets.

'the public interest', which reflected the failure of the statutes to take account of the public interest element and clearly to delineate how it should be interpreted. Against this criticism of the statutes, it has been argued that the broad and vague terminology has allowed for a far more flexible evolution of relationships than could be accommodated within more precise legislation.[1]

It is beyond the scope of this chapter to pursue this point of public administration. It has however raised two issues of central importance to the study of the economics of public enterprise, namely efficiency and social obligations. These two issues recur throughout the next three sections of this chapter, when we shall be considering, from a more theoretical standpoint, pricing and investment policies and social versus commercial obligations. In the final section of the chapter we shall return to UK experience with nationalized industries and consider the development of policies in the last decade or so.

6.3 Pricing policies

Pricing policies are central to the economies of public enterprise. The problem can be posed simply as this. In nationalizing an industry, we are transferring resources from the private to the public sector. This affects the distribution of income; profits earned by these resources will now become a part of public sector revenues rather than accruing to private sector rentiers. It also presents the state with a unique opportunity to influence the allocation of resources. The lower are prices in public sector enterprises in relation to private sector prices, the greater is the demand for public sector products, and the capacity needed to meet this demand, and thus the greater the proportion of total resources pre-empted by the public sector enterprises. The higher prices are set, the smaller the share of resources so pre-empted. Pricing policy in the public sector spills over to affect the allocation of resources in the economy as a whole. Pricing policy in nationalized industries is thus of crucial importance to the whole allocation of resources in the economy. But what is the 'right' pricing policy?

[1] See CD Foster *Politics, finance and the role of economics* George Allen and Unwin London 1972 chapter 3.

Why not profit maximization?

Private sector industry is by and large left to decide for itself in the light of its objectives what its optimal price/output strategy shall be. The state can only influence this by the judicious use of taxes and controls which impose general constraints, incentives and disincentives. Arguably this is what we ought also to do with nationalized industries – tell them to maximize profits and subject them to the same general constraints which we impose upon private sector industry.

One is left however with nagging doubts. What is the purpose of nationalization if the boards of nationalized industries are expected to behave exactly as their private sector counterparts? In the public mind it is clearly 'wrong' for the nationalized industries to use their monopoly position to exploit or 'milk' consumers. They wish to see a more direct redistribution of income to themselves as consumers, rather than indirectly through coffers of the state. But is nationalization only about the redistribution of income and wealth? We have indicated above that pricing policy for public enterprise can have a substantial effect on the allocation of resources. Does the efficient allocation of resources count for nothing? Would a profit maximizing pricing policy promote the most efficient allocation of resources within the economy? We are back to where we started from. Let us approach the question another way. What are the alternatives to profit maximization?

Marginal cost pricing

Many economists advocate the use of marginal cost pricing as the appropriate pricing/output rule for a nationalized industry. This means that industry output should be determined at the point where the marginal cost curve cuts the industry demand curve.

The optimal properties claimed for the marginal cost rule stem from the Pareto conditions for allocational efficiency described in the first chapter. These optimal properties however exist only in the first best world where perfect competition pervades all sectors of the economy; they do not hold in a second best world where some sectors are monopolized, or even where

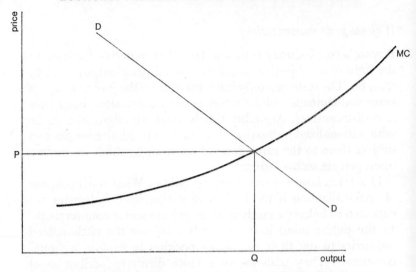

Figure 8. Output determined by the marginal cost principle in a nationalised industry

a system of income taxes or expenditure taxes destroy the marginal equivalences of the first best world. (See chapter 1 p 20 for a discussion of the significance of the concept of second best.)

Nevertheless, even within a second best world, many economists claim that we should adhere to the marginal principle. Mishan[1] argues that we ought to adjust prices towards the price-marginal cost ratio prevalent within the economy as a whole; Farrell[2] that the appropriate second-best rule is that price should not be less than marginal cost. Intuitively this can be explained by the fact that in an imperfect world where the degree of monopoly is positive, prices in general in the economy would be above marginal cost and that in these circumstances to set prices in the public sector at marginal cost would be to encourage over-expansion of the public sector in relation to the rest of the economy; the second-best 'optimal' set of prices would therefore be somewhat above marginal cost.[3] Both of

[2] EJ Mishan *The costs of economic growth* The Staples Press London 1967 pp 45–52.

[2] MJ Farrell 'In defence of public utility pricing' amended version in *Public enterprise* R Turvey (ed) Penguin Modern Economics Series 1968.

[3] In fact it is not quite as simple as this since the 'optimal' price level for each sector depends upon the complex of complementary and competitive relationships with other sectors. See reference cited in footnote 2 above.

these are really a form of marginal cost pricing, amended to take account of second best considerations.

Marginal cost pricing is not without its complications. Although we shall end up suggesting a slightly different approach, it is worthwhile looking at some of these.

COMPLICATIONS OF MARGINAL COST PRICING – WHAT IS MARGINAL COST? Short run marginal cost relates to the cost of those inputs which need to be varied in the short run in order to increase output – usually taken to be mainly raw materials, labour and wear-and-tear costs: but it depends how 'short' your short period is. Long run marginal cost (lrmc) relates to the change in total costs associated with a permanent increase in output which involves costs associated with such items as capital and management which cannot readily be increased in the short period. Short run marginal cost (srmc) tends to rise sharply when capacity is exhausted since there comes a point when, however much extra labour or materials are used, it is physically impossible to increase output without more machine capacity, etc. Thus, while normally srmc is below lrmc, reflecting the fact that srmc does not include the 'capital' and other long run costs, once capacity is exhausted srmc cuts the lrmc curve from underneath and rises above it. Having exhausted initial economies of scale, the lrmc curve may be relatively flat, may rise reflecting long run diseconomies, or may continue to fall reflecting continuing economies of scale. To break-even, price must be at least as high as average cost. In the following figure we have assumed that there are no further economies or diseconomies of scale; both the lrmc and the long run average cost (lrac) curves are therefore 'L' shaped. In such circumstances charging a price equal to lrmc would not enable the enterprise to break even, for lrac, while becoming asymptotic (approaching closer and closer) to lrmc, would always be above it. Price equal to lrmc will only meet a break-even requirement when lrmc rises above lrac reflecting long run diseconomies. Alternatively, charging a price equal to srmc would not 'cover' costs except when the enterprise was working well above capacity levels.

Does marginal cost pricing mean short run or long run marginal cost? The only answer that is given to this question is,

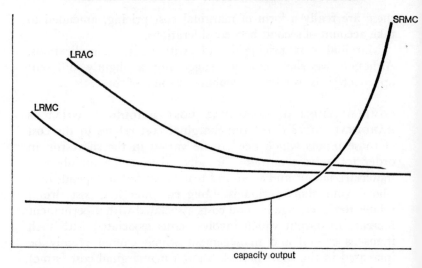

Figure 9. Short and long run marginal cost.

infuriatingly, that it depends upon one's time horizon. If you are concerned with short run pricing policy then it is short run marginal cost; if you are concerned with long run considerations, for example with investment decisions, then it is long run marginal cost. The 1967 White Paper reviewing the economic and financial obligations of nationalized industries[1] suggested that the appropriate criterion was long run marginal cost, except when industries faced major peak demand problems when short run marginal cost was the appropriate concept.

INDIVISIBILITIES: Where the equipment cannot be increased 'marginally' but only in major stages (ie where it is indivisible or lumpy), then long run marginal cost is meaningless. Indeed, there is no such thing as long run marginal cost for the equipment, by definition, cannot be increased 'marginally'. For any given set of equipment, it is possible to distinguish short run costs associated with an increase in output so that it would be possible to set prices equal to srmc, but srmc is likely to be well below lrac which means that pricing at srmc would not cover

[1] Command No 3434 *Nationalized industries: A review of economic and financial obligations* HMSO London 1967.

total costs. The classic example here is the case of Dupuit's bridge (so called after the French economist who first discussed the problem). Once built, the marginal cost of an extra person crossing a bridge is zero until that point when the bridge is so crowded that congestion slows down the traffic stream and marginal social cost begins to increase sharply. Charging a price (or toll) equal to short run marginal cost would mean a zero price until the bridge is used to full capacity. The capital costs involved in building the bridge could not be met. But if a toll is charged when the bridge is not being used to capacity, then it dissuades some from crossing who might otherwise have crossed, and since their crossing would in no way have increased social costs, there is a loss in welfare to the community as a whole. Many public utilities present similar characteristics – heavy and lumpy capital expenditure but low running costs, so that short run marginal costs are very low in relation to average costs. Charging a price equal to short run marginal costs, when plant is operated below capacity levels, may thus entail heavy losses which have somehow to be financed, and poses particular problems where it is stipulated that the enterprise should break-even. (See below section on the problem of the deficit.)

This issue poses a further problem in relation to capital expansion. If plant cannot be increased marginally, but only in relatively large 'lumps', then, while operating at current capacity levels with price (equal to srmc) well above lrac will result in high profits, expansion by the minimum possible amount will mean over-capacity, price dropping below lrac and consequent losses. In such circumstances, when is investment in new plant justified? The answer here requires a calculation of the overall gain or loss in welfare terms – whether the gains resulting from the investment more than offset the costs involved. We shall be discussing this total benefit/cost approach to investment appraisal in the next chapter when we consider cost benefit analysis.

In some cases, where there are indivisibilities, even the concept of short run marginal cost may not be unambiguous. Take the example of a passenger train. The output variable is passenger miles and short run marginal cost is the incremental cost per passenger mile *given* capacity. So far so good. It is the definition of 'capacity' which poses ambiguities. Is the capacity constraint to be *a* the train, given its number of coaches, *b* the potential number of coaches the train can accommodate or *c* the capacity of the rail system between A and B? Here the capacity constraint varies with the time horizon. In the very short run *a* is the relevant constraint, in the not so short run *b* is the constraint, while in the longer run it is *c*. This ambiguity has led some economists to shun the whole concept of marginal cost in favour of the concept of escapable cost[1], distinguishing between those costs directly associated with the operation of a piece of equipment – the direct or escapable costs – and those common to the system as a whole – the indirect or overhead costs. This approach emphasizes that costs are related *not* to the product unit, the extra passenger or the extra unit of freight, but to the extra unit of equipment. The pricing rule advocated is that prices should be set at such a level that revenue obtained from, for example, running a train should, at minimum, cover escapable costs associated with running the train. Given expected usage this leads to a price based upon the averaging of escapable costs over expected usage. The concept of escapable cost is in fact more closely akin to average cost pricing than to marginal cost pricing. This is discussed below.

The problem of the deficit

Since public utilities are industries which, typically, are subject to major indivisibilities, and/or increasing returns to scale, marginal cost pricing – whether long run or short run – will often result in the enterprise failing to cover total costs. How should this deficit be financed?

TAXATION: Some economists have suggested that any deficit that arises should be met from general tax revenues, national or local as appropriate. This involves redistribution from tax-payers in general to the users of the particular good or service. For some services eg the Health Service, or a local public transport undertaking, we may wish to do this. But there seems no particular reason why society as a whole should wish to subsidize telephone or airline users. Where there are no major externalities (see section 6.5 below) then the principle

[1] See Arthur Lewis *Overhead costs* George Allen & Unwin London 1949.

that the industry should aim to break-even is often preferred
on the grounds that 'he who benefits should pay'. This is
indeed the policy which most governments adopt towards
nationalized industries. They are enjoined by statute to break-
even. But the break-even rule should be recognized for the
value judgement that it is – it implies that those who enjoy the
products of the nationalized industry should meet the full costs
of provision. There is nothing implicitly right or wrong about
it.[1]

TWO-PART TARIFFS: This is sometimes referred to as the 'club'
principle, whereby the consumer pays a lump sum annual
membership fee, plus a variable charge related to the amount
he consumes. The price which he pays for each unit can then
be related to marginal cost; capital and other fixed costs being
met by a lump sum payment. This principle suffers from the
disadvantage that the lump sum charge may deter some
customers who would, in other circumstances, be prepared to
contribute something towards overheads and, granted a failure
to cover overheads, any such contribution is welcome. This
method of pricing is commonly used in our public utilities; the
gas, electricity and telephone industries in the UK all use it. It
is not an appropriate method of charging where club membership is easily transferable. For example it is not considered
a suitable method of financing the overhead costs of the railways since 'club' tickets could be easily transferred from one
person to another, while it is suitable where a service is
wired or piped directly to a household, as with electricity or
gas.

DISCRIMINATION: This means charging different users of
essentially the same service, different prices. It is appropriate
where the industry serves customers with differing elasticities
of demand and where trading between customers is impossible,
as for example users of the telephone service at different times
of day, off-peak tickets for shopping which are not valid for
commuter trains, etc. Another method of discrimination that
is sometimes used is described in the phrase 'charging what the

[1] There may be management advantages in the break-even rule. See below
section 6·6 of this chapter.

market will bear'. What it does is to meet overhead costs from consumer surplus. Consumer surplus is the name given to the area between the demand curve and the price line, as shown in figure 10.

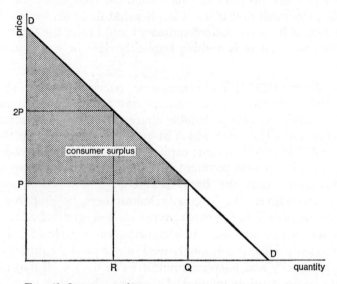

Figure 10. Consumer surplus.

It is apparent that when the demand curve slopes down all but the customer who buys the Qth unit would have been prepared to pay a higher price if necessary for the commodity. Thus if output were limited to R, admittedly fewer people would buy the good, but those who do so would be prepared to pay twice the original price P. Now if you can in fact separate your customers into groups, who are not in a position to exchange the product between themselves, then you can charge one set of customers a higher price than another – you can discriminate between them and, in effect, 'milk' the consumer surplus. A two-part tariff is another method of tapping consumer surplus, the club contribution being paid from consumer surplus. The concept of consumer surplus is an important one in cost benefit analysis and we shall encounter it again in the next chapter.

Under a discriminatory pricing system everyone is charged a

price which, at minimum, reflects marginal or escapable cost, and overhead costs are then met by increasing the charge to those who value the service more highly. Thus passengers on the fast inter-city rail services contribute heavily towards overheads, while suburban commuter services contribute very little. Where there are competing forms of service available, for example rail and air links between cities, a ceiling is provided to the extent of discrimination. The inter-city rail fare cannot be raised above the equivalent air fare without substantial loss of passengers, and vice versa. Where there is no effective competition, as for example with the telephone service or with electricity for lighting, the discrimination could lead to a small group of consumers meeting a substantial part of overhead costs. This could be viewed as a form of redistribution among consumers and, if pursued, it is necessary to make sure that the direction of redistribution does not conflict with the distributional objectives of society as a whole. Granted this, discrimination is probably the most satisactory method of financing the deficit.

It is worth noting at this juncture that a policy of discrimination and 'charging what the market will bear' is, in effect, a policy of profit maximization. When we discussed this briefly at the beginning of this section we dismissed it largely on the grounds that nationalized industries were monopolies, and it would have undesirable effects on both income distribution and the allocation of resources. Where nationalized industries are not monopolies, in the sense that they meet a good deal of competition from other sources, then this argument does not apply. In this sense the only nationalized industry in the UK which could be called a true monopoly is the Post Office, which enjoys a monopoly of both the postal and telecommunication services, the only effective competition for each of these services being from the other.

PEAK AND OFF-PEAK TARIFFS: Some public utilities face major variations in demand according to the time of day and season of the year. For example, the electricity industry faces much higher demand in winter than in summer, and higher demand at those times of day when the domestic cooking, heating and lighting load coincides with industrial and commercial demands. Since electricity cannot be stored, the capacity of the system has to be sufficient to meet the maximum demand put upon it – in the UK, usually between 8 and 9.30 am or between 4.30 and 6 pm on the coldest day of the year. Other industries also face peaking problems. The transport industries have to cope with commuter traffic; the telephone industry faces a daily peak demand during business hours; the postal services face peak pressure at the end of the business day. Some industries face substantial variations in demand but are able to store their product and thus meet the peaks from 'stocks' eg coal and, to some extent, gas. The peaking problem hits most forcibly those industries which cannot store their product like the electricity or transport industries. In these circumstances, it is argued, srmc rather than lrmc is the appropriate pricing concept, for it is peak users who determine capacity and who should therefore bear costs associated with providing such capacity, essentially the capital equipment costs. Off-peak users make no demands for an extension of capacity, but use capacity that would exist anyway irrespective of their demands; they should therefore be charged a price which reflects only the cost of meeting their demands – labour, raw material and wear-and-tear costs. This is illustrated in figure 11. The upper of the two demand curves represents peak demand and the lower, off-peak demand. Charging a price equal to srmc means that consumption is encouraged in off-peak hours and discouraged in peak hours thus helping to reduce the differential usage of capacity.

Average cost pricing

It is sometimes suggested that, given the difficulties of trying to relate prices to marginal costs, the simplest way of meeting the break-even rule is to price at average cost. What this means in practice is unclear. Average cost is an even hazier concept than marginal cost. What method should be used to amortize plant – historic cost or replacement cost depreciation? It may mean the averaging of total system costs across the board and, thus, the *ad hoc* cross-subsidization of one part of the system by another. (Such a practice offers few advantages, and can lead, as it did in the case of British Rail in the 1950s, to the

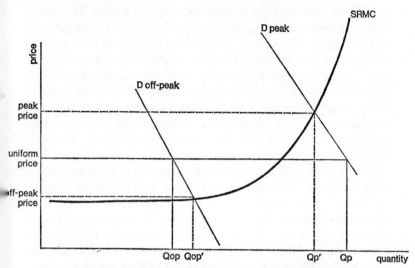

Figure 11. Charging differential prices reflecting the differential short run marginal costs, rather than a uniform price will tend to lessen the differential usage. Qp and Qop represent the differential usage with a uniform price; Qp' and Qop' with differential prices.

accelerating loss of profitable traffic to competitors and the need to raise prices further on remaining traffic as sources of subsidy were lost – a system that is analogous to trying to walk up an escalator going down.) Alternatively, average cost pricing may relate not to the whole system but to the unit of equipment and mean in effect average escapable costs plus a margin to allow for average overhead costs. In such cases, price may bear some relation to escapable costs, particularly where overhead costs are not large in relation to escapable costs. But it can lead to considerable complications over the allocation of joint costs. For example, what part of the chairman's salary is attributable to one particular branch line or colliery? Moreover, like the two-part tariff, such a system has the disadvantage of discouraging potential users who are prepared to pay the direct costs of providing the good/service, but are unwilling to contribute fully to the overheads. The extent to which they are prepared to contribute to overheads, however small, reduces the amount by which others are required to contribute to overheads and there is no reason to spurn their patronage.

183

AVERAGE COST VERSUS MARGINAL COST PRICING: The major virtue of average cost pricing is that it provides a simple way of meeting the break-even criterion. Other than this, average cost pricing has no special status. Above all it has no logical, mathematical rationale. In contrast, the marginal principle owes its rationale to mathematics. Marginal analysis is essentially a mathematical optimization procedure, and since we assume that the government is concerned to *maximize* social welfare, then marginal analysis remains appropriate. The fault of those who advocate marginal cost pricing is to look upon it as a pricing rule, which has to be translated into practical prices, rather than as an *output rule*. If one is looking to an optimal allocation of resources then the most important thing is to secure an optimal level of output in the industry, for it is output that determines the resources, inputs, etc used by the industry. Can optimal levels of output be determined without the introduction into the equation of prices? Of course they cannot, but these need not be the prices actually charged in the market. Output levels depend upon installed capacity. Marginal cost prices (or rather their second best equivalents, for as we have seen marginal cost prices *per se* will not lead to an optimal allocation of resources within a second best world) could then be used as shadow prices for the purposes of the investment calculation (see next section), which in turn would determine the capacity of the industry. Capacity is then optimally adjusted. But the prices used in the investment calculation need not be the actual selling prices. Once capacity is determined, the industry can sell its output for the best price it can get – charging what the market will bear – which does not rule out two-part tariffs, peak and off-peak pricing or other forms of discriminatory pricing. The important thing is not the prices that are actually charged in the market but that output is optimally adjusted. The complications of the marginalist rules need then only affect the planners.

The advantage of this approach, concentrating on output, which determines price, rather than price, which determines output, is that it overcomes the problems involved in the practical definition of marginal cost, or for that matter average cost, and that system constraints, such as the break-even rule, can be accommodated within the pricing framework. Its limitations which are limitations common to all marginal analysis are that it cannot cope with major indivisibilities, where a programming approach (see chapter 2) or a total benefit/cost approach (see chapter 7) (the two being in fact closely linked) would be appropriate. Nor can it take account of what might be described as 'total conditions'. For example, it may be in the interests of the nation that the prices of the products of nationalized industries be controlled in a bid to limit inflation; that the nationalized industries become, in effect, a tool of macroeconomic management. (We shall be discussing this further below.) Such a policy cannot be comprehended within the marginalist framework.

6.4 Investment policies

Present value and discounting

Analogous to the marginal pricing rule is what might be described as the 'marginal investment rule', that no investment will be undertaken unless it yields a return at least equal to its cost; its cost being the rate of interest payable on the capital necessary to finance the investment.

The complication that arises is that the return on an investment is yielded not immediately but over time. £100 ten years hence is not the same thing as £100 today, for, even if you forget about inflation, you can invest the £100 today and let it accumulate at compound interest. Thus £100 today is worth

$$100+100(r) = 100 \ (1+r) \text{ next year } 1$$
$$100 \ (1+r) \ (1+r) = 100 \ (1+r)^2 \text{ in year } 2$$
$$100 \ (1+r)^2(1+r) = 100 \ (1+r)^3 \text{ in year } 3$$
$$100 \ (1+r)^n \text{ in year } n$$

where r = rate of interest

If r = 10 per cent, then £100 invested today would be worth £259 ten years' hence. Similarly, £100 ten years hence is worth today *not* £100, but the sum which invested at compound interest would yield £100 ten years hence. This sum is called the *present value* of the £100 obtained in 10 years time, and is given by the formula $\frac{£100}{(1+r)^n}$.[1] If r=10 per cent, then the present value of £100 yielded 10 years hence is $\frac{£100}{(1+0\cdot10)^{10}}$ or £39. This process is known as discounting, and r, the rate of interest used for discounting, is often referred to as the rate of discount.

Thus, if an investment of £500 with a life of 10 years yields a profit of £100 each year, we should be wary about claims that the investment will yield a total profit of £1,000 over its life, or a return of 20 per cent pa. This 20 per cent pa is the average rate of return, and does not take account of the fact that the present value of each £100 will decrease as time proceeds. Rather, the present value of the profits yielded, assuming an interest rate of 10 per cent, will be as follows

year	profit	present value £ r = 10 per cent
1	100	91
2	100	83
3	100	75
4	100	68
5	100	62
6	100	56
7	100	51
8	100	47
9	100	42
10	100	39

Total present value over
10 year period   614

[1] The compound interest formula is
$$A = I (1+r)^n$$
where A = compound value of initial sum
I = initial sum invested
r = rate of interest
n = number of years
For present value calculations, we have A but wish to know I. Thus
$$I = \frac{A}{(1=r)^n}$$

From this total present value of the profits over the 10 year life of the investment must be subtracted the initial cost of the project, in the example cited £500. This yields a *net* present value for the investment of £114. As long as the net present value is positive, the investment is worth undertaking – the return on the project is greater than its cost.[1]

This method of investment appraisal, since it discounts the 'cash flow' yielded by the investments, is known as a discounted cash flow technique and is a preferred method of investment appraisal since it takes the time pattern of profit yields and costs into account. It is however only a method of appraisal, no better or worse than the data fed into the calculation. This pinpoints the fundamental 'inputs' into any discounted cash flow exercise.

THE FUTURE 'CASH FLOWS' OF THE INVESTMENT PROJECT: To forecast the future 'cash flows' of an investment requires a forecast of future demand and relative price trends for both inputs and outputs. This may be no easy matter, particularly for a long lived investment. For an investment, such as a power station, which is part of a total system and which as it gets older will tend to be used less and less, the forecast should cover not just the life of the power station itself but the long term demands upon the system as a whole, the rate of construction of future power stations and so on. We are involved in a complex 'systems analysis' exercise. As far as price movements are concerned, relative price movements must be taken into account, but general inflation within the economy should be ignored, for while the profitability of an investment will be affected favourably by an upward movement in relative prices of the product concerned, it is important that a project should

---

[1] Another way of looking at this is to say that the investment yields a return which is greater than the cost of borrowing the capital (which we have suggested is 10 per cent). The implicit rate of return yielded by the investment is that rate of discount which yields a net present value of zero – in our current example this is a rate of slightly over 15 per cent (a 15 per cent rate of discount would yield a total present value of the profit stream of £503) – and it is this rate which should be compared with the current rate of interest, rather than the annual average profit as a percentage of capital outlay. This rate of return is sometimes referred to as the 'internal rate of return'. Because in certain circumstances an investment may appear to yield more than one internal rate of return it is simpler to eschew this concept and to stick to the concept of present value.

not show a positive net present value just because general price levels are expected to rise over time. The project should yield a net present value in real terms. The cash flows to some investments can be forecast more accurately than to others, but all will be subject to some degree of uncertainty. Ideally some sort of weighting system according to the probabilities attached to the different outcomes should be used to take account of such differences.

THE DISCOUNT RATE: For a private firm this can be taken as the rate of interest that it has to pay to borrow money (or, if it is using its own resources, the rate it could obtain from lending its cash). Given the complications of the stock market, this may not be as straightforward as it sounds. For a public enterprise it is even less straightforward, for the rate of interest on government stock is influenced by many factors, most of all the monetary policies pursued by the authorities. The discount rate should reflect, not a forecast of interest rates, but the opportunity cost of capital. If the money were not invested by the public enterprise, would it have been invested by private industry and if so what rate of return would it have yielded? Or, is the opportunity cost of public sector investment, private sector consumption? If so, what is the appropriate 'social rate of time preference' that should be applied? That is to say how much extra jam do you have to offer people tomorrow to get them to give up jam today? Are people myopic – do they tend to adopt the line of 'Eat, drink and be merry for tomorrow we die', and thus exhibit an unduly high rate of preference for jam today? We shall explore these questions at greater length in chapter 7. Suffice it to say here that there are no objectively right answers to these questions, and, to this extent, the choice of the rate of discount to be used in the public sector is arbitrary. It is important however that a single rate of discount should be applied to the whole of the public sector for if decisions within the public sector are to be consistent they should be made upon the same basis.

Mutually exclusive investments

So far we have suggested that any investment which yields a positive net present value at the appropriate rate of discount is worthwhile undertaking. Usually however there are alternative ways of achieving the same end, and the choice is between several *mutually exclusive* alternative projects. For example, if the third London airport is built at Foulness, it cannot also be built at Cublington, Thurleigh or Nuthampstead; a decision may have to be taken between building a coal-fired or nuclear power station on a particular site. In such case the decision to be taken is not only, 'Is such and such a project worthwhile?' but also 'Which of a number of possible alternative projects is the best to adopt?' The whole range of alternatives should be considered. One alternative is always to 'do nothing' ie not to embark upon any investment programme, and this should be considered alongside other investment projects. In the case of such mutually exclusive investments, that project which yields the highest net present value should be chosen in preference to the others.[1]

The interdependence of pricing and investment rules

The present value investment rule outlined above is 'optimal' in the sense that it is consistent with profit maximizing. It is more obviously optimal therefore for the private firm than for the nationalized industry. For the latter, given price levels, it will distinguish between projects that will yield a net increase in revenues over time and those that will not, and, given that it takes account of the varying time pattern of revenue flows, it is a superior investment appraisal technique to the use of average rates of return, payback periods, etc. From the point of view of resource allocation, it is 'optimal' only in so far as pricing systems are optimal. In a first best world, it could promote an optimal allocation of resources when used in conjunction with marginal cost pricing policies. In the second best world, as we suggested above in the section on prices, calculations using second best shadow prices might be employed in the investment calculations in order to secure optimal output levels, actual prices being adjusted to clear the market.

---

[1] If the internal rate of return criterion is adopted this procedure is not quite so straightforward, it being necessary to examine the incremental rates of return yielded by more expensive projects.

6.5 Commercial versus social obligations of nationalized industries

So far we have ignored the presence of externalities, that is the possibility that the costs incurred by the nationalized industries and the benefits derived from the services they provide affect not just the producers and consumers in these industries but spill over more widely into society. There are many examples of externalities of production and consumption in the nationalized industries, just as there are in private industry. A railway line may provide a vital communication link to a community, and closure is going to affect more than just those who travel on it. A colliery may be the only source of employment to a mining village and again closure will affect not just the miners and their families, but the prosperity of the whole community. The telecommunications service speeds the passage of information, and results in decisions being taken more quickly and in the light of better information. The list could be infinite.

It is a truism that nationalized industries should look to the public interest and contribute to maximizing social welfare. Nationalized industries should therefore take account where possible of externalities and operate on the basis of social costs and benefits rather than private ones. This applies however just as much to private industry and we constrain and encourage private enterprise to operate in a manner consistent with the public interest by an elaborate mixture of controls, taxes and subsidies. Thus we have created smokeless zones, we have restrictions on development and location, we have investment incentives and the regional employment premium, petrol tax and noise limits on cars and lorries, and so forth. In some instances the government has discriminated towards a particular industry and offered a specific subsidy to encourage it to move in a direction seen to be in the public interest; such subsidies have been paid in the UK to the cotton industry and the ship-building industry. Agriculture is another example of an industry which is subsidized because it is felt to be in the public interest that we should have a rather larger agricultural industry than would survive if left to 'market forces'. Do nationalized industries differ in any respect from these other industries? Is there any reason why the externality problem should not be dealt with for nationalized industries in exactly the same way? The nationalized industries are of course subject to most of the general constraints and incentives provided for private industry, but not all. For example they are not subject to general planning or location of industry controls. Similarly, although it has been generally accepted that there are 'public interest' reasons for preventing the coal mining industry from running down too rapidly, the industry has not, like agriculture, been directly subsidized but has instead received a miscellaneous collection of indirect subsidies, such as capital write-offs, usually given after the event to clear up debts which the National Coal Board has accumulated. The reason for this exemption of the nationalized industries from these forms of control and incentive seems to have been because it was originally assumed that, being nationalized, they would automatically look to the public interest in their actions, although no such obligation was written into the statutes. The result is that it has never been clear who is to interpret where the public interest lies; whether it should be industry itself or the minister responsible to Parliament for the industry. This has led to considerable muddle with, on the one hand, the industries taking onto their own shoulders obligations which conflicted with their commercial interests and, on the other, ministers intervening in the affairs of the industries and persuading them to adopt policies which, although judged to be in the public interest, adversely affected their financial position.

Besides the 'railway closure' type of social obligations which they meet, which might be described as 'orthodox' externalities, nationalized industries also encounter another sort of 'social obligation' which might be described as a 'status obligation', for it derives directly from the public sector status of these industries. Take for example the evidence of Aubrey Jones(then Chairman of the National Prices and Incomes Board), given to the Select Committee of the House of Commons on Nationalized Industries, in which he posed the dilemma of whether it is more inflationary for a nationalized industry to raise its prices to the consumer, or to look to the government to find the necessary resources, either from the taxpayer or from borrowing. He concludes, 'the pricing policies of nationalized industries cannot be divorced from general government fiscal and financial policies'.[1] Again, Lord Diamond, then Chief Secretary to the Treasury, stated in his evidence to the Select Committee, 'The supreme value of the public sector is to enable the government to use it as an instrument for overall economic control'.[2]

If you accept this view of the nationalized industries, then they become a part of the general fiscal machinery, and decisions have to be taken in the light of the public interest in both a microeconomic and macroeconomic sense. For example an industry might be prevented from raising its prices when it wished because the government was trying to encourage the private sector to accept price constraint. Similarly it might be subject to a good deal of pressure from the government to resist a wage claim and to accept the consequences of a strike, whereas in the 'normal' way it would have settled for the higher wage payment. Again its investment may be cut back to levels which it considers below those which would have been commercially justifiable because its investment comes within the definition of public expenditure and the government is anxious to limit the rate of increase of public expenditure. This provides a very considerable extension of the social obligations of nationalized industries; an extension that clearly affects their financial returns but not one where the costs or benefits involved are readily quantifiable, or where, for that matter, the government has shown any inclination to compensate the industries for losses that such policies involve.

There has recently been a move towards compensating the industries for some of the 'orthodox' externality costs which they face. For example, under the terms of the 1968 Transport Act, British Rail now receives an explicit subsidy for each railway line which the Department of the Environment calculate should be kept open on social grounds.[3] Similarly, in 1968–70 the nationalized electricity industry received a subsidy based on the extra costs of using coal rather than oil in power stations, which

[1] Select Committee for Nationalized Industries *Report on ministerial control* House of Commons paper 371 1 1968 Vol II Minutes of evidence p 686.

[2] Select Committee for Nationalized Industries *op cit* question 2351 A p 709.

[3] For London commuter lines, subsidies were provided because of the high social costs involved in shifting travellers from the use of the (public) rail service, to the (private) car – costs which under the present system of road pricing, were not met by commuters. The Conservative government discontinued these subsidies in 1970.

it would have liked to have converted to oil. Compensation so far however has been sporadic and partial. Above all, there has been little move to compensate the industries for the 'status' type social obligations, although there has been no lessening of the extent to which these industries are subjected to pressures of this kind. Indeed, if anything, it has been increased since the Conservative government, eschewing a more formal prices and incomes policy, used the public sector as the front line troops in their attempt to fight inflation in 1970–72.

There are substantial arguments in favour of explicit compensation where it is possible.

a it helps Parliament and the taxpayer to identify the cost involved in pursuing a particular policy and to judge whether the benefits stemming from it justify the cost. In some cases it may be possible to quantify the benefits, in others the judgement has to be qualitative;

b where a nationalized industry is pressed 'in the national interest' to pursue a particular policy, it would seem appropriate that the nation, rather than the consumer of the product of that industry, should meet the bill. (This is a question of income distribution – you may in fact wish to redistribute in this direction);

c it helps to maintain the morale of the industry. Where the industry meets the burden of social costs itself it is impossible to judge the operations of the industry by the normal criterion of the commercial world, namely profit. Yet both management and the public in general do judge industries by this criterion; and on the whole find them wanting. This in turn makes it difficult to attract good management into the industries, and poor management exacerbates losses. The payment of an explicit subsidy to meet social costs which the industry has to bear, plus the adherence to the break-even requirement, helps to keep management on their toes and prevents them falling back on the excuse of social obligations to explain losses.

So far so good. The onus for the recognition of and compensation for social obligations is squarely with the government: the nationalized industry can thus be a strictly commercial enterprise which has to stand on its own feet. The whole exercise depends however upon the ability to quantify compensation for 'social obligations'. It is one thing to calculate the loss which British Rail incurs from running a branch line kept open for social reasons. It is quite another to calculate the costs of more general intervention – the 'status obligations' of the nationalized industries. Consider for example the dispute over miners' pay which led to the coal strike in January–February 1972. Left to itself would the NCB have raised its offer of $8\frac{1}{2}$ per cent to 13 or 14 per cent? Would the miners have accepted this? As it was, after a lengthy and costly strike the final settlement was in the region of 22 per cent. What would have happened without government interference? What in these circumstances is the appropriate level of compensation? The answer to these questions are not clear cut.

This suggests that the calculation of compensation for 'status' social obligations is often impossible.[1] If this is so, then there are two possible courses open. First, it would be quite possible to cease to use the nationalized industries as a tool of macro-economic management, and thus to eliminate the status category of social obligation. Yet is this policy really feasible? These industries have been nationalized and are a part of the public sector. Is it really feasible that any government will not look to them to 'set a good example'? The other possible course is to accept that the nationalized industries are different, and that we cannot expect them to operate as normal commercial enterprises or to meet normal commercial criteria.

6.6 Recent developments in the control of the nationalized industries in the UK

Let us return to the experience of the UK in running its nationalized industries in the post-war period. The major fuel and transport industries were nationalized in the 1945–52 period.

---

[1] In fact the government have announced measures to compensate the NCB for the effects of the coal strike and the subsequent settlement. The sums however were not based upon a calculation of 'what might have happened if' but upon what appeared to be practicable given the desire on the government's part not to increase unemployment by cutting back drastically the size of industry, and the limited extent to which the industry could raise its prices. More closely analogous to compensation for 'status' interventions is compensation being given to certain of the nationalized industries for accelerating their investment programmes in 1972–3. There seems to be no satisfactory basis for assessing compensation in these cases either.

Since 1964 there have been two major new nationalized industries, the steel industry (abortively nationalized in 1949 and subsequently de-nationalized) and the Post Office, for over a century a government department.

The period up to 1960 can be regarded as one of considerable muddle for the nationalized industries. The muddle derived, first, from pricing policies, since the industries had regarded the break-even requirement as justifying average cost pricing, which in the early period of post-war reconstruction led to excess demand for their products and services and, in the later 1950s when their monopoly position had been eroded, to severe financial difficulties. Secondly, muddle came from their social obligations. Ministers, rather than using the 'general direction', preferred the more flexible 'lunch table directive' (as it came to be called) of gentle pressure and persuasion. At the same time the industries themselves assumed social obligations not imposed upon them by statute. The result was that by 1960 few industries were in a strong financial position, and most were failing to put sufficient on one side to allow for adequate depreciation of their plant.

The 1960s saw the development of a much more consistent framework of control for the nationalized industries. Credit for this development should go first to the Select Committee for Nationalized Industries,[1] which did much to uncover the muddle and question the framework under which the industries were operating, and secondly to the Treasury for taking the initiative and setting up the new framework. The first step in this direction was the White Paper of 1961 on the financial and economic obligations of the national industries[2] which created a system of financial objectives for the industries more stringent

---

[1] The Select Committee had been set up in 1957 with the aim of keeping Parliament better informed of the affairs of nationalized industries. Since 1958 it has issued a series of reports on the affairs of the individual corporations as well as a general report on ministerial control (House of Commons Paper 371–1 1968). The Committee has been particularly concerned with the problem of non-statutory intervention by ministers in the affairs of the industries, for ministers were only answerable to Parliament for their actions taken under statutory powers. In so doing the Select Committee has become very much the watchdog of the integrity of the concept of the public corporation and has barked loudly whenever it seemed to it that ministers were encroaching too far on the autonomy of the nationalized industries.

[2] *The financial and economic obligations of the nationalized industries* Cmnd 1337 – HMSO London 1961.

than the break-even commitment in the statutes. In future each industry was to be set a target rate of return, usually expressed as a percentage of net assets, which it was enjoined to achieve.

The introduction of these financial objectives should be seen against the background of many of the industries being in a poor financial position and the simultaneous build-up of investment programmes on the part of the industries, which were having to be financed largely by borrowing. This placed considerable strains on the Treasury's debt management/interest rate policy. To suggest that the nationalized industries should be required to increase their surpluses thus killed a number of birds with one stone. On the one hand, it increased the self-financing ratio of the nationalized industries and lessened calls on the Exchequer for finance, on the other, it enabled the introduction of a more specific objective than the break-even objective for the nationalized industries. It was hoped also that the setting of financial objectives might help to stimulate the management of the industries to greater efficiency. The objective set was to vary from industry to industry to reflect the variations in investment budgets and social obligations of the different industries. Thus the electricity industry with its high rate of investment and low social obligations was set the highest target, 12·2 per cent, while the Coal Board for which the reverse was true was expected to do no more than break-even.

Although the 1961 White Paper was the first attempt to set up a consistent framework for the operations of the nationalized industries, it was widely criticized by economists largely for its emphasis on the average rate of return. What was important was not the rate of return yielded on a collection of assets acquired in the past, but the rate of return on new assets, for even if mistakes had been made in the investment programme in the past, the important thing was not that past mistakes should be made to pay but that such mistakes should not be repeated. Thus emphasis should be on criteria for assessing new investment. Moreover, the White Paper had implied that increasing the degree of self-finance in the nationalized industries would improve the allocation of resources between the public and the private sector. Critics pointed out that this was not so. To expect a higher degree of self-finance was merely to ask present consumers rather than taxpayers or the capital market to contribute towards capital provision for future consumption. This was a question of income distribution, not allocation. There was nothing uniquely right in this strategy. Again varying the financial objective seemed an odd and not very satisfactory way of recognizing the varying social obligations of the industries. Far better, it was argued, to move towards the explicit compensation of industries for such obligations.

The Treasury were not immune to these criticisms and began in the early 1960s to introduce discounted cash flow methods of investment appraisal to the nationalized industries, and to put a good deal of emphasis on the adoption of these techniques. Somewhat later, it also realized that it is not only the methods by which the sums are done that count, but also the figures that go into the sums. If pricing policies are inefficient, then no matter how correct the investment appraisal technique, the resulting resource allocation will also be inefficient. Thus official doctrine moved to advocating the use of long run marginal cost pricing, with short run marginal cost pricing where peak demand problems arose. At the same time, the failure of the 1962 Transport Act,[1] combined with the arrival of a socialist government committed to the co-ordination of transport policy, forced a major reappraisal of the transport sector.[2] One of the distinctive features of the new transport policy was the acceptance by the government that they should explicitly bear the cost of the 'social obligations', which fell upon the Railways Board. Thus for the first time explicit subsidies were paid for maintaining certain branch lines and

---

[1] This had broken down the monolithic British Transport Commission of 1948 origin into its separate and constituent parts, the largest of which was British Railways. Dr Beeching had been appointed head of British Rail with instructions to make it a viable commercial concern. His proposals, which involved the first ever study of the costs and revenues of the different rail routes, came to the inevitable conclusion that viability involved the wholesale closure of branch lines, as well as the discontinuance of many stopping and commuter services. To carry the policy to its logical conclusion was too much even for a Conservative administration, and there was frequent ministerial intervention to 'save' services. In turn this policy vitiated all hope of making British Rail pay, indeed the deficit in 1967 was of the same order as that of 1962, in spite of the suspension of a major part of the capital debt.

[2] *White Paper on transport policy* Cmnd 3057 – 1966. Cmnd 3439 (1967) *Railway policy*; Cmnd 3470 (1967) *The transport of freight*; Cmnd 3481 (1967) *Public transport and traffic*. The policies outlined in these White Papers were incorporated into the 1968 Transport Act.

commuter services. In other words the government had accepted in principle the fact that they should bear the cost of 'externalities' where these fall upon a specific industry.

THE 1967 WHITE PAPER AND THE SELECT COMMITTEE REPORT ON MINISTERIAL CONTROL: These changes were incorporated into government policy in the White Paper, published in November 1967, entitled 'Financial and economic obligations of nationalized industries – a review'.[1] On the one hand it stamped Treasury and government acceptance of the principles of marginal cost pricing policies and discounted cash flow investment appraisal techniques (a test rate of discount of 8 per cent was laid down for all public sector projects – this was later raised to 10 per cent). On the other, it gave official cognizance to the principle of explicit government subsidies for cases where the industries were asked to pursue policies which conflicted with their social interests. However, the Treasury could not bring themselves to drop the principle of financial objectives. The nationalized industries were still major investors[2] and the need for self-finance was in the Treasury's eyes, as great as ever. Moreover, the policy had been successful in increasing both the profitability and the morale of the nationalized industries. There was an element of 'management by objectives' in Treasury policy: if an aspiration level for attainment is set then managers will be stimulated to stretch themselves and their organization to attain this aspiration level. Thus the financial objective was retained side by side with the other two criteria.

What the Treasury seemed to have ignored however was

[1] Cmnd No 3437 HMSO London 1967.
[2] Investment by the Public Corporations

£m Current Prices

	1950	1955	1960	1965	1968	1969	1970
gross fixed capital formation	1700	2797	4105	6319	7798	8121	8886
(As per cent GNP)	(14·6)	(16·6)	(18·1)	(20·6)	(21·2)	(20·6)	(20·8)
gross fixed capital formation	288	570	792	1295	1639	1484	1609
of public corporations	(16·9)	(20·4)	(19·3)	(22·5)	(21·2)	(18·0)	(18·0)
extent of self-finance (per cent of investment by public Corporations finance from internal sources)		(42·0)	(31·6)	(38·1)	(50·5)	(49·0)	(59·0)	(47)

Source: *National income and expenditure Blue Book* 1971 and earlier editions.

that all three criteria provided what economists would call an 'over determined system'. The pricing and investment criteria, if applied, produced a determinate outcome in terms of financial results. It might be possible to think of the financial objective as a forecast of this out-turn, which in itself would provide the aspiration level for managers. But the financial objective was not arrived at on this basis. It was not a best guess as to what the following year's out-turn would be, but a target for a period of years (normally five), agreed between the industry, the ministry concerned and the Treasury, of what it might be reasonable to expect the industry to achieve in the light of trends in profitability, investment levels and so forth. As it was, if an industry was to meet the financial objective, prices might well have to be raised above long run marginal costs or investment limited to those projects yielding a return well above the stipulated test discount rate. It is impossible to meet all three of the criteria concurrently. If one has to give, the question is which one should give. In its evidence to the Select Committee the Treasury was ambiguous, but the Select Committee itself came firmly to the view that the pricing and investment criteria should have priority over the financial objective, and that the latter should not be used to determine the level of prices.[1] If this view were accepted the financial objective could be regarded as the residual, determined by the other two. The White Paper reflecting the Labour government's views, presumably on Treasury advice, on the Select Committee report seemed to accept the residual role of the financial objective, while maintaining its usefulness.[2]

In practice however governments have continued to set financial targets for most industries on a five year forward basis and the industries have given first priority to trying to meet these targets. The targets are not regarded as residuals, but objectives; the residual idea has been, conveniently, forgotten. Nor has there been much effort by the industries to adopt marginal cost pricing; pricing systems remaining predominantly average cost. There has admittedly been some move towards the

[1] Select Committee – Report on ministerial control *op cit* p 291 chapter V especially paras 220–3.
[2] See para 35 Cmnd 4027 – *Ministerial control of the nationalized industries* HMSO London 1969.

use of peak and off-peak tariffs, which might be considered a form of marginal cost pricing. There has also been a move towards more discriminatory pricing, changing 'what the market will bear'. For example, British Rail have deliberately been pushing up fares on the fast inter-city services since they have found price elasticity lower on these than on other routes. Stimulus to adopt these forms of pricing came partly from within the organizations themselves but partly also from various reports of the National Prices and Incomes Board.[1]

Pricing policies, and the overall financial position of the nationalized industries, have been thrown into confusion in the early 1970s by the government's use of the public sector as the front line of defence against inflation. The industries have experienced repeated intervention by ministers on price and wage fronts aimed at limiting all increases. They have been notably more successful in limiting price increases, and the financial results of the industries have suffered accordingly.

The Treasury's emphasis on meeting the financial target is not as illogical as might seem. As we saw when discussing pricing policies above, marginal cost pricing policies are seldom compatible with 'breaking even'. The break-even, 'he who benefits should pay' school of thought is a perfectly valid one, but it requires prices to be adjusted to cover any possible deficit resulting from marginal cost pricing, and the methods of doing this may take prices a good way from reflecting marginal costs. What the Treasury should recognize is that it cannot have the best of all three worlds. If it wishes to stipulate that the industries should break-even, and in addition make some contribution to self-finance, then it cannot also advocate, as in the 1967 White Paper, that these industries adhere to prices based upon marginal cost.

THE OBJECTIVES OF POLICY – MANAGERIAL EFFICIENCY: There have been two important strands of thought which have

[1] In 1967 the NBPI were charged with the responsibility of vetting all proposed price increases by nationalized industries and produced an invaluable series of reports which provided not only an examination of the price increase under review, but also a general commentary on the economic position of the industries.

See for example reports No 58 *Post Office charges* Cmnd 357 1968; No 72 *British Rail fares* Cmnd 3656 1968; No 102 *Gas prices second report* Cmnd 3924 1969; No 153 *Coal prices second report* Cmnd 4455 1970; No 159 *London Transport fares* Cmnd 4540 1970. All published by HMSO London.

underlain policy towards the nationalized industries in the 1960s. One has put emphasis on the optimal allocation of resources, and it is here that emphasis emerged on marginal cost pricing and present value investment appraisal. The other has been a concern with the managerial or dynamic efficiency of the nationalized industries, the instilling of cost consciousness into the managers and generally 'keeping them on their toes'. There are two reasons why the nationalized industries present a problem here. First, because the tradition of low profitability and deficit finance which they inherited from the 1950s (which, as we have seen, stemmed, at least in part, from social obligations which they shouldered) made it too easy for inefficiency to be masked. Secondly, because these industries were immune from the discipline which the takeover market imposes on private enterprise. (See chapter 4.2 above). Efforts to stimulate the industries to greater managerial efficiency can be seen in a number of measures; in the emphasis on target rates of return (though the waters have been muddied here by concern for a greater degree of self-finance on the part of the nationalized industries); in the introduction of the test-rate of discount (which serves a dual role of promoting allocational and managerial efficiency); in the increasing degree of intervention by various ministries in the affairs of the industries; in the 'efficiency audit' responsibilities given to the NBPI in relation to the nationalized industries; even, perhaps, in the support given to the investigations of the Select Committee on nationalized industries. Again the 1968 Transport Act deliberately denied to British Rail the facility of deficit finance and provided explicit subsidies to meet its social obligations, because it was felt by those concerned that deficit financing for over a decade had had a disastrous effect upon managerial morale and efficiency. The success of these measures was considerable. A recent study estimates that, over the period 1958–68, labour productivity in the nationalized industries increased on average by 5·3 per cent, compared with a rise of only 3·7 per cent in manufacturing industry as a whole. Indeed chemicals was the only major manufacturing industry whose output per man hour increased more rapidly than this.[1] In putting emphasis upon

[1] RWS Pryke 'Are nationalized industries becoming more efficient?' *Moorgate and Wall Street* A review issued by Hill Samuel and Company Spring 1970. A

target rates of return, the Treasury were anxious not to surrender a tool which they felt to have been an important one in stimulating these industries to greater efficiency.

It is within the context of trying to stimulate managerial efficiency that two issues raised by the Conservative government that came into power in 1970 should be viewed, namely 'hiving off' and the introduction of private capital alongside public capital in these industries. The 'hiving-off' of peripheral activities of the nationalized industries, for example the brickmaking or chemical interests of the National Coal Board or the hotel interests of British Rail, is mainly a political question. The economic issue involved is one of diversification, and, as we saw in chapter 4, there may be occasions when diversification enables cost savings through spreading indivisible overheads. This is not always so. With the nationalized industries the fear is that diversification may be sheer empire building which, without the constraint on efficiency posed by the takeover market, will diffuse energies and efficiency. There are however no general rules which can be laid down here, and each case has to be judged on its merits. In fact there is remarkably little diversification on the part of the nationalized industries. It should be remembered that all major investment proposals of the nationalized industries are scrutinized by the ministries responsible and required to meet the 10 per cent test rate of discount. From an economic point of view, hiving-off is really a non-issue.

The introduction of private capital poses more difficult problems. It is unclear precisely how private capital should be introduced, but if the aim is to stimulate efficiency by introducing the 'discipline' of the private capital market, then it would presumably have to be in the form of equity capital. This would involve a major departure from the concept of the public corporation and the introduction into this sector of the orthodox company structure. Under such a structure the special features of the relationship with the industries could not survive in the present form; status obligations would have to disappear. The rights and duties attaching to government shareholding could be no different in character from those of

lengthier treatment of the same theme is to be found in his book, RWS Pryke *Public enterprise in practice* McGibbon and Kee London 1971.

private shareholding. During the first two years of the Conservative government there has been no indication that ministers are really intending to face up to these issues in relation to the major nationalized industries.

The question of private capital does however raise the final issue that seems worth discussing in relation to the UK nationalized industries, namely the difficulty of reconciling commercial status with public sector status. As long as these industries are a part of the public sector it seems inconceivable that they should not be used as a part of the armoury of weapons which the government uses to achieve its objectives of economic policy. Therefore, inevitably, they form a part of any campaign to limit price or wage increases; inevitably, they suffer in any moves to limit public expenditure, and so forth. However much, in other respects, they are set apart from the government machine, told to stand on their own feet, subjected to general 'strategic' controls like the target rates of return and test rates of discount, unless and until some method of successfully compensating these industries for such general interventions is found, they cannot be judged by the normal private enterprise success indicator of profits. Yet it is doubtful whether any accurate method of quantification can be devised for such compensation. Is the answer then to cease such intervention? This is a dilemma, upon the horns of which successive governments have hooked themselves – and look like continuing to do so.

6.7 Summary and conclusions

This chapter has aimed, on the one hand, to acquaint readers with some of the main theoretical issues which arise in the field of public enterprise, and, on the other, to relate this discussion to some of the current developments in the control of nationalized industries in the UK. A theme that has recurred throughout is efficiency – efficiency both in its static resource allocation sense, and in its dynamic sense. Static efficiency leads us to consider pricing policies. What is the appropriate pricing policy in a second best world? Has marginal cost pricing any relevance? Do dynamic efficiency or income distribution considerations lead to the introduction of a break-even requirement? We have considered some of the issues raised by these questions and suggested that it is wrong to put too much emphasis upon a pricing rule. If we are concerned about the allocation of resources, then we are concerned with inputs and outputs rather than actual prices, and if we can determine optimal output levels which embrace the constraints of the second best world, then actual prices charged can be fixed at levels which clear the market.

In the UK, the nationalized industries are constrained to break-even, and in addition to provide a surplus that can be used to help finance investment. Since the industries are also required to adhere to marginal cost pricing methods where practicable, there has been a basic conflict of policy which has been resolved, in practice, by dropping the marginal cost pricing requirement. Experience in the 1960s has been dominated by the desire on the one hand to improve the allocational efficiency of the nationalized industries, and thus of the economy as a whole, which explains the emphasis on pricing and investment policies, and on the other to improve their managerial and dynamic efficiency, which explains the emphasis on target rates of return, investment criteria etc. By and large dynamic efficiency has proved the dominant partner, and hence the dropping of marginal cost pricing. Superimposed upon this has been another theme – how to cope with the 'social obligations' of the nationalized industries. We have seen that in some cases they can be quantified and the industry can be paid an explicit subsidy which prevents these social obligations from jeopardizing the objective of dynamic efficiency. In other cases it may not be so easy to define, let alone to quantify, these social obligations, particularly what might be described as general 'public sector status' obligations, and this vitiates attempts to treat the industries as independent commercial enterprises.

Further reading

KG WILLIAM *Transport and public policy* Minerva Series No 11 George Allen & Unwin London 1964 chapters 2–4. This is a good introductory text on pricing policies.

R TURVEY (ed) *Public enterprise: selected readings* Penguin Books Harmondsworth 1968. All the readings are interesting and discuss in more detail some of the issues raised in this chapter, but read selectively according to interests.

R TURVEY *Economic analysis and public enterprises* George Allen & Unwin London 1972. The first part of this book is an excellent (though somewhat mathematical) introduction to some of the pricing policy implications of the second best world; the latter part draws upon his experience with the Prices and Incomes Board to illustrate some of the issues raised in the earlier part of the book.

GL REID and K ALLEN *Nationalized industries* Penguin Books Harmondsworth 1970. A brief description of some of the most important developments in the major UK nationalized industries.

SELECT COMMITTEE ON NATIONALIZED INDUSTRIES *Report on ministerial control* House of Commons Paper 371–1 Vol 1 HMSO London 1968. All the reports of the Select Committee make interesting reading and they have produced at one time or another reports on all the nationalized industries (including the Bank of England). Their two most influential reports have probably been the one on the Post Office, House of Commons Paper 340 – 1967 HMSO London 1967, and the general report on ministerial control which is referenced above. The latter goes into considerable detail on some of the issues discussed in the final section of this chapter.

CD FOSTER *Politics, finance and the role of economics: An essay in the control of public enterprise* George Allen & Unwin London 1972. A discussion, by an economist with experience of working in the field in government service, of some of the issues of accountability, control, and ministerial responsibility for the nationalized industries.

7

Cost benefit analysis

7.1 Introduction

Cost benefit analysis is a decision technique deriving from
several different strands of economic thought. As a decision rule
it derives from the decision theory, programming and game
theory complex; as an application of welfare economics it owes
much to the literature in this field, particularly the fast growing
literature on externalities; and yet again it derives from the
Marshallian concept of consumer surplus. As we shall see, these
strands are woven together into a technique now widely used
and accepted, but which is still the subject of considerable
controversy.

When is cost benefit analysis appropriate?

It is simplest to begin by looking at cost benefit analysis as an
extension to the investment rule discussed in the last chapter.
This rule states that an investment is worth undertaking if the
present value of future revenues exceeds the present value of the
costs involved. The private firm, applying this technique, will
use expected selling prices to calculate future revenues. There
are however a number of reasons why this investment criterion,
as it stands, is inapplicable to the public sector.

PUBLIC GOODS: By definition, public goods are goods and
services which, once provided, shower their benefits indiscriminately on all members of society – where one person's consump-

tion of the good in no way diminishes the amount available for consumption by others. In such cases it is not possible to exclude individuals from the benefits of the good and, therefore, it is not feasible to charge a price for it. A public good is not marketable. (See chapter 1 p 19). In such cases there is no market price which can be used in the investment appraisal exercise and the investment cannot be justified on a normal commercial basis. Yet the question for the state remains – is it worth investing public funds in this enterprise, and, if so, to what extent?

FREE GOODS AND ARBITRARILY PRICED GOODS: Similarly, some goods are provided by the state either free of charge or at a nominal price that in no way reflects the cost of provision. For example, most countries provide education without charge, paying for it from tax revenues; in the UK health services are provided free or at a small nominal charge; roads are frequently provided free by the state and financed from tax revenues. In such cases the commercial investment criterion is clearly inappropriate. Again the question arises – is investment by the state justified?

EXTERNALITIES: The straightforward commercial investment criterion is also inappropriate when important externalities are present and market prices do not therefore reflect the costs and benefits to society as a whole. For example the private cost of motoring in urban areas – the cost of fuel, vehicle and tyre wear and tear, and time – is substantially below the social cost, since it ignores the extent to which the motorist slows down other travellers and pollutes the atmosphere with noise and fumes. Clearly we need a criterion which looks to the welfare of society as a whole and not just to that of one small segment (firm, industry or individual) within it.

INDIVISIBILITIES: We saw in the previous chapter that many of the traditional public utilities are characterized by the 'lumpy' or 'indivisible' nature of their investments, and therefore operate frequently under conditions of increasing returns to scale. If these industries are required to adopt a marginal cost pricing policy deficits result. In some cases, the industry may be able to 'finance' the deficit by means of a discriminatory pricing policy, two-part tariffs, etc, but in other cases this may not be feasible and it may have to look to the state for a permanent subsidy.[1] If this is the case, investment cannot be justified on a commercial basis, and again some other criterion is needed.

In all these cases, there are either no applicable market prices or market prices which do not reflect the costs/benefits deriving to society. Yet the need for some investment criterion in the public sector is clear. In response to this need, attempts have been made to derive 'shadow' prices for use in the investment decision – prices which as far as possible reflect social costs and benefits. This process of deriving shadow prices and identifying and quantifying costs and benefits on the basis of these shadow prices has become known as cost benefit analysis. As its name implies, it is concerned to balance the costs of a project against the benefits which enter into the investment decision of the individual firm. Once these costs and benefits are known and quantified, one can derive present values for them, as in the investment appraisal procedure described in the last chapter, and balance them up against each other in terms of present values. Any project which yields a positive net present value is worth undertaking.[2] In this respect cost benefit analysis does not differ from the investment appraisal method discussed in the last chapter. Where it does differ is in *a* its coverage of costs and benefits, since it takes external effects into account and *b* its technique of measurement, since it attempts to measure costs and benefits which are not priced on the market. Let us investigate these differences in more detail.

[1] The same is in fact true also of a private sector monopolist faced by indivisibilities. He may be able to make a profit by charging a price above marginal cost, or by discriminating between his customers, but in cases where he cannot discriminate there may be no price which he could charge which would produce sufficient revenue to cover costs. In such a situation, he has either to look to the state for a permanent subsidy or go out of business – even though, if he were able to discriminate, sufficient benefit accrued to potential customers to justify production on a commercial basis.

[2] Although primarily concerned with investment decisions, cost benefit analysis can also be extended to other areas where a criterion for economic choice is required, for example it is sometimes suggested that monopolies and restrictive practices might be assessed on a cost benefit basis.

7.2 The main elements of a cost benefit exercise

Objectives

Any procedure for making a choice requires objectives. We cannot choose between alternatives without having some idea, at least implicitly, of what end we want to achieve. For the private firm the implicit objective of the investment rule is profit maximization – profits are maximized when investment is extended up to that point where the marginal return from further investment is equal to its marginal cost. While this may be a satisfactory rule for the private firm (and we saw in chapter 4 that this may be too facile an interpretation of the objectives of the firm), it cannot be a satisfactory rule for the public sector, for the reasons we discussed in the introductory paragraphs to this chapter. What then should the public sector seek to maximize?

This takes us back to the notion of social welfare which we discussed in chapter 1. The practitioners of cost benefit analysis generally adopt what amounts to a simple 'efficiency' criterion, namely to maximize the surplus of benefits over costs, where benefits are measured in terms of prices which beneficiaries would be prepared to pay for the receipt of the goods and services, and costs by the value of the goods and services foregone. The project which then yields the largest surplus of benefits over costs is taken to be the most valuable project from the point of view of society. It is accepted that any project may involve gains or benefits to some and losses or costs to others, but as long as the gains exceed the losses, a net gain overall would be registered.

This simple efficiency criterion ignores, or perhaps one should say remains agnostic to, questions of income distribution. For this reason it is sometimes called the 'Pareto' criterion. It assumes that benefits are of equal value to all, whether they accrue to rich or poor, in London or in Glasgow, on the grounds that as long as a positive net benefit is achieved the possibility exists of making transfers between gainers and losers, so that everyone affected is made at least as well off as before and some better off. The adoption of such a procedure does not however avoid facing up to the necessity of reaching an explicit ethical judgement about the desired distribution of income in society in the form of a social welfare function. (See the discussion on this in chapter 1.) Some economists have sought to introduce what amounts to a form of social welfare function by means of a weighting system whereby benefits derived by, and costs imposed upon, one income group, region, or sector, count more heavily than those derived by other groups.[1] More frequently distributional considerations are introduced by means of a constraint – that such and such a group shall not suffer a cut in their share of national income, etc. An alternative solution, which was used in the most far reaching cost benefit study which we have seen in the UK, namely the Roskill cost benefit study of the siting of the Third London Airport,[2] is to adopt the efficiency criterion and to leave it to the decision takers at a later stage to introduce considerations of income distribution if they feel it necessary to do so. There are some definite advantages in this approach since any attempt to introduce anything by way of a social welfare function is bound to be arbitrary. However, like the adoption of the straightforward efficiency criterion, it can be argued that this just avoids the issue.

Consideration of alternatives

Although, given the rate of discount, any project which yields a positive net benefit is 'worthwhile' from society's point of view, in many cases there are a number of alternative projects that might be adopted. For example a better public transport link between Central London and the Heathrow airport could be provided by railway, underground or overground, a new rapid transit system, or a new road link. All of these considered separately might yield a positive net benefit. There is no reason however to provide more than one of these facilities for they are inter-dependent and if one were provided the others would not

[1] See BA Weisbrod 'Income redistribution effects and benefit cost analysis' in SB Chase (ed) *Problems in public expenditure analysis* Brookings Institution Washington 1966.
[2] *Commission on the Third London Airport* Papers and proceedings Vol VII part I 'Proposed research methodology' chapter 1 para 6. See also Report chapter 12 paras 59–66 in which the Commission refuses to introduce any weighting into the cost/benefit analysis on the grounds that the exercise cannot be expected to include everything relevant to the decision.

be viable propositions. In such a situation, since society is anxious to maximize the net present value of benefits derived, clearly that project which yields the greatest net benefit is the appropriate choice, just as the private firm will use that investment technique which yields the highest discounted profit. It is therefore from society's point of view important not to consider just one project in isolation, but to consider *all* possible alternative strategies, one of which may be to do nothing at all. Some of these may immediately appear non-viable and it is not worth incurring the heavy cost of data collection and analysis in respect of these. For example, the Roskill Commission considered a very large number of possible sites before narrowing the range down to the four on which detailed cost benefit analyses were made. It is important that all alternative projects should be sifted if the best one is to be found.

Identifying and measuring the costs and benefits

At the centre of cost benefit analysis is the problem of measuring overall costs and benefits. There are two problems here. One arises from the need to place a value on goods and services which have no market value and hence can only be approached by roundabout methods. The other is the need to identify those indirectly affected by the project. It is of the essence of cost benefit analysis that not only should the costs and benefits accruing *directly* to the producer or consumer of the goods and services involved be measured, but also those accruing *indirectly* to other members of society. The problem is to identify the latter group, and to decide how widely to take them into account. Identification and valuation are two separate issues and we shall treat them separately here.

IDENTIFYING DIRECT COSTS AND BENEFITS: The problem of identifying where direct costs and benefits fall is fairly straightforward. The direct beneficiaries, for example, of building a new road will be those who use it. The direct beneficiaries of a water resource scheme will be those consuming the electricity generated and those benefiting from the irrigation and navigational facilities provided. Similarly, direct costs are those *directly* associated with the provision of the facility; the building and running costs of for example a new underground line.

IDENTIFYING INDIRECT COSTS AND BENEFITS: Indirect costs and benefits are more difficult to identify. Ideally, we should identify anyone who is in any way affected by the project, so that for example account is taken of the employment of the steel worker who would be unemployed if a new underground line had not boosted the demand for steel sections, of anyone affected by aircraft noise when a new airport is built, of the regional development stimulated by the building of a new motorway or the siting of a new airport, and so on. These indirect effects may spill over very widely into society and it would be an impossible exercise to identify all those affected, let alone to quantify the costs and benefits. A line has to be drawn limiting consideration of spillover effects to those thought to be most important. Where to draw the line is a matter of judgement. In the case of a study of the effects of building a new motorway account is taken of the effects of building a motorway on other road users, those who will find their roads less crowded (because of the diverted traffic) or more crowded (because the road is an approach route to the motorway), but not the effect of a motorway upon the development of urban communities along its route. Water resource schemes will take into account savings from flood control, but not the aesthetic loss in the reduced flow of a river, and so forth. The Roskill Commission research team study went as far as attempting to calculate the amenity loss suffered by fishermen and other sportsmen from the siting of the airport in the four different locations. But even this study found it necessary to limit its consideration of external effects and draw a line somewhere. For example, they took account of the noise nuisance to the residential areas most immediately affected, but not of any nuisance to areas only peripherally affected.[1]

Having identified costs and benefits we have to tackle the problem of measurement. Let us group them into the categories which we identified above.

---

[1] They used a composite index, the Noise and Number Index (NNI) based on both the level and the frequency of the noise as a measure of the noise nuisance. This enabled them to draw contour maps of the noise areas. The area in the airport itself and most immediately surrounding the airport was within the 55 NNI contour. The Commission did not consider those living outside the 35 NNI, a level which social surveys indicated caused 'little' annoyance. See Commission on Third London Airport – Report *op cit* chapter 7.

THE MEASUREMENT OF DIRECT COSTS: Direct costs are those directly associated with any project, construction costs, capital equipment costs and running costs. Usually these are valued at market prices, which, it is usually argued, represent opportunity costs reasonably closely. Adjustment to these prices may be made where *a* monopoly elements push prices above opportunity costs, *b* unemployed resources exist and therefore opportunity cost is lower than market price, or *c* the good is sold subject to tax or its price is set artificially by government control. It is no easy matter to decide just what adjustment to make in these cases. For example, under *b*, if we can be sure that workers on a project would otherwise be unemployed, the opportunity cost involved would be zero, for they would otherwise be producing nothing. But how far can we be sure that this would be so for a period stretching perhaps three or more years ahead? A reasonable guess at the appropriate adjustment has to be made.

THE MEASUREMENT OF DIRECT BENEFITS – CONSUMERS' SURPLUS: Since the project, with which we are concerned by definition produces an output which is either not sold on the market or is sold at an arbitrary price, we cannot value benefits at market prices. Instead, having identified the beneficiaries, we have to value the output *not* by a price that they are paying, but by trying to identify the items of benefit and attempting to value these. In other words for each beneficiary we are trying to identify the price that they would have been prepared to pay for the good or service had they been asked to pay a price which reflects the benefits they feel they have received. Thus the benefit to those travelling on the Victoria underground line was not the advantage of travelling into and around London, for most would have been travelling thus anyway on other underground routes or by other forms of transport, but that of a faster and more comfortable journey. By placing a value on time spent travelling and on greater comfort and convenience we can convert these benefits into monetary values. If we could do this calculation for all travellers then we would find that some, those with the most inconvenient journeys, gained more than others, and we could rank travellers on this basis, as in figure 12.

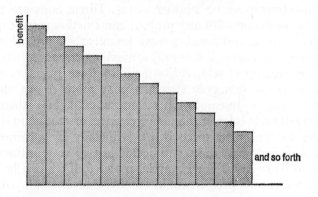

Figure 12. Passengers ranked according to benefit.

To arrive at a calculation of total benefit we would then aggregate the benefits accruing to all passengers. Cost benefit analysis does exactly this. It seeks to identify, quantify and aggregate the benefits stemming from the project. Of course calculations cannot really be made for each individual, and a fair amount of averaging has to be undertaken. For example, in the Victoria Line cost benefit study, users were grouped according to whether they transferred from other underground routes, from the railways, from buses, from private motor travel, or were pedestrians. For each of these categories a calculation was made of the average journey time that would be saved by using the Victoria Line. This was converted into money terms by valuing time spent during working hours at average hourly wage rates, and leisure time saved (which included the majority of journeys since time spent travelling to and from work was counted as leisure time) at a lower rate. (See discussion below on the valuation of leisure time.)[1]

Now this is a very different calculation from that of the firm selling a product on the market. Unless it is able to discriminate between customers (and most firms are not in a position to do this) the firm sells its product at the same price to all customers. At that price the firm's main concern is that the project should

[1] See CD Foster and ME Beesley, 'Estimating the social benefit of constructing an underground line in London' *Journal of the Royal Statistical Society* Vol 126 1963. Series A reprinted in D Munby *Transport-selected readings* Penguin Modern Economics Texts Penguin Harmondsworth 1968.

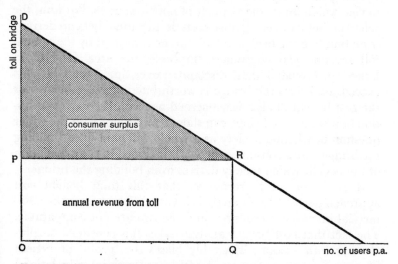

Figure 13. Comparison between consumer surplus and commercial investment criterion. For explanation see text below.

yield a profit, that total revenue yielded at that selling price $(P \times Q)$ should be greater than total cost. The fact that at that price there are some customers who would have been prepared to pay more for the good – who are enjoying consumer surplus – is irrelevant to the firm. It is not however irrelevant to the cost benefit analyst, and this is one important respect in which cost benefit analysis differs from the normal commercial investment appraisal. Take the example of a bridge. Let us suppose that for reasons best known to them the government decides that, if built, the toll to be charged should be fixed at a certain level, OP in figure 13 above. Let us also assume for the moment that it is only users of the bridge who benefit from it being built, that is that there are no external effects.

If a private company were to build and operate the bridge, its concern would be that the toll charged should yield a total revenue (OPRQ × the number of years that the bridge is in operation) which discounted over time is greater than total costs (maintenance, administration and capital costs). If it can make a profit, it is worth its while to build and operate the bridge. In contrast, for the cost benefit analyst assessing whether it is worth building the bridge, the toll is irrelevant except as a rationing device which limits the number of potential users. For him, the relevant item to set against costs is the total benefit derived from building the bridge, which can be measured by the annual toll revenue *plus* consumers surplus – the area ODRQ in figure 13. Provided that, discounted over time,[1] total benefits exceed total costs the bridge is worth building. In other words the cost benefit analyst is concerned not with the narrow question of whether the bridge can show a profit, but with the wider question of whether society as a whole will gain from building the bridge – and consumer surplus is included in the calculation of the benefit which society derives from building the bridge.

It is important to recognize that this total benefit cost approach of cost benefit analysis is very different from the commercial investment criterion, and the two are not comparable. The fact that cost benefit analysis takes this consumer surplus element into account inevitably biases the 'profit' or benefit figures upwards as compared with a commercial calculation.[2]

[1] Another respect in which the public cost benefit calculation may vary from the private profitability calculation is in the discount rate used. The public sector may use a rate which represents the social rate of time preference whereas the private sector will use a rate which reflects the opportunity cost of capital to the firm i.e. the profitability of alternative investment projects. It is likely that these two will differ. See below discussion on the rate of discount (p. 222).

[2] Some economists have been very worried by the 'exaggeration' of benefits inherent in this method of appraisal. See DW Glassborow 'The Road Research Laboratory's investment criterion examined' *Bulletin of Oxford Institute of Statistics* Vol 22 No 4 Nov 1960. There is a further facet to this problem which is discussed by Mishan (EJ Mishan *The costs of economic growth* Staples Press London 1967 appendix C). This is that where cost benefit analysis is considering a facility for which a zero or nominal price is charged, included amongst the beneficiaries are those who, if they had to pay a price which reflected opportunity costs, would not be amongst the users. Take the example of a comparison between a road and rail improvement scheme. The present method of vehicle taxation means that vehicles on the whole do not meet the marginal social costs of road usage. Nevertheless, the appraisal of a road improvement scheme will value the time and cost savings of all users of the road, including those who would switch to other forms of transport if road pricing were introduced. In contrast, the appraisal of a rail improvement scheme with, let us suppose, rail users being charged a price which is rather higher than marginal social costs, would only include amongst its beneficiaries those who were prepared to pay such a price. Even if a consumer surplus criterion were used to assess the viability of both schemes, the benefits derived from the road scheme would be relatively higher because of the differing pricing policies pursued by the two sectors. Thus where two alternatives are being considered, not only is it necessary that the criterion of viability be the same, but, for strict comparability, pricing policies should be based upon the same principle.

There is nothing wrong with this; the aim of cost benefit analysis is to look at a project not from a narrow commercial 'pay your way' point of view, but from the point of view of society as a whole. But it is extremely important that the two exercises are not confused and that the cost benefit rate of return is not regarded as comparable with the commercial rate of return. This is of special importance where the two different methods of valuation are used within one sector. Thus if road projects are assessed by cost benefit methods while rail projects are subject to 'commercial' investment appraisal methods, and funds are rationed and channelled to those projects showing the highest rate of return, there would be a danger that too much investment would go into roads and too little into rail. However, from the point of view of investment appraisal as such (ie assessing whether it is worth undertaking a particular project) this is a non-problem provided that prices in the different sectors are optimally adjusted; the rule that *any* project, whether analysed by cost benefit methods or the normal investment rules, which yields a *positive* net present value is worth undertaking, remains valid. The problem of misallocation through non-comparability of criteria only arises where there is capital rationing or where the prices of one or more of the sectors under consideration are not optimally adjusted.[1]

THE QUANTIFICATION OF BENEFITS: It is the attempt to quantify benefits that raises the greatest controversy. By their very nature these benefits cannot be measured by market prices, and therefore it is necessary to find some means of finding out how much consumers would be prepared to pay for them if they had to – what their personal valuation of the benefit is. It is of little use asking them this question, for if they thought they might have to pay the price they had suggested, they might suggest a low price, and equally, if they thought they might be compensated for the 'cost' (or disbenefit) which they met, they would be tempted to exaggerate.

Where the benefits fall into an *intermediate good* category for which there is a derived demand and a market price, these market prices can be used to convert the benefit into money terms. Thus the benefits from transport projects which result in

[1] For a discussion of this problem see above footnote 2 p 216.

time savings can be measured by using the 'market' value of working time, hourly wage rates; the benefits from irrigation schemes, by the market value of the additional agricultural output; flood control benefits by lowered insurance premiums, etc. On the same basis the value of education can be measured by the extra earnings accruing from extra years of education and the value of health benefits, in the avoidance of loss of earnings through ill health. Neither of these latter examples provide a totally satisfactory method of estimating benefits. Take education; such a procedure may be applied to higher or further education, but could not be applied in relation to investment in new primary or secondary schools, for so many different factors affect the spread of earnings of ex-pupils that it would present an impossible statistical exercise to separate explicitly the influence of, say, new school buildings over old school buildings. Even for higher or further education such calculations fail to value any improvements in the quality of life of the people involved. As far as health is concerned, this type of calculation ignores the cost to the individual from discomfort associated with ill health, health being desired not only because it means a man can work, but in its own right as, so to speak, a consumption good. We shall be discussing the valuation of these 'consumption good' type benefits in the next paragraph. The differential income approach also ignores the external benefits which accrue to society from education and health expenditures.

However, a great many benefits are not in this intermediate good category for which there is a derived demand but may be considered as final *consumption goods*. It is here that the major difficulties in valuation arise. Examples of this 'final consumption good' type of benefit are recreational facilities, beautiful landscapes, leisure time, and the 'disbenefit' of aircraft noise or the pollution caused by the fumes and noise of traffic.

Sometimes an attempt is made to measure such benefits (or disbenefits) by valuing the cost of complementary private goods. Thus the value of recreational facilities can be measured in terms of the 'price' people are prepared to pay in order to make use of the facilities – the cost (including the time cost) of travelling to and from the facilities in question and any entrance fees etc payable. It can be argued that such an approach can at best only provide a lower limit to the benefit because it measures only the cost the consumer actually pays in order to enjoy the facility – and it does not allow for consumer surplus, the fact that the consumer gains a benefit over and above the price he pays for the good. In order to overcome this objection, the Roskill Commission cost benefit study attempted to allow for consumer surplus in their calculations. For example, in the case of the loss of amenity caused by aircraft noise to visitors to Woburn Abbey, they calculated the numbers likely to be dissuaded from visiting the house on account of noise, and the loss in benefit as the amount they would have paid in entrance fees, travel costs, etc. In addition a consumer surplus element was calculated from the differential costs that people were prepared to meet in order to visit the house.[1] Again, in attempting to quantify the costs of aircraft noise to residents, they took differential house prices in areas affected and not affected by aircraft noise as providing a 'minimum' valuation of the noise nuisance, and in addition made allowance for the fact that people obtain benefits from their homes over and above the market valuation, the consumer surplus element. This element was calculated from questionnaire survey which asked people at what price they would be prepared to sell their homes, and the average excess over market price was taken as the measure of consumer surplus.[2]

There are some benefits which elude even those ingenious attempts at measurement. At what price an unspoiled hillscape? A Norman church? Initially, the Roskill cost benefit study valued churches at their fire insurance valuation, which may reflect the value of their physical fabric, but not their aesthetic value. In the final analysis the Commission rejected this approach and preferred not to attempt to place a value on the loss of churches, or, for that matter on another intangible, the loss of wildlife.[3]

One further difficulty which arises in relation to these 'leisure' facilities is that as leisure time increases society's relative valuation of these facilities increases. In such cases, this

[1] *Commission on Third London Airport: papers and proceedings* vol VII part 2 chapters 1, 15 and 16, and chapter 24.
[2] *Commission on Third London Airport: papers and proceedings* vol VII part 2 chapters 1, 13 and 14.
[3] *Commission on Third London Airport: Report* chapter 12 para 7 and chapter 20.

increasing valuation should be written into the calculations, but it is impossible to gauge with any certainty the rate at which the subjective valuation is increasing.

Such attempts at quantification, however ingenious, can become extremely arbitrary, and the question arises as to whether some attempt at quantification is better than nothing. An alternative that has been suggested is that cost benefit analysis should treat these 'consumption' benefits as an unknown dependent value, posing the question the other way round, 'We know the costs. Do we ourselves value the benefits sufficiently highly to justify the outlay?' It would then be left to the decision takers to decide whether they rank the benefits of the project sufficiently highly to justify the cost. Such an approach was explicitly rejected by the Roskill cost benefit study[1] as merely substituting implicit for explicit valuation. However, in opting for the total quantification approach, they inevitably accepted some of the arbitrariness which explicit valuation involves.

THE VALUATION OF LEISURE TIME: An item which enters frequently into the calculation of costs and benefits but which falls between the intermediate and consumption good category is leisure time. It is perhaps because it falls between these two categories that economists have been unable to arrive at any agreed method of quantifying it. On the one hand it is argued that leisure time should be regarded as work time foregone; those for whom overtime is available should value it at the pay they would have received if they had worked (that is, overtime pay less tax). Most studies have however chosen to value leisure time at a rate substantially below that for working time. For example the Roskill cost benefit study valued working time in 1968 at £2·31 per hour, and non-working time at £0·23 per hour.[2] The reason for doing this is that people regard leisure time not as work foregone (ie as a possible intermediate good)

---

[1] *Commission on Third London Airport: papers and proceedings* vol VII part 2 chapter 1.4.

[2] *Commission on Third London Airport: papers and proceedings* vol VII chapter 11 para 8. In view of the uncertainty attaching to the valuation of passenger time, in the final analysis two valuations, high and low, were placed on both business time and leisure time giving an upper and lower estimate of passenger user costs etc. The differential between business and leisure time was however retained. See Report appendix 20 para 4.

but as a final consumption good which they enjoy in its own right, and that they value this (perhaps irrationally) at a relatively low rate in relation to possible earnings. This relatively low valuation of leisure time is supported by work done by Beesley[1] which indicates that the subjective valuation placed on non-working time is as low as one third of earnings during working time.

The valuation of indirect costs and benefits

The sort of problems that arise in trying to measure indirect costs and benefits are very similar to those discussed above under the measurement of direct benefits. Costs falling into this category are often called negative benefits.

The Roskill Third London Airport cost benefit study is a special case here. It is not a cost benefit study proper, for its terms of reference prevented it from inquiring into whether London needed a third airport or whether it would have been better to site such an airport in some other part of the country.[2] The study therefore is not concerned with whether the benefits from an airport outweigh the costs but with finding the least cost site, costs being construction costs and social costs. The main category of indirect cost with which it was concerned was that of the travelling time of potential users. Since Foulness, the coastal site, was the site farthest from the main centres of population, it is on this score that it clocked up its disadvantage. Another important category of indirect cost was that of noise. It was the vociferous objections to the aircraft noise nuisance of the inland site of Stansted that had originally stimulated the setting up of this wide reaching enquiry. In the final calculations, however noise became a relatively minor item, being overshadowed by the very heavy costs involved in differential travelling times.

---

[1] ME Beesley 'The value of time spent travelling' *Economica* May 1965.
[2] The cost benefit study did consider briefly the need for a third London Airport in relation to the question of timing. Rather uncharacteristically, given its commitment to total quantification which we mentioned above, it came to the conclusion that, 'The indirect benefits of an international airport are difficult to quantify, but it seems likely that they would more than offset any costs not covered by air travellers themselves.' *Commission on Third London Airport papers and proceedings* vol VII part II chapter 5 para 60. See also *Report* chapter 5 and chapter 12 para 2.

The choice of the rate of discount

Since the costs and benefits of the projects under consideration
accrue over time, it is necessary to discount them back to their
present value. We discussed the process of discounting in the
previous chapter (see p 188) and indicated that there is no
unanimity on the part of economists over the choice of the
appropriate rate of discount. Economists divide themselves into
two camps on this issue; some favouring the use of a rate of
discount which reflects the social rate of time preference and
others the use of a rate which reflects social opportunity cost.
We must now go into this further.

THE SOCIAL RATE OF TIME PREFERENCE: Those whose main
concern is that the total amount of investment undertaken by
society should be optimal favour the use of a rate of interest that
represents the social rate of time preference. As private individuals we are likely to have a preference for present consumption
over future consumption. This preference will be based partly
upon a feeling that the future is shrouded in uncertainty – we
may be dead and therefore unable to enjoy future consumption
– and partly on the possibility that our incomes will rise, in
which case we shall be better off in the future, and will place a
relatively lower valuation on what we could buy with our
savings than we would place on the equivalent consumption
now.[1] This explains why, as private individuals, we are likely to
have a positive rate of time preference. Such a philosophy on
the part of the individual cannot be applied directly to society
as a whole, for what I am prepared to save 'for future genera-
tions' may be affected by what others do; I may be prepared to
make a bigger sacrifice if I know everyone else is making an
equivalent sacrifice. Thus the savings-consumption decision on
the part of society has certain 'public good' characteristics. For
this reason the social rate of time preference may be quite
different from, and lower than, the private rates of time preference and we cannot calculate it from any set of market rates
(even duly adjusted for inflation and uncertainty). As we saw in

[1] This assumes that we have diminished marginal utility for income – as income
rises we gain less utility (benefit) from equivalent expenditures.

chapter 1, the savings-consumption decision is a collective one which has to take its place amongst the other objectives of economic strategy and one possible way to calculate the social rate of time preference is from the decisions made on these issues by the politicians and administrators. But it would seem wholly tautological to use this implicit social rate of time preference to help make investment decisions which themselves affect the total of investment undertaken by society.

Emphasis on the use of the social rate of time preference in cost benefit analysis comes from economists who feel that it is important that the *total* amount of investment undertaken as a whole by society should reflect an explicit choice between present and future consumption. If a higher rate of discount is applied, the amount invested will be less than is optimal from society's points of view, and similarly, if the rate of discount used is too low, investment will be above optimal levels.

THE SOCIAL OPPORTUNITY COST OF CAPITAL: The other group of economists is concerned not with the optimal distribution of resources between investment and consumption, but with the optimal distribution of investment resources between the public and private sectors. Taking the stance that it is undesirable from society's point of view that projects in the public sector should yield a social return lower than the equivalent social return available from private sector projects, this group favours the use of the social opportunity cost of capital, which is the rate of return yielded by the stream of social costs and benefits from the best alternative private project. This is the opportunity cost to the community of output foregone if it pre-empts resources for the public sector. It is not the same thing as the financial return yielded by such a private investment for it is concerned with *social* costs and benefits and these may differ from the private financial return both in taking account of the presence of externalities and in being calculated pre-tax, whereas the financial rate of return is a post-tax rate of return.

There is no agreement among economists as to which of these two rates is the appropriate one to use as the discount rate in public sector projects. This difference of opinion would not matter were it not that where more than one alternative is being considered the ranking of projects may vary with different discount rates. Thus for example thermal power stations are superior when a high discount rate is used, and nuclear power stations, which are capital intensive but low cost and long lived, are superior when a low rate of discount is used. The whole debate however is somewhat academic, since there is also no agreement as to what rates of discount might represent the two concepts. It is generally agreed that the social rate of time preference is the lower of the two and for the reasons discussed above is likely to be somewhat below current rates of interest.

For what it is worth, the discount rate used by the UK government in cost benefit analysis is the same as that laid down for use by the nationalized industries in their investment appraisal exercises, at present 10 per cent. This it is claimed, is a figure 'broadly consistent, having regard to differing circumstances in relation to tax, investment grants, etc, with the average rate of return in real terms looked for on low risk projects in the private sector'.[1] This would appear to embody the 'social opportunity cost of capital' approach.

The relevant constraints

An investment decision is an optimization procedure. As we saw in chapter 2 (p 56) linear programming is a method of optimizing. The linear programming framework of objectives and constraints is a relevant framework for the investment decision. Indeed many firms use programming methods to help investment decisions and in allocating resources within the firm. Cost benefit analysis borrows much from this framework. For example, the concept of an objective function is a programming concept. It would be nice to think that if we could feed into a computer the relevant constraints combined with the objective function not only could the computer tell us which projects were worth undertaking but it could also provide a set of shadow prices for scarce resources, so solving the valuation problem as well. Unfortunately the programming approach

[1] Command No. 3257 *Nationalized industries: a review of economic and financial objectives* para 10 HMSO London 1967. The rate then 8 per cent was raised to 10 per cent in 1969.

cannot be applied directly to cost benefit exercises. As McKean says, 'Such calculations have turned out to be relatively success-ful in connection with blending problems for which the objective function and inter-relationships can be specified with con-fidence and completeness. For entire economies or sectors of economies, however, it is almost impossible to conceive of com-plete and appropriate preference and production functions. Shadow prices from a pretend economy have a good chance of being no more relevant than shadow prices from the economy on Mars.'[1] Nevertheless the approach has its value for cost benefit analysis in emphasizing the constraints which need to be taken into account. These are of various types.

PRODUCTION CONSTRAINTS: These are constraints on physical inputs to and outputs from a project. In most cases these con-straints will have entered directly into the calculation of costs and benefits, but there may be so called 'external' production constraints, such as limitations on physical size, which have to be taken into account at a later stage.

LEGAL AND ADMINISTRATIVE CONSTRAINTS: Projects have to fit into the legal framework. For example, road projects require lengthy preliminary public hearings where all affected may voice their objections and which may affect the siting of the project. Administrative constraints impose limits on the speed with which work can be handled and on the type of project itself; eg, air traffic control problems limited the number of possible sites for the third London airport.

BUDGETARY CONSTRAINTS: Ideally the public sector ought to undertake any project which yields a positive net benefit (with the exception of mutually exclusive projects) on the grounds that this adds to social welfare. Within the second best world however this is not so, and many projects either have a sum of money specifically allocated for them or, perhaps more generally, form a part of the sub-budget of a department of state. Where a number of projects compete for limited funds, one method of rationing is to rank projects in order of net benefit/capital ratio, those yielding the highest ratio within the budget total being

[1] RW McKean, 'The use of shadow prices' in SB Chase (ed) *Problems in public expenditure analysis* The Brookings Institution Washington 1968 p 49.

chosen in preference to others.[1] Budget constraints often also impinge in terms of strict costs limits, so called 'standard costings'. For example, in the UK the Department of Education and Science lay down strict cost criteria for school and university buildings; the Department of Health and Social Security lay down cost limits for hospital construction.

DISTRIBUTIONAL CONSTRAINTS: As mentioned at the beginning of this chapter most cost benefit studies adopt an 'efficiency' objective; namely that as long as the gains exceed the losses, whosoever it is who gains or loses, the project is worthwhile. Distributional objectives are sometimes introduced not into the objective function but instead by introducing a distributional constraint into the exercise – limiting the detriment which may be imposed on any particular income group or geographical region etc.

RISK AND UNCERTAINTY:[2] We do not live in a world where we can predict with certainty the outcome of events. Many factors over which we have no control – the weather, political events, changes in tastes and preferences, future developments in technology – will affect the relative success or failure of a project, and this applies just as much to public sector projects subjected to cost benefit analysis as to private sector projects. Take the example of the siting of a new airport. One of the fundamental elements in the calculation of both costs and benefits is the projected rate of growth in the demand for air transport. The noise nuisance is going to be affected by the number of aircraft movements, and this in turn depends upon the developments in aircraft size. Another factor affecting noise will be developments in aircraft technology, and this will be responsive to government pressure itself reflecting the success or otherwise of the environment lobby; and so on. All these are uncertain. We can make projections based upon past experience and the best available information on future trends. But we can

[1] This ratio ranking method only works in fact under rather restrictive assumptions, and cannot be used when capital expenditure is spread over two years or more. For a fuller treatment of this issue see J Hirschliefer 'Theory of optimal investment decision' *Journal of Political Economy* 1958.

[2] This section does not purport to be more than a brief resumé of some of the problems presented by risk and uncertainty. For a fuller treatment see EJ Mishan *op cit* 1971 chapter 38–44.

never be certain and our estimates of costs and benefits are, for this reason if no other, bound to be subject to some degree of error.

We can however take certain measures which will limit the effects of uncertainty. These fall into two distinct categories. On the one hand are techniques aimed at elaborating and clarifying the implications of uncertainty; on the other hand are techniques which affect the methods of appraisal. In the former category comes much of the information research which might loosely be described as 'narrowing down the area of uncertainty'. For example, it may be possible to present the data as a range of possible outcomes according to the relative pessimism or optimism of the assumptions adopted, which would involve work in clarifying the precise implications of adopting this or that particular assumption. A variant of this is what is known as 'sensitivity analysis' where the basic model is tested to see what difference changing the values of some of the most important elements or parameters in the model makes. This helps the analyst to identify how much uncertainty is involved, how sensitive are the results he has obtained to changes in some of the most important parameters of the model. The Roskill cost benefit study, for example, tested the sensitivity of its findings to changes in a number of important variables, including the valuation of business and leisure time, and in the noise parameters it employed (which in effect meant assuming that more or less people were affected by noise).[1] It may be possible to go one step further and not only to identify different possible outcomes according to different assumptions, but actually to assign probabilities to these different outcomes. In a few cases past experience may give a fairly good 'objective' assessment of risk. For example mortality records can give us the actuarial probabilities of death at different ages. But in most cases past experience and other information available (eg experience from overseas) can only give a fairly rough idea of the probability that might be attached to different outcomes.

Uncertainty will affect appraisal techniques in different ways. Where it has been possible to assign probabilities, the various outcomes may be weighted according to their probabilities. For

---

[1] *Commission of Third London Airport: papers and proceedings* vol VII part 2 tables 29.10 to 29.28.

each alternative project considered the costs and benefits entering into the appraisal calculation will then be the weighted average of possible outcomes, and that project yielding the highest net benefit after discounting will be the preferred one. In this case the appraisal technique as such is not affected, merely the method by which costs and benefits are calculated. Where it is not possible to assign probabilities to different outcomes, then different choice techniques may be used.[1] The results may be presented as a range of possible outcomes, and it may be left to the politicians to decide whether they are prepared to accept the risk of the most pessimistic assumptions. Another method frequently employed is that of adding a risk premium to the discount rate. This technique can be justified when uncertainty is primarily a function of time, but may discriminate against long-lived investments where uncertainty arises from other sources. Another method employed is arbitrarily to limit the life of a project below its probable technical life, a somewhat crude method of adjustment but which may be justified where sudden and total obsolescence is feared.

The probability approach, though acknowledged logically to be the most satisfactory method of allowing for risk and uncertainty, presents considerable problems in its practical application. For this reason it is not a method that has been used much in cost benefit studies, where the most frequent method of allowing for risk and uncertainty has been either to add a risk premium to the discount rate or arbitrarily to limit the life of the project.

The arbitrary element in cost benefit studies

It should be evident from the above discussion that cost benefit analysis is no 'wonder technique', no answer to all the imponderable decision problems in the public sector. Its great virtue is that it does require ministers, administrators and planners to adopt a rigorous decision-making framework, but there is no escaping the fact that to be operational it requires a

[1] Strictly speaking, situations of risk are defined as those where objective probabilities can be assigned, and situations of uncertainty as those where no such probabilities can be assigned. In most states of knowledge, however, the two merge: we have some information from past experience which gives us some idea of probabilities, but not sufficient to assign objective probabilities.

series of assumptions to be made all the way along the line, assumptions which, though plausible, are nevertheless arbitrary. The most important of these are the assumptions about social objectives, the necessary limitation of spillover effects (externalities), the proxy methods of valuing benefits, and the choice of a discount rate. For the technique to be workable, assumptions have to be made, and the cost benefit analyst will adopt what seem to be the most plausible assumptions. But they are nevertheless assumptions, and like any edifice built on such a foundation, if you undermine the assumptions, it can fall to the ground. For example the UK government chose the coastal site at Foulness, the least favourable of the four sites investigated by the Roskill Commission, in preference to an inland site. In so doing it apparently judged that it was politically not feasible to choose an inland site; implicitly it was putting very much higher value on noise nuisance and very much lower value on travel time than the Roskill Commission. In addition it disputed the Roskill assumption that airport policy would remain neutral in relation to the use by airlines of different airports. Airlines would be positively encouraged to use Foulness by both a pricing policy which made the use of this airport relatively cheaper than others and by strict physical controls over the use of the other airports in the area.[1] This 'bouleversement' of the findings of the Commission is a splendid illustration of how the acceptance of the findings of a cost benefit analysis requires the acceptance and understanding of the assumptions incorporated within it.

7.3 The use of the price system – charging for road space

Properly undertaken, a cost benefit exercise is costly, requiring the gathering and processing of huge amounts of information. The Roskill Commission investigation, at the centre of which was the cost benefit exercise, cost over £1m and took more than two years to complete. It is not possible or feasible for every project in the public sector to be subjected to this sort of

[1] Roskill had argued that the total noise nuisance created by Foulness would in fact be greater because airlines would continue to use heavily existing airports in the region, which were badly situated from a noise point of view, whereas an inland site would be able to channel off a good deal of this usage and thus relieve the noise nuisance at existing airports.

examination. It is sometimes suggested, as a means both of avoiding some of the arbitrariness of cost benefit analysis and of achieving greater simplicity, that prices should be adjusted by a system of taxes and subsidies to reflect marginal social costs, and investment decisions then made on a 'normal commercial' basis. If the facility yields a surplus or 'profit' at this price, it should be expanded, and, conversely, contracted if it yields a loss.

One example which is frequently cited as an application of this principle is that of road pricing. At present in the UK roads are financed from general taxation. The use of road space is subject to two types of tax; the vehicle licence fee, which is a lump sum tax imposed upon all vehicles using public roads, and petrol tax payable at a flat rate per gallon. The latter can be regarded as a marginal tax on road use. On average, it is higher than the wear and tear, maintenance, policing, etc, costs imposed by an extra vehicle on uncongested roads, but fails to reflect the high social costs imposed by an extra vehicle on congested roads; the costs imposed, in terms of time and vehicle running costs, by slowing down the whole traffic stream, and the costs of pollution from the noise and fumes emitted by a slow moving traffic stream. It has been suggested that the present tax system be replaced by one which incorporates a tax on road use in congested areas.[1] This tax would in fact only reflect congestion costs; pollution costs would not be taken into account. It is possible to calculate the costs of congestion from knowledge of the relationship between traffic flow and speed. The more vehicles there are, the slower the pace of the whole traffic stream. Each additional vehicle slows all the other vehicles marginally. Suppose, for example, that a car joins a traffic flow of 2000 vehicles per hour, moving at 10 mph. The extra car will slow down the whole stream marginally; say by the order of 5/1000th minute for each mile travelled. For each person concerned this is minimal, but for the whole stream (assuming for the present that each car unit contains 1 person and therefore that a vehicle flow of 2000 passenger car units (pcu's), represents 2000 people) it amounts to 2000 × ·005, that is 10 minutes. If time is valued at say £1·00 per hour, then

[1] GJ Roth *A self-financing road system* Institute of Economic Affairs Research Monograph 9 1966.

10 minutes is worth £0·17. On top of time costs are the extra vehicle costs – petrol and wear and tear costs – arising from the slower traffic speed. On this sort of basis it is possible to calculate the congestion costs per vehicle mile. A study in the early 1960s for London calculated these costs as follows

Table 6
congestion costs caused by an extra car in Central London

traffic speed mph	costs per extra vehicle mile £
20	0·02 (5d)
18	0·03 (7d)
16	0·045 (11d)
14	0·065 (1/4)
12	0·11 (2/2)
10	0·17 (3/5)
8	0·30 (6/0)

Source: *Road pricing: the economic and technical possibilities* HMSO 1964.

A tax imposed on vehicles which approximated to these costs would go a considerable way towards ensuring that the charges reflected the marginal social costs they imposed. The charges would be higher still if account were taken of the pollution costs caused by traffic congestion.

The advocates of road pricing schemes argue that such a form of taxation could be used to solve not only the environmental problem of traffic congestion but also the 'investment problem' in roads.[1] The price charged would reflect short run marginal social cost. A congested road would make a surplus over its cost of construction etc and it would be worth improving the road, and the road system, until this surplus disappeared. Improvement would reduce congestion and lower tax receipts; thus as the road was improved the surplus would automatically disappear. Such a procedure is akin to the normal investment process in private industry; investments which would yield a profit are undertaken.

It is worth pausing at this point to consider whether the procedure suggested for road pricing provides a way of avoiding problems involved in cost benefit analysis. Have we been

[1] See GJ Roth *op cit* p 73.

barking up the wrong tree? Rather than these elaborate, and necessarily arbitrary, exercises in shadow pricing which cost benefit analysis involves, would it not be simpler to return to the pricing mechanism?

Let us consider how far the road pricing approach is applicable to the other areas which we identified at the beginning of this chapter as offering candidates for cost benefit analysis. One category was that of *indivisibilities*, where our reason for looking to cost benefit analysis was that the pricing mechanism broke down. We would therefore not expect to be able to substitute the road pricing approach for cost benefit analysis, and this is indeed so. Take the example of building a motorway. The existing trunk road system serving an area may be grossly overloaded and a congestion tax, the road pricing solution, would yield a handsome profit; this argues for building some relief road. Improving the trunk road system bit by bit – a section of dual carriageway here, straightening there – which gradually relieves the congestion, can be accommodated within the road pricing framework. Each improvement scheme is justified up to the point where no 'surplus' was yielded by the congestion tax. However, if the congestion were relieved at one blow by the building of the motorway, the motorway itself would yield no revenue in congestion tax and could not be justified *per se* on a profitability basis within a road pricing framework. This is not to say that a road pricing system is not applicable to motorways as a means of rationing scarce road space. Once a motorway becomes congested, tax revenue begins to rise but, if the motorway achieves its objective and relieves congestion for some substantial period, then it will not be able in that period to justify itself in terms of the surplus it yields. Thus a pricing system cannot replace cost benefit analysis where a major indivisible item of investment is being considered. It is only applicable to marginal improvements to the system.

Another category where cost benefit was appropriate was that of *public goods*. Here again the market mechanism breaks down. It is impossible to charge a price equal to marginal social cost and see whether a sufficient number of people are prepared to pay the price to justify the investment, for once provided we cannot exclude people from benefiting from the provision of public goods; for example from the provision of a defence force, or a police force, street lighting and so on. (See chapter 1 p 19.) We have therefore no alternative but to look to the total benefit/cost approach of cost benefit analysis to justify investments in this category of good.

A third category, goods at present provided *free of charge* or at *arbitrary charge* which does not reflect the costs of provision, are clearly candidates for turning over to the market mechanism provided that the externality elements are not too diverse. However, where the government has deliberately chosen to eschew the price mechanism in the allocation of resources, such as in the health and education fields, although it might be perfectly feasible to substitute the price mechanism for a cost benefit approach, it will not always be judged to be in the social interest to do so. This is a problem which we shall be discussing further in chapter 8.

The case of *externalities* is a little more complicated. The adjustment of prices by means of a system of taxes and subsidies to reflect marginal social costs is the classic solution put forward by Pigou to the externality problem, indeed the road pricing example we discussed above is essentially an externality problem. In order to be able to adjust prices correctly, to take account of externalities we need to be able:

a   to identify those on whom the costs (or benefits) fall,
b   to quantify these costs (or benefits), and
c   to attribute these costs (or benefits) to their sources and to tax (or subsidize) accordingly.

In the road pricing problem we had a clearly identifiable group who were affected, the road users themselves. We also had data which enabled us to calculate with some accuracy the marginal social costs imposed by an extra vehicle joining the traffic stream (although these calculations were based upon the same methods of time valuation as used in cost benefit analysis). It is significant however that no attempt was made to measure pollution costs, for those affected by pollution from congested roads are a wide and diverse group within the community, and the same problem of identification and measurement of spill-overs (external effects) arises as in cost benefit analysis.

The Pigovian tax/subsidy solution is only feasible where the externality elements are readily identified and quantified.

233

Where the spillover effects are widely diffused among the population, and not easily valued, then such a solution, requiring as it would a complex system of taxes and subsidies which would have to be collected and redistributed, is likely to be both arbitrary and administratively complex. There are, in fact, relatively few cases where the external effects are sufficiently limited in their coverage for such a solution. The majority of the environmental spillover effects associated with industrialization – noise, air and water pollution, nervous diseases and so forth – cannot be dealt with by a tax/subsidy solution within a market framework. In those cases too we have to look to other solutions, including cost benefit analysis.[1]

It is worth noting that in cases where the external effects are widely diffused among the population and generally acknowledged to be detrimental, the simplest solution may be to pass a law which prohibits the nuisance. We have, for example, laws establishing smokeless zones, which in the last 15 years in the UK have done a great deal to improve the cleanliness of the atmosphere in urban communities; we have limits imposed on aircraft noise at airports, noise limits on road vehicles; we have by-laws which prohibit the playing of transistor radios in parks; we have established pedestrian precincts, and so on. This total prohibition of the nuisance is not costless, smokeless fuel is more expensive than house coal, quieter diesel engines for lorries cost more than noisy ones, but in these cases, it is judged that the benefits so far outweigh the costs that a total ban is justified. Cost benefit analysis has a role to play here in

[1] Mishan regards road pricing as an example of 'internalizing the externality', which is essentially creating a market in spillovers where the gainers and losers from external effects can bargain with each other on the appropriate level of bribe/compensation required to make good the detriment. He points out however that for such a market to operate certain conditions have to hold, first the victim has to have clear property rights which can be traded, secondly these property rights have to be able to be clearly demarcated and thirdly it must be impossible for a monopsonistic situation to arise, that is the 'properties' demarcated by the rights must be close substitutes one for the other. Now while it is relatively simple to establish property rights and demarcate property in relation to physical property, this is clearly not so in relation to metaphysical property, peace and quiet and privacy, for example. In the case of a majority of environmental spillovers there is difficulty in identifying both trespasser and the extent of trespass, and it is clearly difficult to establish a market – let alone (since the third condition is not satisfied either) a competitive market. See EJ Mishan *Cost benefit analysis* George Allen and Unwin London 1971 chapter 15.

attempting to quantify in advance the costs and the benefits of such laws.

7.4 Summary and conclusions

In the normal functioning of the market mechanism activities yielding above average profits are expanded and those yielding below average profits or losses are contracted. This profitability investment criterion runs into difficulties where it encounters major indivisibilities, externalities or when the goods or services concerned are provided free of charge or at an arbitrary price. In these circumstances some criterion is needed which can be used to judge whether it is worth extending an activity. Cost benefit analysis is an attempt to provide such a criterion. As its name implies, it attempts to balance the costs of a project against the benefits; but these costs and benefits considered are the *social* costs and benefits, that is, externalities are taken into account.

This exercise is by no means straightforward, and this chapter has explored some of the problems that it encounters. The most important of these centre around the identification and quantification of costs and benefits. The identification problem arises because we are considering those indirectly affected as well as those directly affected – the externality elements. Where the effects of a project spill over widely into society it may be no easy matter to find out who is affected and in most cases it is necessary to limit consideration to those most immediately affected – a necessary but nevertheless arbitrary limitation. The quantification problem arises because in most instances we are considering benefits (and sometimes costs) which are not subject to a market valuation, and we have to try to place some valuation upon them by roundabout methods which provide some means of valuation, but frequently involve far-reaching assumptions which need to be written into the analysis. For example, when a project involves a faster journey to work, we can value the benefit by valuing the time savings; but to do this we have to be able to place a valuation upon time, both working time and leisure time, and there is no agreement on how this is done. This method of valuing benefits involves another complication. It includes a valuation of consumer surplus; we are weighing total benefits against total costs. This makes the whole exercise very different from the normal private sector invest- ment criterion which involves balancing total revenues which the firm can obtain (which exclude the consumer surplus element) against total costs: cost benefit analysis is therefore not directly comparable with the private sector profitability criterion.

There are other features of cost benefit analysis which involve the acceptance of fairly far-reaching assumptions. We have to introduce into the exercise some income distribution objective. In most cases it is assumed that all costs and benefits are of equal weight to whomsoever they accrue. Is this a fair assumption, or do we want to introduce some bias which favours certain regions or certain income groups? Again, since benefits and costs accrue over time, we need some rate of interest to discount these back to present values. But what is the appropriate rate of discount for the public sector? On these, and other issues, there is no consensus – no 'objectively right' answer – and arbitrary assumptions have to be introduced.

A possible way to avoid such arbitrariness is instead to adjust prices in the market to reflect marginal social costs and benefits, and leave the provision of facilities to the 'normal' working of the market mechanism. We discussed this idea in relation to road pricing and saw how such a solution is only applicable to a small proportion of the 'candidates' for cost benefit analysis; it does not provide a general alternative to the cost benefit approach.

We are left therefore to make up our minds whether cost benefit analysis, with all the arbitrariness involved in the exer- cise, is any improvement on the rule-of-thumb methods used generally by the politico/administrative machinery. These rule- of-thumb methods often mean that decisions are reached on a somewhat similar, but essentially qualitative, basis. The advantage of cost benefit analysis over such qualitative decision making is that it forces upon decision takers a more rigorous and consistent framework for decision. For example, although, as we have seen, there is no agreement about the valuation of leisure time, a common measure is now used throughout the government machine. The very need to attempt some quantifi- cation forces the decision taker to consider the ranking of different categories of benefit. Cost benefit analysis is not the answer to all imponderable problems, but it can help towards clear thinking about such problems. It is of prime importance however that those presenting cost benefit exercises to the public be duly humble about its limitations, and make quite explicit the assumptions on which their calculations are based. It is the sheer arrogance of some cost benefit analysis that detracts most from its findings.

Further reading

EJ MISHAN *Cost benefit analysis* George Allen & Unwin London 1971. This is not an easy book for the non-specialist economist to read, but it explores at some depth many of the issues raised in this chapter.

EJ MISHAN 'The ABC of cost benefit analysis' *Lloyds Bank Review* 1971. A simple introduction to the subject.

AR PREST and R TURVEY 'Cost benefit analysis: a survey' *Economic Journal* 1965. Reprinted in *Surveys of economic analysis* vol III Macmillan London 1966 St Martins Press New York. A useful and comprehensive survey.

O ECKSTEIN 'A survey of the theory of public expenditure criteria' in JM Buchanan (ed) *Public finances: needs, sources and utilization* Princeton University Press Princeton 1961. This remains one of the best introductions to the analytical content of cost benefit analysis.

GH PETERS *Cost benefit analysis and public expenditure* Eaton Paper No 8 Institute of Economic Affairs London 1968. A good introduction to the subject.

COMMISSION ON THE THIRD LONDON AIRPORT (ROSKILL) *Papers and proceedings* vol VII particularly part I Proposed Research Methodology HMSO London 1970. The detail is interesting and illuminating. The Proposed Research Methodology provides one of the clearest expositions available of the purpose and methods of cost benefit analysis.

D MUNBY (ed) *Transport – selected readings* Penguin modern economics texts Penguin Books Harmondsworth 1968. Contains many of the seminal articles on cost benefit analysis in the transport field.

8

The social services and redistribution

8.1 Introduction

The term 'the social services' is used in the UK to denote a group of services provided by the state for the community. This group is commonly regarded as embracing the state social security system,[1] the health and education services, and the local authority based welfare services. It is also sometimes extended to cover state provision in the housing sector. In this chapter we shall exclude housing and also the local authority welfare services and shall be mainly concerned with some of the economic issues arising in the provision of social security and the health and education services. Here too we shall be selective for, within one chapter, it is not possible to deal comprehensively with this subject. We shall on the whole be concentrating on issues which link up with the themes of allocation and redistribution which have run through the other chapters of this book.

Why is there state provision of these services? In chapter 1 we suggested that, within the framework of a market economy, the state has three functions

[1] The term social security is used here to cover both national insurance provision (mainly sickness, unemployment and retirement pension) which is financed in the UK on a substantially self-supporting basis through the National Insurance Fund, and national assistance/supplementary benefit provision which is financed by the Exchequer and paid on a means tested basis to those who for some reason or other 'fall through the net' of the insurance scheme (eg fatherless families) or to supplement the basic national insurance payments. It also includes family allowances and the income-related Family Income Supplement (FIS) introduced in 1971.

a to redistribute income in accordance with society's wishes;
b to provide goods and services which the market either fails to provide (public goods) or provides inefficiently (where externalities or indivisibilities are prevalent);
c to steer the economy along a stable growth path.

With the social services we are not primarily concerned with the third function of stabilization, although it is worth remembering that the government's macromanagement function is not wholly unaffected by the provision of social services.[1] It is the first two functions, the redistributive function and the 'public goods/ externalities' function, which might be called the 'want satisfying function', with which the provision of the social services is involved.

At first sight it is tempting neatly to divide the social services between these two categories, the cash transfers of the social security programme fulfilling the redistributive function and the 'provision in kind' of the health and education services fulfilling the 'want satisfying' function. Such a simple categorization rapidly breaks down. Taken together with the tax system, the social security programme does, it is true, provide the main vehicle for redistribution within society, but it also has an important 'want satisfying' role, correcting distortions which arise in the allocation of resources between individuals.[2] For example, both Keynesian (demand deficient) and structural unemployment in an industrial society can be seen as a by-product of the process of industrialization, an ill which society has wrought upon the individual and for which society ought to accept some responsibility. Similarly, poverty in old age is in part caused by the break-up of the nuclear family, again a

[1] Expenditure on social services as a whole counts as a part of public expenditure. There are those who see the complexities of the government's macromanagement function to increase in direct proportion to the total of public expenditure. This is misleading; macromanagement involves a good deal more than the control of public expenditure. Moreover, the social security programme (roughly 45 per cent of expenditure on social services in the UK) does not constitute a direct claim on resources, but a transfer of claims on resources. Even so it presents its macromanagement problems. Consider for example, the influence on the propensity to save of the introduction of a national superannuation scheme.

[2] See R Titmuss *Commitment to welfare* George Allen & Unwin London 1968 for a wider view of the objectives of the social services, especially chapter 5 pp 64–5.

product of the process of industrialization, and in part the result of individuals being short-sighted and failing to put sufficient on one side to meet the needs of their old age, a general myopia which causes the private rate of time preference to be higher than the social rate of time preference (see chapter 7.2). In both these cases it could be claimed that the social security programme was in part correcting for externalities within the economy.

Just as the social security programme does not fit neatly into the redistributive role, nor do the health and education programmes fit into the 'want satisfying' function. Admittedly, both these services are characterized by public good/externality characteristics – consider, for example, the benefits which society derives from literacy, or from vaccination programmes, but neither service could be claimed to be a pure public good in the sense defined in chapter 1 (namely that provision does not vary with the number of users and that 'more for me means no less for you'), and wholly free provision cannot be justified on these grounds. It is only when we recognize as well the redistributive aims of these programmes, in creating greater equality of opportunity and thus contributing in the long run to a more equal distribution of income, that we begin to see the justification for provision in kind free of charge.

Dual purpose programmes of this kind immediately run us into difficulties. The state is no longer involved only in furnishing services which the majority has voted to satisfy its own wants (namely public good services such as police, defence, street lighting, roads and bridges), but in providing some people with services which they would not necessarily have bought had they been handed the equivalent amount of cash. From the point of view of the majority, this could well be the most effective form of redistribution, it ensures that the transfer is not squandered on drink, or gambled away, but is directed to a purpose which in the eyes of the majority is deemed worthy. But can this attitude be justified, or is it the tyranny of the majority over the minority?

We shall explore this question further in the final part of the chapter. On the whole we shall be concentrating upon the redistributive function of the social services, which is probably their dominant function. There are two main aspects that we shall explore here. The first concerns objectives. Redistribution to what purpose? What are the underlying objectives of redistribution and how have policies to this end evolved in the UK? The second aspect is effectiveness. How far does the pattern of social services evolved in the UK over the last fifty years meet these objectives? What limitations are there upon the use of taxation and the social services to redistribute income?

Before we can begin to talk about redistribution however we must consider the distribution of income. This is what the first section of this chapter is about. The next section takes up the theme of redistribution, and the final section the issue of redistribution in cash or redistribution in kind.

8.2 The size distribution of income

What do we mean by the distribution of income? In essence we mean the share of national income which goes to each member of society. In a capitalist economy the share accorded to each member depends upon their ownership of factors of production. Most members of society between the ages of 16 and 65 are in a position to provide 'labour' and the rewards of labour, earnings, are the most important constituent of income. Some members of society also own other factors of production, capital and land (often referred to as wealth), and derive income from these. The ownership of wealth is largely a matter of history. As we shall see however it has an important effect upon the personal distribution of income.

Each member of society is also a member of a large number of overlapping sub-groups within society. Thus one can think in terms of regional groupings, or industrial groupings and look at the shares of income going to these groups. Another method of grouping is by factor group (labour, capital, land), and economists have evolved various theories to explain the relative share of income going to the different factors of production.[1] One of the most usual groups for discussing income shares is by income group – the share of national income going to people with different levels of income. Here people are grouped according

[1] For a very readable discussion of these theories see EHB Phelps-Brown *Pay and profits* Manchester University Press Manchester 1968.

to the size of their income; hence this grouping is known as the size distribution of income. This is what is usually meant when people refer loosely to the distribution of income.

Frequently for the family group there is only one source of income, the earnings of the father, and there is little purpose in trying to attribute shares of this income among family members. Income distribution figures for this reason often relate not to persons but to family or household units. Indeed, the main primary source of data on the distribution of income in the UK, the Inland Revenue tax statistics, aggregate husband and wife incomes together. The Family Expenditure Survey, another primary source, goes further and aggregates all household income, including the earnings of any relatives living with the household, even where they constitute separate tax units. It is therefore much easier to obtain figures for family or household distributions of income, than for the personal distribution of income.

A family of four living on an income of £30 per week is, however, obviously better off than a family of six living on the same income, and attempts are made to extrapolate a 'personal' or *per capita* distribution of income from the family or household figures by dividing it by the numbers in the family. One recent study even made allowance for 'economies of scale' in family size by reducing families to equivalent adults. For example, a husband, wife and four children counted for 3·2 adult equivalents.[1] A family of six living on £30 per week is 'better off' than an old age pensioner living on £5 per week, because there are economies of scale in the provision of accommodation and food. While a family needs more accommodation than a single person, it does not need an additional room for each member of the family and therefore the cost of accommodation will not rise proportionately with size. The distribution of income derived for these equivalent adults is as shown in table 7.

[1] AR Prest and T Stark *Some aspects of income distribution in the UK since World War II* Manchester School September 1967. This study also attempted to overcome some of the deficiencies in the basic Inland Revenue/cso data which had been highlighted by Professor Titmuss. See RM Titmuss *Income distribution and social change* Allen & Unwin London 1962 and T Stark *The distribution of personal income in the UK 1949–63* Cambridge University Press 1972.

Table 7
percentage distribution of income* by
percentiles of equivalent adults—UK 1963

equivalent adults	percentage distribution of income
top 1 per cent	7·33
top 5 per cent	18·54
top 10 per cent	27·65
top 20 per cent	41·21
top 30 per cent	52·06
top 40 per cent	61·45
top 50 per cent	69·87

* Income here is income *before* tax
but *after* the receipt of social security
and assistance payments

Source: table 3 AR Prest and T Stark *op cit*.
For a full discussion of the data from which these figures are derived
see Prest and Stark *op cit*.

It is apparent from these figures that the size distribution of income in the UK is not equal. The top 1 per cent of equivalent adults have 7·33 per cent of income, the top 5 per cent, 18·54 per cent of income. Over all, in 1963 approximately 29 per cent of people had incomes above average and 71 per cent had incomes below average. A method of illustrating the inequality in the distribution of income is the Lorenz curve. The cumulative percentage of income received is measured on the horizontal axis and the percentage of income recipients on the vertical axis. The closer the curve is to the 45° line, the more equal the distribution of income. The 45° line is the line of complete equality where 10 per cent of income recipients receive 10 per cent of income.

The shaded area between the Lorenz curve and the 45° line gives an idea of the degree of inequality in the distribution of income. The larger the shaded area, the further the Lorenz curve is from the 45° line and the more unequal the distribution of income. It is possible to measure this area by means of a Gini coefficient (which is the ratio of the shaded area between the 45°

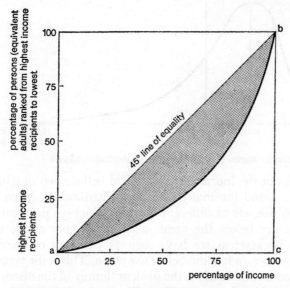

Figure 14. The Lorenz curve of income distribution. If income were completely equally distributed then the distribution would be represented by the 45° line–10 per cent of people would receive 10 per cent of total income. The more unequal the distribution, the further the Lorenz curve from the 45° line.

line of perfect equality and the Lorenz curve to the area of the triangle abc subtended by the 45° line). This coefficient varies between 0 and 100; the closer the coefficient is to 0, the more equal the distribution of income, and vice versa.[1] For the UK, the Gini coefficient for the income distribution quoted above is 32·83. The Prest and Stark study shows the distribution of income in the UK becoming more equal during the post-war period. The Gini coefficient for the 1949 distribution, calculated on a similar basis, is 34·36, and the 1959 distribution, 33·35.[2] We shall be looking in more detail at trends in the distribution of income later in this chapter.

Another way of showing the same data is by means of a frequency diagram, which shows the number of persons with incomes of different levels. The shape of such a frequency diagram for the distribution of income is distinct. The distribution

[1] It is sometimes quoted in decimal terms, varying between 0 and 1. In this case a coefficient of 0·32 denotes a more equal distribution of income than a coefficient closer to 1, say 0·83.

[2] Prest and Stark op cit.

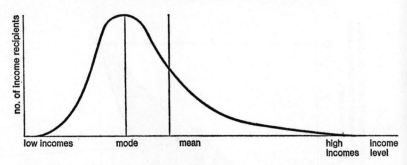

Figure 15. The size distribution of income – frequency distribution diagram.

in the UK is not the 'normal' symmetrical bell-shaped distribution that is found for many statistical distributions (such as height, shoe size, etc at different ages) in which 50 per cent of distribution are below the mean and 50 per cent above the mean, but is skew: as we have seen 71 per cent of income recipients receive an income below the mean. This is the typical shape of income distribution, the peak or 'hump' of the distribution coming below the mean. Mean income is above the modal income (the most frequent income/figure group appearing in the distribution); moreover below modal income the distribution is compact, but the distribution has a long tail in its upper reaches. This is illustrated in figure 15.

One of the significant features of this shape of distribution is that a majority of the population have incomes below the mean. Since this is the typical shape of the size distribution of income both historically and in other countries, it is interesting to consider the factors influencing the distribution of income.

The distribution of earnings and the distribution of wealth

Income comes both from labour earnings and from unearned income derived from wealth. A majority of people derive their incomes from earnings. In 1970, 79 per cent of personal income in the UK derived from employment or self-employment, 11 per cent from rent, dividends and interest, and 10 per cent from social security and assistance payments.[1] The distribution of wealth in the UK is extremely unequal. It is estimated that the

[1] *National income and expenditure* HMSO London 1971. Income from self-employment contains an element profit on capital which the self-employed have put into their own businesses.

top 1 per cent of wealth holders in the UK own 43 per cent of wealth, the top 5 per cent own 68 per cent of wealth, and the top 10 per cent, 79 per cent of wealth. The estimated Gini co-efficient for this distribution is 87.[1] The distribution of earnings from wealth mirrors the distribution of wealth – if anything it is even more unequal since the very wealthy get better investment advice than the less wealthy. However, although the skewness of this distribution 'pulls' the distribution of personal income to be more skew than the distribution of earnings, the distribution of earnings is itself skew. We cannot find a total explanation for the skew distribution of personal income in the highly skew distribution of wealth.

THE DISTRIBUTION OF EARNINGS: How can the skew distribution of earnings be explained? The distribution of earnings reflects pay differentials both within and between occupations. There are a great many factors affecting these differentials. Here we only mention some of the more important of them, and do not attempt to provide anything by way of a total theory of the distribution of earnings.[2]

There are two important sets of factors influencing pay differentials. We may call the one 'market' factors and the other 'institutional' factors. Market factors influence differentials through their influence over the supply and demand for labour. In the extreme 'textbook' model of the labour market, labour is homogeneous, and differentials exist only as a temporary phenomenon reflecting temporary disequilibrium between supply and demand in some labour submarket, a disequilibrium which is rapidly eliminated by the mobility of labour between submarkets. Labour is not however homogeneous. People vary in ability and skill and this variation provides one clear explanation for differentials. Ability derives partly from inherited characteristics.[3] Where an ability, such as that of an actor,

[1] These figures are taken from HF Lydall and DG Tipping 'The distribution of personal wealth' *Bulletin of Oxford Institute of Statistics* 1961. The distribution of wealth has probably changed very little since then. See AB Atkinson *Unequal shares* Allen Lane: The Penguin Press London 1972 chapter 1 pp 3–24.

[2] Readers interested in this may like to look at HF Lydall *The structure of earnings* Oxford University Press 1968. See in particular chapter 4.

[3] But it also derives from early family and social environment and is influenced by education. Thus measured ability is not wholly innate, but may be influenced by environment.

singer, pop-star, etc, is unique and highly regarded it commands a high price. Supply is inelastic in relation to demand, and price is 'demand determined'. In such a situation the factor commands an 'economic rent', or what is sometimes called a *real* differential. By contrast to innate abilities, skills can be acquired, but it takes time and teaching to acquire skills. From this derives the concept of human capital; it is worth investing in a skill as long as the reward (the differential earnings over time) justifies the initial investment. Differentials for different acquired skills are called *compensating* differentials, for they compensate for the investment in training etc. The same idea can be applied to other types of differential. A job which entails a high degree of risk, scaffolding erectors, steeplejacks, may pay a differential to 'compensate' for the risk involved. Similarly jobs that involve working underground or in very dirty conditions command compensation in the form of differential earnings. Differentials over and above those necessary to compensate workers for skills, and which do not reflect innate differences in ability, tend to be eroded over the long period, for they attract labour into the occupation. The long run elasticity of supply of labour is greater than the short run elasticity.

Institutional factors tend to lessen the impact of market forces. On the one hand they affect the market itself. For example professional or trade union requirements on minimum training periods and minimum entry qualifications create barriers to entry into certain occupations and constrain long run supply elasticity. On the other hand, these institutional factors by-pass the market; a man's rate of pay, in part at least, reflects the social position he is expected to maintain while, in turn, social status determines pay. Differentials, once established, thus become a part of the social system and are 'institutionalized' and perpetuated by it. Superimpose on top of this the presence of trade unions, with their firm ideas of the appropriate 'rate for the job' and 'differential' between jobs, and it can be seen that market forces, though perhaps dominant in the very long run, are muted in their impact over a shorter period of time.

The interplay of these market and institutional forces in the labour market fashions the pattern of earning differentials which we observe. One of the features of this distribution is that, although it does not conform to the 'normal' bell-shaped distribution, it has been found to conform reasonably well to a 'log-normal' distribution. This means that if the intervals on the horizontal axis were measured not in equal absolute steps, but on a logarithmic scale in steps of equal proportion,[1] then the distribution assumes the 'normal' bell-shaped pattern. This log-normality of the distribution of earnings has been shown to persist both over time and across industry groups.

The log-normal distribution has certain interesting statistical properties. In a log-normal distribution, each member of the distribution is the product of a number of separate influences *a* which are independent of each other and *b* each of which tends to raise or lower the size of each member of the distribution by a given proportion. There are certainly a large number of separate influences at work affecting an individual's earnings. It is more difficult to claim that they are independent of each other – ability and training, for example, are frequently closely related to each other, as are age and seniority, health and environment, etc – let alone that each influence has an equiproportionate effect upon earnings. The truth of the matter is that although we can identify various influences operating upon earnings, we have no satisfactory explanation as to why this particular distribution should result.

8.3 Redistribution and the social services

In the previous section we saw that the size distribution of income is skew. This means that a majority of people receive an income which is below the average income level. In these circumstances it is hardly surprising that the growth of democracy has meant pressure for a more equal distribution of wealth and income. Such an objective is, however, tempered by other objectives in society with which it comes into conflict, for example, the freedom of the individual and his right to privacy, and the desire for full employment and a fast rate of economic growth. Under such influences, pressure for a more equal distribution of income has frequently been transferred into a concern to alleviate poverty, and it is this objective, sometimes called the

---

[1] That is, rather than in steps of say £2.50, in steps of 50 per cent – viz interval marks *not* of £5, £7.50, £10, £12.50 . . ., but of £5, £7.50, £11.25, £16.52. A scale with intervals of equal *proportion* is a logarithmic scale.

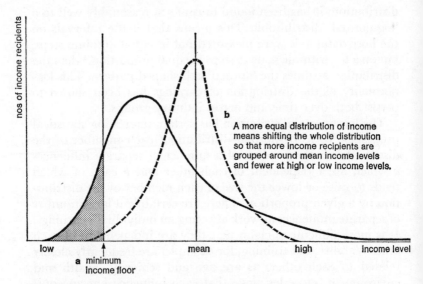

Figure 16. A comparison of the effects on the size distribution income of (a) a minimum income floor, and (b) a more equal distribution of income.

'anti-poverty objective', which can be seen to lie behind much of the development of the social services.

It is important to distinguish between the objective of alleviating poverty and the desire for a more equal distribution of income. The alleviation of poverty is concerned with providing a floor below which incomes shall not fall; it is not concerned with the shape of the size distribution of income above this floor. In the diagram the aim would be to eliminate the shaded portion of the distribution.

Those who seek to establish a more equal distribution of income wish to effect a redistribution which would cluster incomes more closely around the mean, as in the dotted distribution in the diagram. To the extent that the minimum income level was established by taxing the rich and giving the proceeds to the poor, then the elimination of poverty would *de facto* have brought about a more equal distribution of income. But the alleviation of poverty can also be achieved by taxing those just above the poverty line and redistributing to those below the poverty line, which would leave those in the upper part of the income distribution unaffected.

250

Distinguishing between the anti-poverty objective and the desire for greater equality in this manner helps to show that while the social services can be seen as the main vehicle for alleviating with poverty, it requires a combination of progressive taxation and progressive benefits to achieve a more equal distribution of income. Here, indeed, we come to the two themes which recur throughout this section. On the one hand we shall be looking at the interaction of poverty and the development of the social services; on the other the interaction of notions of social justice, particularly equality, and the redistribution effected through the combined tax and social service system. Each of these four concepts interacts with the other, and therefore rather than two separate themes, they form what might be regarded as the four corners of a square.

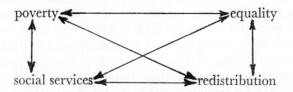

This four-fold relationship underlies a good deal of this section, and it is worth keeping it in mind when we explore some of the more detailed issues which arise in this field.

The problem of defining poverty

The establishment of a minimum income floor or poverty line is not easy, for what are regarded as minimum subsistence standards of nutrition, housing, and so forth vary according to the state of development of the economy, the social structure etc. The first attempts in the UK to measure poverty in any systematic way were those of Booth and Rowntree in the late nineteenth century. In his definition of 'primary' poverty, Rowntree sought to establish a scientific standard of poverty.[1] He calculated the minimum nutritional needs of families of different sizes and translated these into terms of food and hence

[1] BS Rowntree Poverty – a study of town life Macmillan London 1901. See also his subsequent surveys in 1936 and 1950 *Poverty and progress* Longmans London 1947 and *Poverty and the welfare state* Longmans London 1951.

money. To this he added rent and an allowance for the minimum quantities of clothing and other items which he considered to be necessary 'for the maintenance of merely physical efficiency'. However, this attempt to establish an objective standard of poverty was not satisfactory. When using the concept of the 'minimum necessary for physical efficiency' in his subsequent surveys in 1936 and 1950, Rowntree's list of minimum necessities grew longer. This is the problem. Even for food it is difficult to determine minimum requirements with any exactitude, and clearly in the case of housing, clothing, etc, the idea of a basic physiological standard is impossible. What is considered to be the 'minimum necessary' will depend upon the subjective judgement of the investigator, and his judgement will be conditioned by current living standards. Incomes providing what would be considered a good standard of living in an underdeveloped country are considered to be below the poverty line in developed countries. This applies even between developed countries. Households of two adults and two children living on an income equivalent to average earnings in the UK (£32 pw in 1971 equal to approximately $4000 pa) would be considered as living 'in poverty' in the US. Poverty is an entirely relative concept relative to the standard of living in the economy under consideration. As the standard of living rises, so the definition of poverty changes.

The recognition that it is impossible to establish any 'scientific', objective standard of poverty has led investigators to move away from poverty standards of their own creation to the adoption of an 'official' standard of minimum subsistence. For the UK, this has become the standard applied by the government to determine eligibility for Supplementary Benefit. The justification for this is that, 'granted the standard adopted is a relative one, the nearest that any investigator can get to a consensus on what constitutes poverty is to take the "official" operational definition of the minimum level of living at any particular time' and one that has been 'approved by Parliament'.[1] As we shall see this is now the most frequently used measure of poverty in the UK, but it is not without its shortcomings.

---

[1] B Abel-Smith and P Townsend 'The poor and the poorest' *Occasional papers in social administration no 17* G Bell & Sons London 1965.

Poverty in the UK 1900–70

In the UK social surveys since those of Booth and Rowntree of the late nineteenth century have been concerned to establish both the extent and causes of poverty. All have found poverty to exist, though its extent has varied from survey to survey, reflecting the growth of real living standards, the cyclical pattern of economic growth, and the relative 'poverty' standard adopted by those conducting the survey.[1] During the first half of this century the general rise in real wage levels, combined with welfare measures and the adoption after 1940 of a full employment policy brought a substantial reduction in the incidence of poverty. For the period since 1950 the evidence is less conclusive. Abel-Smith and Townsend in their study 'The poor and the poorest'[2] found a rising incidence of poverty with an increased proportion of the population dependent for long periods on sickness benefit (itself reflecting the larger number of old people in the population), and with an increasing number of large families in the population. Their study was based upon Family Expenditure Survey data. Another study by Gough and Stark based on Inland Revenue data found, on the contrary, that the incidence of poverty decreased over the same period, though showing some slight tendency to increase during the early 1960s.[3]

[1] For a brief summary of the earlier surveys see W Hagenbuch *Social economics* Nisbet and Cambridge 1958 chapter 6.

[2] For later surveys see B Abel-Smith and P Townsend *op cit* and AB Atkinson *Poverty and the reform of social security* University of Cambridge Dept of Applied Economics Occasional Paper No 18 Cambridge University Press 1969.

[3] I Gough and T Stark *Low incomes in the UK* The Manchester School June 1968. Their data was based upon the income distribution data used for the Prest and Stark analysis discussed in section 8.2 of this chapter which involved correcting the basic Inland Revenue/CSO data for its most serious deficiencies. Using this adjusted distribution, Gough and Stark have estimated that the number of people with incomes below national assistance scales were:
1954 – 12·3 per cent of total population
1959 – 8·8 per cent of total population
1963 – 9·4 per cent of total population
The difference between 1959 and 1963 can be explained in part at least by the different state of the economy in the two years, 1959 being a year of rapid expansion while 1963 was a year of recession.
The explanation for the very much higher 'level' of poverty found in this study, as compared with the Abel-Smith and Townsend study (which found an incidence

The balance of the evidence supports the view that the incidence of poverty decreased slightly over the period. Abel-Smith and Townsend had considerable difficulty with the income data for 1954, and in the end used expenditure data to estimate income levels for their sample. Because there is a well established tendency in surveys of this type for expenditure to exceed income and for income to be understated, this probably contributed to an underestimate of the incidence of poverty in 1954. Both surveys used supplementary benefit (sb – at that time it was called national assistance benefit, nab) support levels as their 'poverty line'. The period 1950–65 saw a considerable increase in the real value of these assistance levels, but 1954 was below trend, which would again tend to deflate the estimate of poverty for that year used by Abel-Smith and Townsend. By comparison, Gough and Stark took trend values of the sb support levels over this period.

This latter point highlights one of the major difficulties with taking supplementary benefits or similar 'official' scales as a measure of poverty. Since a large number of families are to be found living just above the 'poverty line', any relative increase in the poverty standard, will bring a large number previously outside, within the definition of poverty. The very means by which the state is trying to alleviate poverty, namely increasing assistance scales, in itself causes an increase in the measured incidence of poverty. This seems very unsatisfactory. Since the sb scale is increasingly used and accepted as a measure of poverty, it is worth bearing this point in mind.

Turning to the 1960s, a survey by Atkinson[1] based on the 1967 Family Expenditure data finds a level of poverty close to that of Abel-Smith and Townsend, 3·5 per cent of persons living on incomes below the Supplementary Benefit Level. He points out, however, that two surveys by the Ministry of Social

in 1960 of 3·5 per cent of persons), lies partly in the different definitions of 'household' adopted by Inland Revenue statistics and the Family Expenditure survey. In the former, the household refers to the *income unit* (ie husband, wife and dependent children etc) and adult working children or elderly relations who have their own incomes are considered as separate units. In contrast in the Family Expenditure Survey the household is taken as the group living together, and all incomes coming into the household are included. Since it is young workers and the old who have the lowest incomes, one would expect to find a considerably greater incidence of low income households in the Inland Revenue data.

[1] AB Atkinson *op cit* chapter 2.

Security[1] of the two groups most vulnerable to poverty, old people and families, provide a 'minimum' estimate of poverty which is slightly above this – 3·7 per cent.[2] Atkinson concludes that the proportion of the population living on incomes which are below the amount they would have received had they been dependent on National Assistance/Supplementary benefit 'lies towards the upper end of the range 4 per cent–9 per cent,'[3] constituting in all about 5 million people. In spite of the greater attention paid to the social security programme of the Labour government of 1964–70, it would appear that the position was little altered in the early 1970s.[4]

Poverty and the development of the welfare state

In all these poverty surveys, poverty is defined as income insufficiency in relation to needs, and the surveys were concerned both to measure the extent of poverty and to uncover the causes of the income insufficiency. Broadly speaking they found that either income was, for one reason or another, below average levels, or needs were above average levels. Sometimes, both insufficiencies coincided, as in the case of large families living on below average incomes. Delving a little further below the surface, the most prevalent causes of poverty revealed by the surveys were old age, unemployment, sickness, large families, single parent families and low wages.

Since the first decade of the twentieth century successive measures have been introduced which aimed to counter these causes of poverty, and what we now term 'the welfare state' gradually emerged. Its development has retained very much the same pattern; measures are introduced as one cause or another is shown to be an important element in poverty – a very *ad hoc* pattern of development. Indeed, the Beveridge Report,[5]

[1] Ministry of Pensions and National Insurance *Financial and other circumstances of retirement pensioners* HMSO 1966 and Ministry of Social Security *Circumstances of families* HMSO 1967.
[2] Again the discrepancy between his figures and those of Gough and Stark can be explained by the differences between the Family Expenditure survey definition of household and the Inland Revenue definition.
[3] AB Atkinson *op cit* p 38.
[4] See chapter by AB Atkinson in P Townesnd and N Bosanquet (eds) *Labour and inequality 16 Fabian essays* Fabian Society London 1972.
[5] *The Beveridge Report social insurance and allied services* Cmnd 6404 HMSO 1942.

which is regarded frequently as the foundation of the welfare state in the UK, can be seen as much as the consolidation of earlier measures introduced somewhat randomly, as the laying down of a pattern for the development of the welfare state in the post-war period.

Granted the association between the revealed causes of poverty and the development of the social services, it might be useful briefly to indicate the relationship between the two. The following table, in a somewhat crude fashion, maps some of the more important developments:

causes of poverty	welfare measures
old age	1908 Old age pensions provided a means tested non-contributory pension at age of 70.
	1925 Contributory pensions from 65 available for certain categories of worker.
	1946 National Insurance Act made compulsory contributory but flat rate retirement pensions payable for women at 60 and men at 65.
	1970s Earnings Related retirement pensions financed from earnings related contributions are projected in plans formulated by both political parties.
unemployment	1944 The commitment to a full employment policy has been the most effective general remedy. More specific measures aimed to alleviate poverty caused by unemployment include:
	1911 Partial and variable insurance against unemployment introduced for some industries, the coverage being gradually extended until the
	1946 National Insurance Act made unemployment insurance under the national scheme compulsory for all workers, benefit being paid at same flat

rate as for other national insurance benefits, viz old age and sickness.

1965 Earnings related unemployment benefit for first 6 months of unemployment.

sickness

There are two separate items that cause poverty in sickness *a* loss of earnings

b the costs of medical care.

After 1946 these were tackled separately.

1911 Health insurance for some categories of worker providing both free medical care through a panel arrangement and income benefits when sick. Coverage was gradually extended but it was not until the

1946 National Insurance Act, that all workers were compulsorily insured against loss of earnings when sick, and entitled to claim sickness benefit at flat national insurance rate; and the

1946 National Health Service Act that free medical care was provided for all paid for largely from Exchequer funds (although there is a small contribution towards its costs from payments made to the National Insurance Fund). Charges, in general unrelated to cost, have been subsequently introduced for dental and optical treatment and for prescriptions, both to help defray costs and to contain demand.

1965 Earnings Related Sickness Benefit for first six months of illness.

1971 Constant Attendance Allowance – a small allowance paid to those who need constant nursing attendance.

large families

1945 Family Allowances Act made provision for a flat rate allowance to be paid for second and subsequent children, financed from Exchequer funds. The

257

payment was universal, that is to say it was paid as of right irrespective of parental income. Payments, although periodically revised, did not keep pace with inflation and in real terms by 1968 had fallen well below original levels. The allowances were increased in 1968 to a level which restored their 1945 purchasing power, but at the same time the *clawback* principle was introduced whereby those paying the full rate of income tax gained nothing from the increase.

1971   Family Income Supplement which allows a payment of 50 per cent on the shortfall of income below £18 per week (raised to £20 per week in 1972). The limit is raised according to the number of children in the family, the maximum payment being £4 (£5 from 1972).

single parent families 1925   Widow's pensions introduced as part of contributory pension scheme for many workers but not universal until

1946   Widow's pensions introduced as part of national insurance scheme, benefits being claimed on husband's contribution record.

1945   Family Allowances ⎱ see above
1971   Family Income Supple- ⎰ under
ment   large families

low wages 1971   Family Income Supplement. (See above under large families.) This is the only measure specifically introduced to counter the effects of low wages, although family allowances can be seen as a method of alleviating the effects of low wages for families with 2 or

more children. More generally the
health and education programmes,
providing free health care and education can help low wage families in so
far as they provide greater equality of
opportunity. This is an aspect we shall
be taking up later.

In addition to these specific measures, there has always been
available the fall back of 'public assistance' administered prior
to 1945 by the local Poor Law authorities, and after 1945 by the
National Assistance Board (becoming the Supplementary
Benefits Commission in 1967). Claims for such assistance have
always been subject to a means test. Under the old Poor Law
administration being on public assistance carried the implica-
tion of being destitute, a stigma which the National Assistance
Board and the Supplementary Benefits Commission have long
been trying to live down. Since the 1948 National Assistance
Act benefits payable under national assistance, contrary to
the Beveridge recommendations which were that both insurance and assistance benefit should be at subsistence level,
have consistently been slightly higher than the equivalent levels
of benefit payable under national insurance. Those totally
dependent upon national insurance benefits (for example, old
people dependent upon state retirement pensions) have been
eligible to 'top up' their national insurance benefits by claiming
assistance. This has become one of the more important functions
of 'public assistance', which explains the change of name to
supplementary benefit.

The pattern that emerges is clear. It is a pattern which
underlay the Beveridge report and which has remained more or
less unaltered since. The rationale behind it is as follows. Many
of the causes of poverty are risks that can be insured against, and
thus the first line of defence against poverty is a compulsory
national insurance scheme covering old age, sickness, unemployment and widowhood combined with a family allowance
scheme and free medical care for all. (These latter two pro-
visions help to provide for situations where needs are above
average because of family size or ill health). Benefits under
these schemes are paid as of right in return for contributions,

which may be considered as insurance premiums. The element of redistribution involved here might be said to be one of redistribution over a lifetime rather than between persons, a man putting aside income during periods when he is working to help finance periods when, for one reason or another, he is not working. But even if all contributions were calculated actuarily on this basis, a 'national' insurance scheme would involve some redistribution between persons, in so far as the good risks would subsidize the bad risks. In fact, the UK National Insurance Fund is not run on normal insurance reserve finance principles (on which a man's contributions would be invested and kept in 'reserve' until outpayments were necessary), but is run on 'pay as you go' lines, which means that there is little element of redistribution over time, but a substantial element of redistribution between persons, those in work subsidizing those out of work.

For those who, for some reason or another, fall through this first line of defence against poverty, for example unmarried mothers or those whose contribution record is deficient, there is a second line of defence, the national assistance/supplementary benefit programme, whose benefits are means tested. As we saw above, this second line of defence has had to cope with a large category of people, those who have no other source of income than the flat rate national insurance benefit, for whom the first line of defence, though it catches them, is inadequate, a contingency not envisaged by Beveridge.

How effective is the welfare state?

This apparatus of the welfare state, combined with rising real living standards, has undoubtedly done a good deal to alleviate the gross poverty which observers like Booth and Rowntree recorded at the end of the nineteenth century. Booth, for example, suggested that one in three Londoners then lived in poverty and Rowntree found only a slightly lower proportion in York. As we have seen, standards of poverty change and we can make no clear comparisons over the last 70 years. Yet, that somewhere between 3·5 and 9·5 per cent of the population should still be living below what is 'officially' judged to be an acceptable minimum standard of living (namely below the supplementary benefit levels) indicates that the welfare system that we have created to combat poverty is far from perfect.

The main pockets of poverty that exist in the early 1970s spring from three sources, low wages, the setting of national insurance benefits and family allowances at levels below 'subsistence' level (ie below the equivalent supplementary benefits level), and the failure of those entitled to means tested benefits to claim them.

The *low wage problem* is not an easy one. Solutions range from substantial increases in family allowances combined with the abolition of income tax allowances for children, through negative income tax, a scheme under which a family would automatically receive a subsidy when its income fell below the taxable level in the same way as tax is automatically paid through PAYE as income rises above taxable levels, to minimum wage legislation. Each scheme has its advantages and its disadvantages.[1] Raising family allowances, particularly where combined with some element of *clawback*, does provide a method of helping large families with low incomes and does not run up against the work disincentive problem that income related payments encounter, but it fails to help the low wage earner with only one child, or without children. Minimum wage legislation would cope with this problem, but might have undesirable employment and inflationary effects. Under the terms of the 1972 budget, it is proposed to introduce a 'tax credit' scheme which amounts to a form of negative income tax, which will replace both family allowances and the family income supplement.[2] The family income supplement (FIS) is the only measure so far introduced specifically to help the low wage earner, but it has not been a success. It has run into problems both over takeup (in spite of an extensive advertising campaign only 60 per cent of those eligible have claimed the benefit to which they are entitled) and over its inflationary effects upon wage claims as workers try to shift the 'burden' of the equivalent tax on to employers. (See below p 271 the discussion of tax incidence.) Within the relevant income ranges, a man earning an extra £1 stands to lose a half of it through the loss of FIS, which amounts

[1] For a comprehensive survey and critique of the schemes see AB Atkinson *op cit* chapters 8–10.
[2] For a discussion of this, see below p 264.

to the equivalent of a 50 per cent tax rate. As the miners pointed out during the 1972 strike, a man earning £18 per week with two children of school age may, by the time he has forfeited FIS, rate rebate and other means tested benefits such as free school meals, be very little better off for a £2 per week rise in pay.[1] The tax credit scheme provides an ingenious method of getting over the 'means test' take-up difficulties, but is likely to run into the same disincentive/inflationary effects, particularly when aggregated with other means-tested benefits.

The category of low wages is however a most unsatisfactory one, a catch-all for many more subtle explanations of poverty. Probing deeper reveals problems over lack of education, mental and physical handicaps, discrimination and obsolescence of human skills. It is an old adage that poverty begets poverty. Poverty is not just a question of income insufficiency, which we have regarded it as being up to this point, but is a far more complex association of 'deprivations' involving the total household environment. If poverty has many dimensions, so the attack upon poverty needs to be multi-pronged. Anti-poverty programmes need to be directed not just at redistribution to provide sufficient income to meet current needs, but at changing the whole environment. Cash redistribution is only a temporary palliative; the longer term solution requires health, education and training programmes which will increase skills and productivity, together with community care and support. Hence the emphasis on compulsory and free state education, the provision of free medical care etc. More recently has come the idea of 'positive discrimination' whereby relatively more resources are put into these programmes in poor areas than in better-off ones. Here we see the education, health and welfare programmes contributing to effect a long term redistribution of income in a way which money redistribution alone cannot achieve.

Yet a multi-dimensional concept of poverty runs us into even greater difficulties over definition, for there is no obvious method of measuring cultural or environmental deprivation, and it seems most unlikely that any operational definition or index can be found. If we are to be forced back into using, as a measure of poverty, income (and/or asset) insufficiency, then it

[1] See 'The miners' case' summary of Ruskin memorandum for NUM *The Guardian* Saturday 15 Jan 1972.

is important to establish how closely related this is to these various concepts of deprivation. Another corollary of this wider concept of poverty is that the necessary multi-pronged attack splits the dichotomy between the redistributive and want-satisfying functions of the state which we discussed in the introduction to this chapter. Redistribution in kind, free health and education services and so forth, become a necessary concomitant of an effective anti-poverty programme.

Let us now turn to the other two contemporary causes of poverty, namely that of *national insurance benefit levels and family allowances falling below subsistence level* and *the low take-up rate* amongst those eligible to 'top up' these payments by means-tested benefits. There would seem a simple and straightforward answer to this problem. This is to adopt a 'back to Beveridge' policy of raising all the national insurance benefits to a level equivalent to the supplementary benefit level and to abolish the differential which has existed ever since 1948. The difficulty with so simple a solution is cost. In 1969, Atkinson calculated that, if the whole cost of raising national insurance benefits to subsistence level were met from the Exchequer and financed through an increase in income tax, it would mean raising income tax by 11p in the £, about 25 per cent.[1] Moreover, we should be increasing benefits not only to those who are poor, but also to many who have incomes well above the poverty line. The answer may be to raise these benefits selectively; to concentrate resources upon those 'in need' who fall below the poverty line. This costs much less and hence, for a given increase in public expenditure, we can go much further to eradicate these pockets of poverty. In effect, by setting supplementary benefit levels above those of the national insurance benefits and encouraging those who have no other source of income to 'top up' their national insurance receipts, the policy has been to allow selective increases in benefits and the 1971 Family Income Supplement extended this selective approach to low wage earners as well. But the 'take-up' rate has consistently been disappointing, in spite of extensive advertising campaigns, changes of name and other attempts to remove the 'stigma' of public assistance.

[1] AB Atkinson *op cit* p 188.

THE SOCIAL SERVICES AND REDISTRIBUTION

The new tax credit scheme,[1] when in operation, will go a long way to solve these difficulties. It is a form of negative income tax, but by separating the taxation and benefit payments it creates a relatively simple piece of machinery for redistribution. All income, including all national insurance payments, will be subject to tax at 30 per cent (with higher rates applicable to earnings over £5000). Tax allowances, which at present limit liability to tax and are therefore of more value to those whose incomes are above the tax threshold than to those whose incomes are below it, will be combined with family allowances and paid explicitly as, what are called, 'tax credits'. These may either be used to offset tax liabilities, or, where the total tax payable is less than the appropriate credit, to supplement income. Since nearly all employees[2] and all those receiving national insurance benefits will qualify for tax credits automatically, the scheme overcomes the problems of take-up which have bedevilled FIS and the use of supplementary benefit for 'topping up' national insurance payments. In this respect it is an ingenious method of providing additional assistance selectively but painlessly. It still has to be seen how far it will go towards solving the basic problem of national insurance payments below supplementary benefit payments. It will certainly raise the income of those entirely dependent upon national insurance payments, but whether it raises it up to the level of supplementary benefit will depend upon the rates at which the tax credits are fixed, the movement of supplementary benefit payments and other factors such as rents. Until more definite details are announced, it is not possible to come to a judgement here.

Financing of the social services

In 1970 we spent £8953 or just about one-fifth of GNP on the social services.[3] During the previous decade expenditure on the social services had increased at the fast rate of 10 per cent per

[1] See *Proposals for a tax credit scheme* Cmnd 5116 HMSO London 1972.
[2] Excluded are all those earning less than £8 per week and the self-employed. The latter in particular constitute an important category amongst the poor and it is unfortunate that it should be necessary to make this exclusion.
[3] These and subsequent figures are derived from *National income and expenditure* HMSO 1971.

annum. Part of this is accounted for by inflation, but even in real terms expenditure was increasing by slightly over 6 per cent per annum, at a time when GNP was increasing in real terms by only 3·0 per cent per annum—indeed in the latter half of the period the rate of growth of GNP had slowed down to only 2·5 per cent. It is not surprising therefore that the social services should have been taking an increasing 'share' of GNP – 1970 expenditure on the social services was 21 per cent of GNP compared with 15 per cent in 1960. In the period 1970–5 it is projected that the rate of growth of expenditure on social services should be considerably slower than in earlier years, 4·4 per cent per annum in real terms.[1] Even so, this is likely to be faster than the average rate of growth of GNP which official forecasts would appear to put at about 3 per cent per annum.

There are two reasons for this fast rate of growth in expenditure on the social services. The first is rising population, and an increasing proportion of the population in the two age groups that make most use of the social services, the young and the old. In 1961 there were 9·0 m. persons over sixty years of age in the population; by 1971 this had risen to 10·5 m. and by 1981 it is estimated to reach 11·1 m., more than 19 per cent of the population. In 1961 there were 12·3 m. children under the age of 15, by 1971 there were 13·5 m. and it is projected that there will be 14·1 m. in 1975.[2] A good part of the increased expenditure is expenditure necessary for the services just to keep still and provide the same standard of service for an increased population. Another complication is that these services, particularly the teaching and health services, are labour intensive. It is to be expected that wages in these sectors rise roughly in line with wages elsewhere but, unlike manufacturing industry, increased wage costs cannot be offset by increased productivity. Therefore, as time proceeds, these services become relatively more expensive in relation to the economy as a whole. In their projections of expenditure the Treasury allow for this factor; they call it the 'relative price effect'. When this factor and population changes are taken into account, very little is left over for any rise in standards. Yet there has been some raising of standards

[1] *Public expenditure to 1975–76* Cmnd No 4829 November 1971 table 1.2.
[2] See *Social trends* No 1 1970 table 9.

and improvement in the quality of service provided, which has also been another factor pushing up costs. This is a response to public pressure. People, used to an increasing standard of living in their own homes, look to increased standards in these public sector services. They want better schools, smaller classes, modern hospitals. They want the opportunity to stay on at school after the school leaving age, to go on to higher education and equip themselves with degrees or equivalent qualifications. They want pensions that provide for a 'decent' standard of living rather than pensions which force old people to live at bare subsistence level. As in the case of many other services, hair-dressing, restaurants, cleaners, car servicing etc, increasing income brings a disproportionate increase in demand as there is a high income elasticity of demand for these services. Public pressure may indeed force expenditure above the projected limits during the next five years.

The major problem lies in meeting the costs of expansion. The choice lies between increasing the proportion of GNP taken by the government in tax revenues to pay for them, and 'return-ing' a part of the provision of these services to the private sector. In 1971, 69 per cent of the cost of the social services came from central and local government taxation, 28 per cent from contri-butions and 3 per cent from charges.[1] In its widest sense all three methods can be thought of as 'taxation', levies made by the government upon the public, for they are really just different ways of levying taxes. However, it is useful to retain the distinc-tion for the present, and to consider why it is considered to be difficult to increase revenue from these three existing sources.

TAXATION: It is a commonly held belief that we have reached the limit of our 'taxable capacity'. Precisely what this means is unclear. Some people think of it in terms of an international league table. But by this standard the UK does not do badly. Taxes, including social security contributions, as a proportion of GNP, totalled 40·1 per cent in the UK in 1968, a proportion which was exceeded in a number of countries including France (42·5), Austria (43·2), Sweden (48·4) and the Netherlands (42·2). As regards direct taxes (income and corporation tax),

[1] These figures are estimated from the January 1971 White Paper on Public Expenditure (Cmnd 4578).

the US and the Scandinavian countries all levied a larger proportion of GNP in direct taxes than did the UK, while the UK was exceeded only by Austria and Denmark in the proportion of taxes levied on expenditure (indirect taxes – customs and excise, purchase tax, SET, rates, etc).[1]

It might be argued that we should look *not* at the total proportion of taxes levied, but at the marginal rates of tax, since what is meant by reaching our 'taxable capacity' is that so much of additional earnings are taken in tax, that it is not worth the effort of working harder. (This implies that taxation is a major disincentive to work effort, which is a view we shall be examining in more detail below.)

A comparison of our marginal rates of tax on earned incomes with those of other countries marks us out in the lack of progressivity in our income tax structure. Between income levels of about £1000 and £5000 the marginal tax rate on earned income is unchanged at 30 per cent (for a married man with two children: given the present structure of allowance, he would not be liable for tax under about £1000; exact allowances vary according to number and age of children, mortgage and insurance commitments, etc). A man earning £1300 will be paying a higher marginal rate of tax than most of his counterparts in other countries. At £5000 however he pays a lower marginal rate than his counterparts in the Netherlands, Germany, Australia and Scandinavia. It is only at the £10 000 mark that the UK marginal rate of tax begins to rise above all others.[2] The two groups who are hardest hit in relative terms are those on and around average earnings (£32 per week in 1971) and the higher executive earning above £10 000. While we hear a great deal about the effects on long term industrial dynamism of 'penal' rates of taxation on higher executives, it is the former that presents the more important obstacle to increasing taxation to finance the social services. Inflation and rising real wages have put the man with the average wage packet into the income tax range. If we retain our present tax structure, where the

[1] These figures taken from *Economic trends* August 1970 International comparison of taxes and social security contributions 1968.

[2] See *The Times Business News* 12 August 1968. The extent to which UK marginal rates of tax soar above other countries has been substantially curtailed by the Budget changes of 1971 and 1972 which has reduced the highest rate of surtax on earned incomes to 75 per cent.

marginal rate jumps at about the £1000 mark (depending upon allowances) from zero to 30 per cent, then it is not surprising that 'an increasing number of people are becoming convinced that, since extorting more and more from the taxpayer will merely cause revolt, we must look for alternative sources of revenue'.[1] One obvious alternative would be to change the pattern of income tax and introduce much greater progressivity between £1000 and £5000. Surprisingly enough, this is not an alternative that has been given much consideration. Indeed, the abolition in 1969 and 1970 of the 'intermediate' tax rates which applied to the first £300 of taxable income moved in exactly the opposite direction, and the changes in tax structure announced in the 1971 and 1972 budgets, involving the merging of income tax and surtax, have left this plateau unchanged.

An alternative is of course to finance an expansion of the social services by an increase in indirect taxation (taxation on expenditure). As we saw above, Britain ranks high in the league table of the proportion of GNP going in expenditure taxes. Indirect taxes and local authority rates (which amount to a tax on housing) are both regressive, that is to say take a larger proportion of the income of low income earners than of high income earners, and it is not clear that those who wish to see higher expenditure on the social services would wish to see it financed in this way.

CONTRIBUTIONS: National Insurance contributions meet 28 per cent of the cost of the social services. Most of these contributions go to finance the National Insurance Fund from which national insurance benefits are paid (unemployment, sickness and retirement benefits). A small element goes towards the cost of the Health Service. The National Insurance Fund is kept separate from the general Exchequer funds, although the Exchequer contributes to the fund to the tune of about 15 per cent. With this Exchequer contribution, the aim is that the Fund should pay its way. Its main source of income is therefore from contributions. At present, 1972, these are mainly flat rate contributions paid half by the employer and half by the employee.[2]

---

[1] RHS Crossman 'Paying for the social services' *Fabian tract* No 399 1969 p 18.

[2] A small graduated element was introduced in 1961 to finance the graduated pensions, and later increased to finance earnings related benefits for unemployment and sickness. By far the largest element at present is the flat rate payment.

The flat rate system has presented a major obstacle to increasing national insurance contributions, since it is a regressive system with the less well off paying a very much larger proportion of earnings in contribution than the better off.[1] To raise all national insurance benefits to supplementary benefit levels, whilst retaining the flat rate principle, would mean either a very substantial increase in flat rate contribution (which would hit low income earners very hard), or a sizeable increase in the Exchequer contribution and hence taxes (and we saw above that our tax system is far from progressive). The only long run solution, as indeed envisaged in the pension plans of both political parties, is the abandonment of the flat rate principle and the recognition that the national insurance system is part of the redistributive machinery of the fiscal system. It is clearly easier to gain public acceptance of such a change if it is accompanied by a switch, at least in part, to earnings related benefits so that he who pays more in contribution will get more in benefits. This is however not essential; indeed flat rate benefits financed from proportional contributions constitute a more radical redistribution than earnings related benefits financed in the same way. It is somewhat paradoxical that it should be a Conservative government which implements such a policy.[2]

The pension proposals of both political parties do however envisage a switch to earnings related contributions.

The principle of a flat rate contribution yielding a flat rate benefit was dear to the heart of Beveridge. He believed that the National Insurance Fund should be no charitable institution. Benefits should be earned by contributions and paid as of right to those who had contributed. Since he also thought that benefits should be thought of as providing a minimum subsistence living (those who wished to live above this standard could make private provision to do so), benefits should be flat rate at subsistence level. Flat rate benefits meant flat rate contributions. As we have seen, we have already moved some way from Beveridge principles in introducing earnings related benefits for sickness and unemployment, and in the 1961 graduated pension scheme (which only provides for a very small graduated element). The current Conservative government's pension plans and the Labour party's national superannuation plan mean the total abandonment of the Beveridge ideas, for they involve earnings related pensions and earnings related contributions.

[1] This assumes that the 'burden' of the tax is met by those who actually pay the tax, and that the employees do not shift the burden by demanding higher wages to compensate them for their contribution. See brief discussion of this issue on p 276 below.

[2] See the proposals set out in the White Paper *Strategy for pensions* Cmnd 4755 HMSO London 1971. These proposals envisage a flat rate basic pension to be topped up by an occupational or reserve pension. The Labour party proposals, see Cmnd

The new tax credit scheme would, depending upon the rates adopted and the movement of rents, supplementary benefit levels etc, 'top up' the basic flat rate pension, and remove from some pensioners the need to look to SB for such topping up.[1] However it is fairly clear that the basic flat rate pension envisaged will not be equal to the supplementary benefit level of provision, and, although in the long run the occupational or reserve pension payable in addition to this will raise pensions above SB levels, the long run does not emerge until the 1980s, and short term 'topping up' will remain a necessity.

CHARGES: Thirdly, revenue for the social services might be increased by raising charges. These are obviously not appropriate to the social security field, where the contribution may in any case be considered as an insurance premium, but might be appropriate in the health and education field. Indeed, charges already exist here; they are levied on prescriptions, spectacles, and for dental treatment. These charges bear little relation to cost and can be considered really as taxes levied upon the users of these services. At present they contribute 8 per cent to the cost of the Health Service.[2] They are moreover extremely costly to administer, since the complex rules about exceptions to charges mean considerable administrative expense in sorting out who is and who is not eligible. If such exceptions were not made, the charges would be highly regressive, hitting most severely the old, the chronic sick, and those with children.

Potentially charges could be used to bring in a good deal of revenue and the proportionate cost of levying them would decrease as more revenue was raised by this means. The argument against raising more revenue by increase of charges is philosophical rather than economic. We shall be examining below in section 8.4 the whole issue of providing services such as the health and education services free of charge.

3883 HMSO 1969, in contrast proposed a system with both contributions and benefits related to earnings, with no basic flat rate pension.

[1] See *Proposals for a tax credit scheme* Cmnd 5116 HMSO London 1972 pp 26–7.

[2] Health and welfare charges were estimated in Jan 1971, White Paper on Public Expenditure (Cmnd 4578) to yield £175 m 1971–2. The current cost of the Health Service is about £2200m (Cmnd 4829).

Taxes, contributions and the supply of effort

Before proceeding further we ought to tie up one loose end which we have left trailing, namely the question of the disincentive effects of taxation on incomes.

Traditionally economics treats work as unpleasant and its counterpart leisure as pleasant and desirable. In order to induce a man to work, it is necessary to compensate him for the loss of leisure, and the greater the amount of work required, the higher the rate of compensation required. A man, free to choose how much he wants to work, will allocate his time between work and leisure so that at the margin he values the leisure foregone at the same rate as he is paid for work; if he valued his leisure more highly, then he would be 'better off' if he gave up some work and opted for increased leisure, and vice versa. This treatment of the work/leisure choice suggests that the imposition of an income tax, which lowers his net reward for work, will cause him to substitute leisure in place of work. Thus it is argued that all income taxes have a disincentive effect on work effort; the higher the proportional rate of tax, the greater the disincentive.

In fact, it is not quite so simple as this. Each man's relative valuation of work and income will be different, and some may value income relatively more highly than others. The effect of a proportional income tax may be to induce these people to work harder, in order to maintain previous net income levels, rather than to work less hard. Leisure is in these cases an 'inferior' good, and the negative income effect outweighs the substitution effect. The traditional view that income tax has a disincentive effect on the supply of effort is thus maintaining that leisure is normally not an inferior good.

Empirical evidence has failed to produce any clear support for the disincentive effect of income tax.[1] This is perhaps hardly surprising. The traditional theory runs into major conceptual problems when one tries to apply it. What is meant by the 'supply of effort'? Is it the number of hours worked, the intensity or quality of work, attitudes on promotion or training? Similarly, it is now recognized that income is only a part of the

[1] For a comprehensive review of the empirical evidence see CV Brown and DA Dawson *Personal taxation, incentives and tax reform* PEP 1969.

rewards from work, and that prestige, promotion prospects, status, responsibilities and security are also important 'rewards'. The ambiguity of both these concepts in itself makes it probable that the incentive effects of a tax change will vary from person to person. It is hardly surprising in these circumstances, that empirical work has proved inconclusive.

DISINCENTIVE EFFECTS OF SELECTIVITY: As we saw earlier, it is frequently suggested that a more effective way of redistributing income would be to make benefits payable under the present national insurance and family allowance schemes dependent upon income and variable according to income; payment would go to those in need rather than to those whose status qualifies for benefit. Council rent and rate rebate schemes are increasingly of this form, as is the qualification for free school meals, school uniform allowances, etc. Such suggestions run up against the difficulties of administering a means test. A painless method is the *negative income tax*, which would involve the automatic payment of benefits as income fell below taxable levels in the same way as PAYE involves the automatic payment of tax. Such proposals would mean that, as income rises, benefits fall. At the extreme, if benefits fall by the exact amount that income rises, it is equivalent to a 100 per cent marginal rate of tax; what is gained in extra income, is lost immediately in benefits. Because of the disincentive effects that this 100 per cent rate of tax would entail, most schemes propose that the rate of benefit should be well below 100 per cent. But many proposals nevertheless involve fairly high equivalent rates of tax. For example, Professor Lees's proposals[1] for a negative income tax to replace the present family allowance scheme would involve a marginal rate of tax equivalent to 38 per cent, which is higher than the standard rate of income tax on earned incomes. Moreover, when other forms of selective payment such as rate rebate are added to this, the whole can rapidly build to very high equivalent marginal rates of tax.[2]

[1] DS Lees 'Poor families and fiscal reform' *Lloyds Bank Review* October 1967.
[2] Even without the addition of a negative tax, those earning somewhat below average wage levels in the UK already meet very high equivalent tax rates from the existing selective charges, when these are superimposed on income tax and national insurance payments. For example a family with two school age children and earning between £15 and £20 per week would find itself, as it moved up the income

To the extent that there is a disincentive effect from income tax on work effort, then there is no reason to suppose that the same effect would not be present in the case of 'negative income taxes'; indeed it is the likely disincentive effects of such schemes that have been considered their most serious disadvantage. However, as we indicated above, the evidence on disincentive effects is sufficiently inconclusive that it is dangerous to try to generalize. For what it is worth the New Jersey experiment where a community has been subjected to a negative income tax scheme for the payment of welfare benefits, has so far revealed no serious disincentive effects. However, the experiment has not been running for long and we have to be cautious of reading too much into this 'controlled experiment'.[1] The UK government is sufficiently convinced of the merit of a version of the negative income tax to suggest the tax credit scheme which we discussed above.[2]

The combined redistributive effect of taxes, contributions and benefits

Although the desire to eliminate poverty may have been instrumental in the initial development of the social services, in the background was the wish to effect a greater equality in the distribution of income. To examine the effect of the social services upon the distribution of income we must look at the combined effect of taxation on the one hand and benefits on the other.

An attempt to measure the total effect of our tax and benefit system and to gauge how far those in different income brackets and household sizes gain more or less in benefits than they pay overall in taxes has been pioneered by JL Nicholson and the

scale and ceased to be eligible for rate rebate and free school meals, paying equivalent marginal rates of tax which varied from 35 to 80 per cent. See Piachaud 'Poverty and taxation' *The Political Quarterly* Vol 42 No 1 January–March 1971. The introduction of Family Income Supplement and income related rent rebates since Piachaud's study has increased substantially these 'equivalent rates of tax', so that the gain from extra earnings at certain critical income levels is actually negative and the equivalent rate of tax is more than 100 per cent.

[1] See HW Watts 'The graduated work incentive experiments: current progress' *American Economic Review* Papers and proceedings of 1970 conference May 1971 vol. LXI No 2.

[2] See above p 264.

Central Statistical Office.[1] It is based upon detailed surveys of family income and expenditure undertaken by the Government, from which it is possible to make an estimate of the total of all taxes paid and benefits received by each household and thus to calculate whether each household paid more in taxes than it received in benefits. The calculations include estimates not just for direct and indirect taxes (which vary according to the composition of household expenditure), but also the element of intermediate taxes (rates on business premises, fuel oil tax etc) met by the household as consumers. Similarly calculations of benefits include not only the cash social security benefits, but in addition the benefits the household receives from the health and education services. These are calculated in terms of average expenditure *per capita* or per child. Calculations are also made for the value of the indirect benefit received from housing subsidies. The resulting figure from all these calculations is expressed as a percentage of original income. Thus 100 is the 'breakeven' figure where total taxes paid just equal total benefits received. Over 100 indicates that benefits exceed taxes and less than 100 that taxes exceed benefits. The sample of 3000 households is then broken down into household/income groups. Table 8 which is based on the 1970 Family Expenditure Survey illustrates the general nature of these calculations.

These same calculations have been made for over a decade now. In general terms they indicate that 'households with low incomes on average gain much more from benefits than they pay in taxes, and households with high incomes pay more in taxes than they receive in benefits. Within a given income range, the largest households gain most and the smallest gain least (or lose most) on balance from all taxes and benefits combined.'[2] Such findings indicate a much greater element of redistribution than seemed likely on an intuitive basis. However, this approach has come in for a good deal of criticism from a number of sources.[3]

---

[1] JL Nicholson *The redistribution of income in the UK in 1959, 1957 and 1953* Bowes and Bowes Cambridge 1964. See also *Economic trends* November 1962, February 1964, August 1968, February 1969, February 1970, February 1971 and February 1972.

[2] *Economic trends* HMSO February 1972 'The incidence of taxes and social service benefits in 1970' p viii.

[3] See, for example, A Peacock and T Shannon 'The welfare state and the redistribution of income' *Westminster Bank Review* August 1968. A more recent and

Table 8
income after all taxes and benefits as a percentage of original income 1970

percentages

	range of original income: £ per year															average over all income ranges
	under 260	260–	315–	382–	460–	559–	676–	816–	988–	1196–	1448–	1752–	2122–	2566–	3104 and above	
all households in the sample	726	227	189	178	141	130	113	104	89	86	81	78	78	74	70	84
retired households																
1 adult	775	159	150	133	114	108	97	80								219
2 adults	693	243	216	176	144	137	129	108	90		79	74	72			150
non-retired households																
1 adult	398	178	133	123	110	84	77	70	68	60	61	56	65		65	74
2 adults	409	245	190	184	129	124	97	91	78	72	69	68	66	66	63	71
2 adults, 1 child							116	92	90	81	75	73	75	72	70	77
2 adults, 2 children								117	93	89	83	81	81	77	73	83
2 adults, 3 children								128	112	104	98	90	90	83	74	92
2 adults, 4 children										120	105	102				108

Source: *Economic trends* Feb. 1972 table A p vi.

275

The main criticisms are as follows:

a   The definition of income The definition of income used excludes all capital gains and most income in kind. However such income accrues on the whole to the rich; it may lead to some overestimate of the 'tax burden' on the better off; it should be borne in mind, however, that such income is not a major constituent of national income – at a maximum about 2 per cent of GNP – and its exclusion is not likely to affect the direction of redistribution revealed by the CSO studies.

b   The definition of benefits Four points here; first, the calculations assume that the population gains no benefit at all from some 50 per cent of public expenditure, expenditures on defence, police, roads, administration, museums, parks, libraries, etc, which amounts to some £300 per household. As long as one can assume that all households benefit to an equal extent from these expenditures then the effect of including these is just to shift the breakeven point upwards by £300; it does not affect the direction of redistribution. Secondly these calculations ignore the implicit subsidies that are paid through tax relief. For example payments to owner occupiers. Thirdly, the calculations of the value of health and education benefits are based on the assumption that all income ranges benefit to the same average extent. If there is any tendency for the higher income ranges to make greater use and thus benefit more from the health and education services than lower income ranges,[1] this is ignored in this type of approach. Finally, the calculations assume that the benefits obtained can be measured by input costs, whereas one ought perhaps to look at expenditures in the health and education fields as investment expenditures whose benefits accrue over the course of years.

c   The incidence of taxes The calculations assume that all direct

detailed critique of Nicholson's methods is to be found in AL Webb and JEB Sieve 'Income redistribution and the welfare state' *Occasional papers in social administration* No 41 G Bell & Sons London 1971.

[1] H Glennerster in 'Education and inequality' No 6 in *Labour and inequality 16 Fabian Essays* P Townsend and N Bosanquet (eds) Fabian Society London 1972 indicates that the very substantial increase in education expenditures in the 1960s benefited the middle classes disproportionately. This is a commonly held view also about the benefits stemming from the National Health Service. See R Titmuss *Commitment to welfare* part III, and M Feldstein *Economic analysis for Health Service efficiency* chapter 8.

taxes are met wholly by the supplier of the service (that is, for example, that income tax is borne by the income recipient and profits tax by the recipients of profits) and that indirect taxes are met wholly by the purchaser (namely that no part of the 'burden' of purchase tax or excise duties are met by the supplier, only by the purchaser). But, although eg the obligation to pay social security contributions is upon employers and employees, the actual burden may not rest there. Employers may be able to recoup the costs either through raising prices, or through not increasing wages in line with productivity increases. Similarly, employees may demand increases in wages to compensate for their increased contributions. It is not possible to say where the process stops, increased prices leading to increased wage demands and increased wage demands to higher prices, but it seems likely that groups that hold some form of monopoly power (employers as sellers in the product market or as buyers in the factor market, or employees/unions in the labour market) are more likely to be able to 'pass the buck' to someone else.[1] A recent American empirical study comes firmly to the conclusion that when a payroll tax is imposed upon employers (and social security contributions are a form of payroll tax) they reduce the wage by roughly the amount of the tax. Thus the real burden of such a tax falls on labour.[2] The cso studies in *Economic Trends* exclude the possibility of such 'shifting' of taxes from one group, those who initially meet it, to another.

d *The average approach* Inevitably a study of this nature deals with averages, with the average effect on broad groups of households or families, and therefore ignores the wide disparities which exist within each group. Even though the cso studies give the break down by both household and income group, there can be marked differences within each group caused by, for example, different types of housing provision, or varying access to local authority welfare services. This averaging is inherent in the nature of this type of global study.

These criticisms lead to some caution in the interpretation of the results of these exercises. Indeed, one is left with the question

[1] For a more detailed discussion of these issues see GL Reid and DJ Robertson *Fringe benefits, labour costs and social security* George Allen & Unwin London 1965 pp 106–17.

[2] JA Brittain 'The incidence of social security payroll taxes' *American Economic Review* vol. LXI No 1 March 1971.

of whether, granted the very major limitations of this type of approach, the whole exercise is worthwhile. As with cost benefit analysis, it is a beginning, an attempt at quantification in a field where qualitative judgements are frequently made. The criticisms that have been levelled at it have led to refinements in technique, which are likely to continue, and to the realization that this type of quantitative approach cannot provide all the answers. For these reasons, although such studies need to be supplemented by other more detailed work they cannot be condemned as totally useless. But we have a long way to go before we can feel that we can assess with any accuracy the overall redistributive effect of the 'welfare state'.

In this context it might be useful to look at the effectiveness of the different types of service in achieving redistribution. In his continuing study for this work JL Nicholson has made calculations of the effect on the Gini coefficient (see above section 8.2 p 245) of income distribution of the different types of tax and benefit. These are given below in table 9.

Table 9
effects of taxes and benefits on Gini coefficient of inequality

Gini coefficient[1]	1969	1970	1971
1 Original Income[2]	33·3	33·4	33·9
Percentage reduction in Gini coefficient from:			
2 Direct benefits	23·7	23·1	23·7
3 Direct taxes and benefits	31·8	31·5	31·0
4 All taxes and benefits	25·4	26·1	26·3

[1] The Gini coefficients given here are weighted averages (fixed weights) for the six main types of family where over three-quarters of income does not come from old-age pensions, national insurance pensions or supplementary benefits. The families (roughly three-quarters of non-pensioner households) comprise one- and two-adult households without children and two-adult households with one, two, three or four children.

[2] The estimated standard error of the Gini coefficient of original income shown here is of the order of 0·5.

Source: JL Nicholson 'The Distribution and Redistribution of Income in the UK' in Dorothy Wedderburn (ed.) *Poverty, Inequality and Class Structure* Cambridge University Press (forthcoming).

This indicates that direct benefits (social security benefits, health and education services) are a more important element contributing towards equality in the distribution of income than our present income tax system. In view of what we have said above about the 'progressiveness' of the UK income tax system, this conclusion is not surprising. However, it is necessary to remember that Nicholson's calculations on Gini coefficients are subject to the same limitations as the rest of the exercise. If you are prepared to overlook these limitations, the calculations lend support to those who claim that within the present tax/benefit framework redistribution through direct benefits is 'cost effective', in that the egalitarian effect of £100 distributed in these benefits is greater than £100 collected through income/surtax.

8.4 Redistribution in cash or redistribution in kind

We now return to the dilemma we posed at the beginning of the chapter. The social security programme can be seen as a method of redistributing income and although, as we have indicated, there are other aims to the programme, government intervention can be justified on these grounds even within a *laissez-faire* framework. But what about the health and education services where provision is made in kind? Can we justify these? We have seen that their function is also, at least in part, redistributive. But why provide these services in kind? Why not provide a cash grant to cover such expenditures? Can we justify a situation where, in effect, the government decides for consumers how much of these services they should enjoy? Is there any reason why these services should not be provided through the market mechanism?

The great virtue of the price system as a rationing device is that it enables us to tell how much users value a good or service in comparison with other goods or services that they might obtain. If we also have production cost data, we are in a position to judge whether too little or too much of a service is being provided; assuming that there are no externalities, the service should be expanded, when consumers' valuation exceeds production cost, and contracted when consumers' valuation is less than production cost. Where no price is charged, then there is no clear cut method of determining the appropriate amount to supply. Take the position of the National Health Service. Treatment generally is provided free of charge, and the demand for treatment is therefore equivalent to demand at a zero price. Production cost however is positive. Some consumers of health services are therefore 'consuming' services on which they place a valuation which is lower than the cost of providing these services. Is it appropriate to aim to meet the demands of all these consumers? Is supply to be determined by demand at a zero price? If supply is less than this then some other means than price has to be found to ration the service among consumers.

This situation is further complicated by the fact that as citizens we are both taxpayers and users of the National Health Service. As taxpayers we are aware that the greater the provision made under the Health Service the greater the tax bill reflecting the required diversion of resources from other uses to the health sector. We weigh up the relative benefits to be obtained from an expansion of the health sector with the other uses that might be made of the resources, and we are loth to vote resources into a use upon which we feel society places a relatively low value. As consumers however we are confronted with a zero price and we would be irrational if we limited the demands we made upon the service; others do not, so why should we? This schizophrenia creates an inevitable conflict. The supply of health services is determined arbitrarily by the political/ administrative process at a level less than demand at zero price because as taxpayers we are not prepared to vote resources to this sector sufficient to meet that demand at zero price. This means that there is always excess demand for these services and some sort of rationing system has to be used, thus we have queues for hospital beds, in doctors' surgeries, etc. Arguably our impulses as taxpayers are too mean, and we limit the supply of these services to a level at which our valuation as consumers is higher than their production costs. But with a zero price there is no way in which we, as consumers, can show how much we value them. Our only method of influencing supply is through the indirect route of the ballot box, and here, as we have said, we run into schizophrenia between our taxpaying and consumer egos. Supply is not determined, as in the case of goods or services supplied under market conditions, by the interaction of consumer preferences and production constraints, and we have no direct method of making our preferences as consumers felt; rather decisions on how much to supply, both of the service in total and of the individual parts of the service, are made by the political/administrative system.

It is because of the unsatisfactory nature of the supply side decisions that some economists[1] have argued that these services should be charged for at a price which reflects marginal costs. Services which then make a profit should be expanded and those which make a loss contracted. Alternatively, it is suggested that the provision of these services should revert to the private sector where competition between suppliers would ensure that those services which were highly valued by consumers (and for which they would be prepared to pay a high price) were expanded and services on which consumers placed a low valuation in relation to their costs, were contracted.

This is a hoary issue and one to which there is no simple answer. There is some logic in the 'marginal cost/free market case' even if one thinks it is based upon too facile an interpretation of the traditional welfare model. After all, we advocate marginal cost pricing (or something akin to it) for the nationalized industries. This approach could be interpreted as treating the education and health services as nationalized industries, requiring them to pay their way and to expand those sectors that are profitable and contract those that are not. There are advantages, too, in the allocation of resources to these sectors being determined by the 'objective' criterion of profit, rather than by power struggles between the Treasury and respective departments.

The trouble is that the virtues of the price system as a means of allocating resources cannot be upheld where the provision of the good or service in question involves the provision of public goods or where there are important externalities. As we saw in the introduction, the state has a 'want satisfying' role as well as a redistributive role. Both the health and education services involve elements of the public good/externality case. It could not be claimed that either good constituted anything like a 'pure public good', such as street lighting, lighthouses or even a TV or radio transmission where 'more-for-you-means-no-less-for-me'. Clearly the health and education services are more closely related to private goods in that a 'more for you means less for me' – if you wish to see the doctor, then there is less time available

[1] See JM Buchanan *The inconsistencies of the National Health Service* Institute of Economic Affairs London occasional paper No 7. R Harris and A Seldon *Choice in welfare* Institute for Economic Affairs 1965.

for me to see the doctor; the larger the number of pupils in a class, the less time has the teacher to devote to each of them individually – and *b* it is perfectly feasible to charge each individual according to the use he makes of the service. However, both services possess important 'public-good characteristics'. (We noted in chapter I the overlap between the categories of public goods and externalities and there is also a good deal of overlap here.)

Consider the example of the hospital service. The existence of a casualty department provides insurance for a whole neighbourhood that, if an emergency is met with, there are medical facilities available to cope with it. There is a necessary minimum of facilities which need to be provided and which do not need to be extended in proportion to the population of the neighbourhood. The same argument can be applied also to the general practitioner services which in the event of an emergency should be available within a fairly short time. In both cases, the public good element is provided by the existence and ready availability of these medical services, in exactly the same way as in the transport field a regular scheduled service which people know will be available if they want to use it increases the public benefit derived. Other more straightforward externalities on the health front stem from things like the vaccination and inoculation programmes which limit the prevalence of infectious diseases. Through vaccination not only do I limit the chances of my catching a disease but I also reduce the probability of others getting it. Public sanitation is another example of a programme with major externalities.

The education service too exhibits externalities. The public lecture is a classic case of public good. Until the lecture hall is full, an extra student listening to the lecture in no way detracts from the benefit derived by others: closed circuit television can extend these benefits indefinitely. If all teaching took the form of lectures, then one might argue that once a school is established one extra pupil adds little to costs and gains benefit equivalent to that gained by all the other pupils. Fortunately most teaching is not conducted by public lecture, but is more personalized. Then education becomes more clearly a private good. An extra pupil joining a class absorbs teaching time which would otherwise be devoted to the remainder of the class.

However, there are other externality elements. My learning to read and write is not only to my own advantage, but also to the advantage of all those who wish to communicate with me other than by means of direct speech. This in turn means that we can base a good part of the running of our society upon the written word. If you try to imagine running a complex industrialized society without literacy, then you can gauge the immense benefit that society gains from literacy. It is not surprising that education is a high priority in less developed countries.

So far, what we have been discussing have been examples of *production* externalities in the health and education field, that is spillover effects from the production of those services. In addition, there is an important class of externality prevalent in these services associated not with production but with *consumption*. It gives people pleasure to see others benefiting from good health or a good education; our consumption of them benefits others as well as ourselves. Evidence of the existence of consumption externalities in health and education is seen in the support given by individuals to voluntary groups and charitable trusts working in these areas and in the successful functioning of such agencies as the British blood transfusion service[1] which relies entirely upon voluntary donation of blood. Economists have been much perplexed by the existence of consumption externalities. Some find in them an argument for state provision; others, a cause for nihilism towards welfare economics.[2] What is certainly true is that when they are present, even under the most ideal circumstances, price can no longer measure the contribution of a good or service to social welfare; it measures the contribution it makes to private welfare which may be a quite different thing.

The existence of these production and consumption externalities in the provision of health and education means that in seeking a set of prices to help allocate resources within these sectors we cannot look to marginal production cost to provide the relevant price criterion. However the existence of externalities *per se* does not argue for state provision, but rather for the

[1] See R M Titmuss *The gift relationship* George Allen & Unwin London 1971.
[2] See D Collard *The new right* Fabian Tract No 387 and J de V Graaf *Theoretical welfare economics* Cambridge University Press 1967.

adjustment of prices to take account of them. Let us suppose, for the sake of argument, that we could sort out the various externalities and the constraints of the second best world, and that we could arrive at a set of prices which were more nearly optimal. This is a big assumption; unravelling the inter-dependencies in production is difficult enough as we saw in chapter 7, for consumption it is well-nigh impossible. However, even if we could solve these difficulties there would still be some who would argue in favour of the free provision of these services by the state.

Their argument is based on equity and social justice. Health and education are basic human 'rights' and should be available to all according to their needs and abilities, irrespective of their income or position within society. Now the 'free-marketeers' argue that if these are your sentiments there is no reason why income should not be redistributed through the tax/social benefit system so that all can be placed in a position to purchase these services. In order to ensure that the money is spent on these services rather than, for example, gambled away, it is suggested that it can be provided in the form of vouchers, which can be cashed only at 'approved' educational institutions or on 'approved' health insurance schemes. (The element of un-certainty in health expenditures means that some sort of insurance scheme has to be envisaged if redistribution is to be in cash.) Such a scheme constrains consumer freedom of choice – redistribution may be in cash, but the cash can only be spent on certain services. It has the advantage over provision in kind in so far as it allows the consumer directly to influence the type of service that is provided since he is able to spend his vouchers as he wishes; a popular school or health insurance scheme will accumulate more voucher income than less popular ones, and this will provide an incentive to expand popular services and to contract unpopular ones. The system will therefore conform more closely to consumers' preferences than one which is dictated by those in charge of the organization who, though they may be influenced by consumer votes cast in the ballot-box and through political pressure groups, do so at considerable remove.

The advocates of provision in kind have two answers to these arguments. First, they point out the difficulties inherent in any

THE SOCIAL SERVICES AND REDISTRIBUTION

attempts to redistribute income selectively (as we saw above in the discussion of redistribution and selectivity on p 272). They argue that administratively, if you wish people to have access to health and education, it is more effective to provide them free of charge for all than to fiddle around with voucher schemes or the like. In the case of education for example which, as we have seen, can have long run redistribution effects, the ability to 'top up' vouchers would mean that better off parents were able to give their children better education, thus perpetuating or exacerbating existing class and income differentials through the education system, and vitiating any long run redistributive effect. Secondly, the advocates of free provision argue that we should not necessarily always try to provide those services which the consumer thinks he wants, for the consumer (parent, pupil or patient) is often in no position to judge what 'benefit' he will obtain from his purchase and therefore in no position to weigh up costs and benefits.[1]

Here lies the crux of the issue. It is an argument about *consumers' sovereignty*, whether the over-riding objective of society should be to try to meet consumers' wishes as far as is technically feasible. Once you admit that in certain sectors of the economy, for example the health and education sectors, resources should be allocated not on the basis of consumers' wishes but by standards that the doctors or the educationists think best, then you are over-throwing consumer sovereignty. Some feel that when consumers' preferences are founded not upon knowledge, but upon ignorance, uncertainty and prejudice, and liable to be easily swayed by admass, the allocation of resources in accordance with consumer wishes should not be the over-riding objective. Others, such as Hayek, argue that once you allow any chink in the bastion of consumer sovereignty, you open the door to paternalism and big brother. They claim that logically there is no distinction between health and education and all the other goods and services which we buy. If you want to provide health and education free, then why not food and clothing? All goods and services will then be allocated not according to preferences

---

[1] How, for example, is the patient in a position to judge what benefit he is likely to derive from medical advice. This problem of uncertainty and consumer ignorance is highlighted by Arrow in his article, 'Uncertainty and the welfare economics of medical care' *American Economic Review* December 1963.

but according to what the 'big brother' of the state thinks is appropriate for you.

It is not possible to say that the one view or the other is right, for this is a matter of ethical judgement. Many feel that in any society it is necessary to compromise between objectives which seem equally ultimate and that in a democracy there are built in constraints which prevent the exploitation of paternalism, the benefits to be gained in terms of social justice and equity offsetting the dangers of paternalism. Others see paternalism as a Giant Evil to be resisted at all costs. The choice between the two is, as we have said, one of ethics and not one of logic.

8.5 Summary and conclusions

The theme of this chapter has been redistribution. We have looked at the social services as a method of redistributing income, on the one hand to alleviate poverty, and, on the other, to achieve a more equal distribution of income, and we suggested that the development of the welfare state has been primarily stimulated by the desire to eradicate poverty. The wholly relative nature of the concept of poverty and the difficulty of devising any really satisfactory way of measuring it makes it difficult to reach any firm conclusions on how far these objectives have been achieved, but it is clear that in spite of the development of the welfare state, there still exists in the UK today a sizable minority in the population whose standard of living the majority regards as falling below tolerable limits.

There are two constraints which limit the effectiveness of further action in this field. The first is the difficulty of channelling resources to those who need them. To provide benefits universally to all whose status (ie as old, unemployed, etc) qualifies them for benefit may well be the most effective way of ensuring that those in need receive these benefits, but it also means that many whose standard of living is well above the 'poverty line' receive the same benefits. Moreover, as general standards of living rise, so too do what are regarded as tolerable minimum standards, and thus any programme of universal benefits becomes increasingly expensive. Recent moves towards greater selectivity have posed however as many problems as they have solved. Take-up rates for means tested benefits remain low, so that these benefits are not effectively reaching the poor, while the aggregation of a series of means tested benefits has resulted in marginal effective tax rates of in some cases 100 per cent or more. Even if this presents no dis-incentive to work effort, and the evidence here is inconclusive, its effect is certainly cost inflationary, as workers try to shift the burden of tax by demanding relatively higher wage increases. The new tax credit scheme, which is a form of negative income tax, should help to sort out the jungle that has grown up here, but it is not yet clear how comprehensive its coverage will be, and there will still remain a problem in the proliferation of means tested benefits, such as rent allowances, rate rebates, free school meals, free medicines, etc.

The second constraint to a more effective anti-poverty pro-gramme lies in the nature of poverty itself. Poverty is not just income insufficiency, but involves the whole environment of the household. It is a more complex and elusive concept than ever we had thought. Yet if we find difficulty in defining poverty in income terms, how much more difficult is it to define this multi-dimensional concept of poverty? How can we expect effec-tively to deal with poverty if we have not yet really decided what the problem is? One thing is clear. If poverty has many dimensions, so the action needed to remedy poverty needs to have many dimensions. Income redistribution is only a tem-porary palliative; we need to look also to longer term pro-grammes of education and training, health and medical care and the wider support of the personal social services. It is here that we run into the other problem that has occupied us in this chapter. For once we begin to attack poverty by providing these sorts of service, we run into the problem of paternalism; we are telling people what is good for them, rather than letting them decide for themselves.

There can be debate on all these questions, whether income insufficiency is best dealt with through universal or means tested benefits; whether resources should be devoted to tackling income insufficiency or to dealing with the other facets of poverty; what role benefits in kind should play. But underlying debate on these issues is a more fundamental question of how important we, as individuals or as society at large, consider it to be to tackle the problem of poverty and the allied problem of equality. Some feel that the development of existing provision, with growth kept in line with the growth in real GNP, is all that is needed; others that a massive shift in emphasis by society as a whole, involving a radical redistribution of income through the combined use of taxation and benefits, is needed in the pursuit of a fair society. The economist at this point has no contribution to make; it is for society as a whole to choose.

Further reading

R A MUSGRAVE *The theory of public finance* McGraw Hill New York 1959 chapters 1 and 3. A useful introduction to the public finance issues raised in this chapter.

A B ATKINSON *Poverty and the reform of social security* University of Cambridge Dept of Applied Economics Occasional Paper No 18 Cambridge University Press 1969. A thorough survey by an economist of the UK social security system and various schemes for reform.

R TITMUSS *Commitment to welfare* George Allen & Unwin London 1968. A collection of Titmuss's essays containing, amongst other things, his response to the welfare marketeers. It is interesting to contrast his essentially administrative viewpoint with the narrow economic viewpoint of the marketeers.

A CHRISTOPHER *(et al)* *Policy for poverty* Institute of Economic Affairs Research Monograph No 20 IEA London 1970. An indictment of the ineffectiveness of the present social service provision and a plea for its replacement by a system of selective cash benefits paid through a negative (or reverse) income tax.

P TOWNSEND and N BOSANQUET (eds) *Labour and inequality 16 Fabian essays* Fabian Society London 1972. A critical assessment of the record of the Labour government of 1964–70 on social policy.

Index

detergents, 124, 160, 161; films for exhibition, 160, 161; matches, 132; petroleum distribution, 124, 131, 160

Monopolies and Mergers Act, 157, 160

Monopolies and Restrictive Practices Act, 148, 149, 153; definition of the public interest, 153

Monopolies and Restrictive Practices Commission, 148–52; report on collective discrimination, 151

Munby, D, 214n

mutually exclusive investments: investment criteria, 188, 189; in cost benefit analysis, 209, 210, 235, 236

National Assistance Board, 254, 259

National Board for Prices and Incomes, 158, 163, 164, 191, 200, 201

National Economic Development Council, 82–4

National Economic Development Office, 82, 83

National Health Service, 178, 270, 276n, 279, 280

National Health Service Act, 257

National Income and Expenditure: Blue Book, 198n, 264n

National Insurance: Act, 256, 257; benefits, 256–64 *passim*, flat rate, 256, 257, earnings related, 256, and relation to supplementary benefits, 258, 259, new proposals, 266–70 *passim*; contributions: flat rate, 268, 269, earnings related, 256–60, 269, new proposals, 266–70 *passim*

National Plan, 85–8

nationalized industries, 168–204; investment criteria, 185–9; management by objective, 97; pricing

policies, 172–84; statutory framework, 169–72; social obligations, 190–5, 204

Neale, AD, 145n

negative income tax: disincentive effects, 272, 273; and the proposed tax credit scheme, 264

Net Book Agreement: Restrictive Practices Court case, 155

Nicholson, J L, 273, 274n, 278, 279

noise: measurement and evaluation of, 212, 219

Noise and Number Index, 212n

Nove, A, 44, 50, 51

organizational slack, 97

overhead costs, 179–85 *passim*

Peacock, A, 274n

pensions: contributory, 256; earnings related, 256; flat rate, 256, 270; old age, 256

perfect competition, 14–29 *passim*; and Pareto optimality, 16; and the general theory of second best, 20–3

Permanent Magnets: Restrictive Practices Court case, 155

per se rule: and the UK restrictive practices legislation, 153, 166

petroleum distribution, 124, 131, 160

Phelps-Brown, EHB, 242n

Piachaud, 273n

Pigou, AC, 233

planning: capitalist, 67–91; in Britain, 67, 81–9; in France, 67, 75–80; indicative, 68–71, 75–90 *passim*; and input-output analysis, 53–6; Hungarian reforms, 59–62; and linear programming, 53, 56–8; the National Plan, 85–8; the NEDC Plan, 83, 84; negative and positive planning, 71–90 *passim*; Soviet 5 year and